PRAISE FOR

Obsessive Compulsive Disorder Demystified

"If you or ... *OCD*
Demystifie... ...ey
through t... ...es, this
book illu... ...variety of
symptom... ...ence and
treatment ...ou have
OCD, thi...

—R... ...fessor
of P...
Hoa ...*eas-*
ures.

"OCD is ...tive treat-
ment is a... Cheryl
Carmin i... ...es her ex-
perience ...possible
causes, an... ...y illustra-
tive exam... ...s in each
chapter a... ...a 'must
read' for ... ...suffering
from this

—J... ...ociate
Ch...
Chapel Hill, Director, Anxiety and ... linic

Obsessive-Compulsive Disorder Demystified

AN ESSENTIAL GUIDE FOR UNDERSTANDING AND LIVING WITH OCD

A LYNN SONBERG BOOK

Cheryl Carmin, Ph.D.
Consulting Editor: Anne Coulter

Da Capo
LIFE LONG

A MEMBER OF THE PERSEUS BOOKS GROUP

Set in 11.5 point Bembo by the Perseus Books Group

Cataloging-in-Publication data for this book is available from the Library of Congress.

First Da Capo Press edition 2009
ISBN: 978-1-60094-064-4

Published by Da Capo Press
A Member of the Perseus Books Group
www.dacapopress.com

Note: The information in this book is true and complete to the best of our knowledge. This book is intended only as an informative guide for those wishing to know more about health issues. In no way is this book intended to replace, countermand, or conflict with the advice given to you by your own physician or treatment provider. The ultimate decision concerning care should be made between you and your doctor. We strongly recommend you follow his or her advice. Information in this book is general and is offered with no guarantees on the part of the author or Da Capo Press. The author and publisher disclaim all liability in connection with the use of this book. The names and identifying details of people associated with events described in this book have been changed. Any similarity to actual persons is coincidental.

Da Capo Press books are available at special discounts for bulk purchases in the U.S. by corporations, institutions, and other organizations. For more information, please contact the Special Markets Department at the Perseus Books Group, 2300 Chestnut Street, Suite 200, Philadelphia, PA, 19103, or call (800) 810-4145, ext. 5000, or e-mail special.markets@perseusbooks.com.

10 9 8 7 6 5 4 3 2 1

CONTENTS

FOREWORD

OBSESSIVE-COMPULSIVE DISORDER is a challenging problem and one that is not easy to overcome. But it is also an anxiety disorder that we understand pretty well and, even more important, we have some treatments that work quite well to address the problem. Let me introduce this very helpful book that answers many sufferers' questions by beginning where I began.

I was fortunate to study under Dr. Edna Foa beginning back in 1977 when effective behavioral therapy for OCD first began to filter into the United States. This treatment, developed in England in the mid-1960s, was pioneered by clinical researchers like Victor Meyer, Jack Rachman, Ray Hodgson, and Isaac Marks. It soon became clear that these astute practitioner researchers were onto something that was really making a difference for people who heretofore had been unable to function effectively because their OCD had taken over their lives. It was an honor to work on testing their intensive treatment methods in Edna Foa's clinic; what a pleasure to see it work remarkably well.

I will never forget one of my first patients. He was a doctor who wanted to dedicate his life to pediatric oncology. He was a very committed man and a very smart one. OCD had begun to affect his life early in his medical career. The not-yet-doctor found himself struggling during medical school with contamination fears that stemmed from a chemical spill in a laboratory where he was studying biochemistry. His fears spread—slowly and surely. First he worried about the people who had been in the lab when the spill occurred. Perhaps they had not cleaned up properly and some of the contaminants leaked out. He saw some of them in the library and that became off limits. They used the dining hall and soon that was verboten. Eventually even the campus newspapers could not be touched. Wherever he could see or imagine that the lab inhabitants had gone became a contaminated place he had to avoid.

At the end of the day, after entering his home through the basement where he shed his working clothes, he washed long and hard, showered for 45 minutes, and finally emerged upstairs into his "clean" home. Completing medical school involved great personal sacrifices like never taking medical books to study at home, or never sitting down in seats at work that others might have contaminated. Remarkably, he finished his MD degree and went on to an internship. It was here that the OCD took over, gradually constricting his life and his movement until there were no options left. He quit his internship and took a different job in another city.

Not long after, he heard of Dr. Foa's work and sought help at our clinic, enrolling in her research study to see if the treatments developed in England would work in the United States. He became my patient and we worked together, using cognitive behavior therapy including exposure and response prevention, a treatment you'll learn about in detail in the coming pages. Through much work, the young doctor was able to manage his fears so that obsessions no longer controlled his life. The experience was remarkable, especially watching his face and body language gradually change from gripping fear to hesitation to resignation and eventually pleasure at his accomplishment. It took a while longer for him to master the fears and for his automatic behaviors to return to normal, no longer restricting what he did and washing and cleaning extensively. I was hooked on this therapy method and have continued to find it useful for so many clients over the years. The behavioral treatments and newer cognitive ones really are effective for the vast majority of those who truly work at it.

What I learned in the course of my work with this client and many others after him was that OCD has many forms, but they all make sense. There is a logic to the symptoms, once one understands the misguided premise the person is following. In fact, the symptoms are predictable—the thoughts, feelings and behaviors follow rules. This makes OCD very responsive to the treatments that target the source of the problem.

This appealing and extremely useful book truly does demystify OCD. With clear language, many examples and frequently asked questions that are right on target, Dr. Carmin explains this seemingly complicated problem so it makes sense. The treatment strategies described here are strongly evidence based—they have been shown to work in repeated research studies with scores if not hundreds of patients. I wish you good speed in using the methods described in this book.

GAIL STEKETEE, PHD
Dean and Professor
Boston University School of Social Work

PREFACE

TWENTY YEARS AGO, when I was caught in the grip of obsessive-compulsive disorder, no one talked about OCD. Now, it's common to hear people say things like, "I'm a little OCD" or, "That's so OCD." Somehow it's become part of our culture's daily vocabulary, even though the vast majority of people have no idea what real OCD is like.

The reality of OCD is that it robs us of our most precious resources—time, energy, and self-confidence. Left untreated, the symptoms can worsen to the point where they take over our waking hours, leaving little room for the important things in life.

Obsessions and compulsions waste time. A lot of time. I accomplished nothing in the countless hours I spent stuck in loops of anxiety and rituals over the years, checking stove burners, door locks, alarm clocks, window screens, and many other things over and over. And not one second of it was ever fun. That's time I'll never get back.

Obsessions and compulsions squander energy. When I was anxious, I broke into a sweat, my heart raced, my stomach twisted in knots, and I felt like the world was closing in on me. As the list of things I checked grew longer and my checking rituals became increasingly elaborate, I fell into bed later and later at night. Then I repeated the checking in the morning before leaving for work—getting out of the house felt like a Herculean task every day. I arrived at work already tired, and by the time I got home in the evenings I felt used up.

Hiding OCD symptoms also requires an incredible amount of energy. Those of us who have it often become terrific actors: We're so busy trying to make sure other people don't notice the odd things we're doing that we actually come up with rituals to hide the rituals! I never wanted anyone to realize that I was checking something to the point of obsession. Take the anxiety that's at the heart of OCD and add the stress of trying to keep your symptoms a secret—it's draining beyond belief.

Obsessions and compulsions erode self-confidence. It's pretty hard to feel good about yourself when you think you're losing your mind. One of the most insidious things about OCD is that most of us who have it *know* that our thoughts and behaviors are irrational, but the anxiety is so intense that we feel powerless to make it all stop. No matter how accomplished we might be in other areas of our lives, feelings of shame and weakness drag us down.

The good news, however, is that there's also *another* reality of OCD—that the right kind of treatment can help most people with this disorder regain control of their lives. I'm a walking, talking example, and I hope that my own story, which runs throughout this book, will provide insights and comfort to those who are ready to make the journey to recovery.

If you have OCD, reading this book can mark your first step on that path. In clear and sympathetic language, Cheryl Carmin explains what OCD really is—and isn't—and how it's treated. You'll learn that OCD is a medical condition that causes your brain to function differently from that of someone who doesn't have the disorder. You'll discover that effective treatment can teach you how to manage your anxiety and change your life for the better. And the personal stories recounted here, including mine, will help reassure you that you are not alone in facing this devastating, but ultimately treatable, disorder.

Getting smart about OCD is important, but it's not enough. My greatest hope is that this book will motivate you to seek treatment from a qualified professional so you can get the relief you deserve.

If someone you care about has OCD, these pages will help you understand what causes your loved one's strange behavior, why it may be difficult to persuade that person to seek treatment, and what you can do facilitate the recovery process. Living with someone who has this disorder can be challenging, but I hope that what you learn from *Obsessive-Compulsive Disorder Demystified* will increase both your patience and your compassion.

ANNE COULTER
Consulting Editor
Former Board Member of OCD Chicago

INTRODUCTION

I HAVE SPECIALIZED in treating anxiety disorders, including OCD, for over twenty years and have not lost my fascination for these conditions or my admiration for those patients who choose to face the things that terrify them the most as they engage in the very hard work involved in recovery. I am writing for those individuals who are choosing the hard road of helping themselves by taking the first steps to recover or are using this book as a reference as they work with a therapist.

My introduction to cognitive behavior therapy (CBT) and working with anxiety disorder patients during my post-doctoral fellowship training was like coming home—I'd found my niche. I was drawn to this approach to psychotherapy because of its fundamentally pragmatic nature and the way it functions to constantly test our hypotheses about the possible causes of anxiety disorders.

In the past several years I've also benefited from training with some of the luminaries in the fields of cognitive therapy and cognitive behavior therapy. To those who are just now learning about anxiety disorders, let me say that CBT is a type of treatment that addresses both the cognitive and behavioral aspects of a disorder: In CBT, patients change their dysfunctional thought patterns and learn healthy new behaviors to reflect their new ways of thinking. It's the foremost treatment for OCD as well as the approach I practice in my clinic and in this book.

Over the course of my career I've dealt with a fairly broad range of patient populations and diagnoses. However, the majority of my career has been dedicated to working in anxiety disorder specialty clinics located in university medical center/medical school settings. It is in this area that I now have the unique opportunity to teach and supervise psychology graduate students and post-doctoral fellows as well as psychiatry residents, do research, run a clinic, and see patients. On some days wearing all of those hats is a juggling act, but it is always a rewarding one.

One of the most enjoyable aspects of working with people suffering from anxiety disorders and OCD is that no matter how severe their symptoms may be and how miserable the disorder makes their lives, anxiety patients do not seem to lose their sense of humor. And, they can get better. It is exceptionally rewarding to be able to tell someone who is desperate for help and calling our clinic that OCD is a treatable condition.

Yet I've found that the biggest challenge occurs when, after years or even decades of struggling with their condition, patients suddenly grasp that they actually *can* get better. I know it seems paradoxical—one would expect this realization to bring about a huge sigh of relief and a burst of motivation. For some of my patients it's just the opposite. They realize just how much of their life was robbed by OCD. They are at a loss as to how to fill up time no longer being spent undergoing the rituals that have been destroying their lives. They have lost friends and possibly alienated family members. They have been forced to leave their jobs or were fired—all because of their OCD. As they recover, they find they are facing a huge and often overwhelming void that once was filled by their obsessions and rituals. It's clearly an example of "Be careful what you wish for," because they are so unprepared for the consequences of recovery. Indeed, if treatment is to conclude successfully, the recovering OCD sufferer must be helped to deal with these broader life issues of career, relationships, and self-worth.

What I hope people glean from this book is a better sense of what OCD is at its most human level. It's easy to be entertained by how

OCD is depicted on TV or in the movies. But the media don't really portray the human cost. I have colleagues who refer to people with anxiety disorders, including OCD, as the "worried well." OCD patients are neither worried nor well. They are tortured by their intrusive obsessions and held captive by their rituals. Thus, above all, I want people to gain a sense of hope. OCD is a treatable condition, and readers of this book will learn not only how cognitive behavior therapy can help them get better but also how medication can play a supporting role during their treatment. This is a comprehensive guide to conquering OCD, and it is directed both to OCD sufferers and to the people who love them. People *do* get better and reclaim their lives. Recovery doesn't happen overnight and a considerable amount of work is involved, but it is entirely possible for people who suffer from this disorder to get their lives back on track.

It is my sincere hope and intention that this book will help in that endeavor.

CHERYL CARMIN, PH.D.
Professor and Director
Stress and Anxiety Disorders Clinic
University of Illinois at Chicago

ONE

OCD: It's No Laughing Matter

If all of your information about obsessive-compulsive disorder comes from movies and television shows or even literary classics (Lady Macbeth, for example, is constantly washing her hands), you've no doubt thought that people with OCD are either funny or downright bizarre. In a sense, it's fortunate that OCD is in the spotlight, as this provides an opportunity for people to learn about the disorder. But too much of the attention currently being paid to this condition shows OCD sufferers in an unrealistic, usually unflattering light.

Hollywood likes to play OCD for laughs, giving characters obvious symptoms—most often excessive cleansing habits and a fear of germs—and treating OCD-related rituals as if they were quirky personality traits. It's amusing to see someone opening a medicine cabinet to reveal dozens of bars of soap or wearing gloves to read a magazine, right?

But if you were to spend a day in my clinic, you would see how OCD tortures people who suffer from this anxiety disorder. For them, and for their families and friends, OCD is nothing to laugh at. Indeed, people with OCD live in fear that others may find out they are having disturbing, intrusive thoughts—or, worse, may think that they are crazy and should be locked up in an institution for the mentally ill.

Fictional characters seem to overcome their OCD relatively easily, and some even parlay it into a successful career. In *As Good as It Gets*, Jack Nicholson's character finds the love of a good woman, and his OCD symptoms begin to disappear. In *Matchstick Men*, Nicholas Cage's character gets relief from his OCD when he takes a placebo. And in the award-winning TV series *Monk*, the popular detective gets into comical predicaments and ends up catching the bad guys *because* he has OCD.

It would be wonderful if falling in love or taking a sugar pill could cure OCD or if OCD symptoms could be leveraged into greater success on the job. But the truth is, those plot lines are like fairy tales, and real-life OCD is more like a horror story. Neither I nor my colleagues have ever seen a movie or TV show that realistically portrayed the struggles we see in our practice. Our patients' stories are anything but entertaining.

What OCD Is and What It Is Not

OCD involves experiencing repetitive thoughts that range from annoying to extremely distressing and responding to those thoughts with similarly repetitive behaviors or thoughts—also called *rituals*. Some of my colleagues view OCD as a medical disorder caused by an imbalance of chemicals in the brain; others of us believe that a chemical imbalance may contribute to the disorder. But the jury is still very much out as to whether the behaviors associated with OCD are biologically based or learned and then reinforced over time. Given the large number of patients for whom there is no apparent genetic predisposition or whose disorder seems to have arisen in response to an ineffective attempt to manage anxiety-producing thoughts, many experts in the field lean toward a behaviorally based understanding of what causes and maintains OCD. Regardless of whether they believe the source is biological or learned, however, many OCD sufferers—though they know their obsessions and compulsions are irrational—cannot control their intrusive thoughts or the resulting rituals. Moreover, there are still many people who are unaware that effective treatments are available and thus don't seek help.

That's the short explanation of what OCD *is*. We may use the word "obsessive" to characterize perfectionists, stubborn people, workaholics, or bossy friends, but OCD is not a personality trait. In mild cases, OCD prevents people from living full and satisfying lives. In moderate to severe cases, careers, marriages, friendships, educational pursuits, self-confidence, and even the ability to experience joy are crippled or ruined.

If Hollywood were to show realistic portrayals of life with OCD, these are the kinds of scenarios we would see:

- A successful young attorney whose life is overwhelmed by her fears of contamination and by cleaning rituals that involve taking showers that last for hours. We'd watch her buy isopropyl alcohol, cleanser, and disinfectant by the case because she uses cleaning materials to sterilize her kitchen every day. We'd witness her quitting her job because she can no longer tolerate the anxiety she feels when she leaves her house and losing control over even some of the simplest areas of her life to the point where she stops functioning and has to be hospitalized.

- A man who doesn't fall asleep until 3:00 A.M. every night because he spends hours "evening up" things in his house—the fringe on his living room rug, the cans in his kitchen cupboard, the books in his bookcases, the hangers in his closet. We'd watch his family life disintegrate and his performance at work slip so far that he gets fired because he's perpetually anxious and exhausted.

- A bright teenager who constantly asks his teachers for reassurance that he has correctly understood his homework assignments and who then spends so much time writing and rewriting them until they "look right" that he rarely finishes them on time. We would watch him erase his writings so often that every page in his notebook is torn. His grades and his self-confidence soon plummet and he becomes increasingly isolated from his peers.

We came across a blog written by an anonymous OCD sufferer that illustrates some of the mental contortions the disorder can impose on a person. In an entry dated May 2008, the writer was evidently trying to find the correct spelling of "Asperger's syndrome," another disorder marked by restricted, repetitive behaviors: "I try to get online to check whether I should include the S. . . . I have to now go downstairs to check this out in a book. . . . This book has a peculiar smell so I will need to wash my hands after looking up the correct way of writing Asperger."

He went on in this way for an entire page, waffling between various spellings of the word "Asperger." "I am now ruminating if Asperger should be capitalized," he continued. "And now of course I have brain fog which is causing me to feel doubt all over again about the S so just to be sure I will check again." After checking two more times, and writing on and on about his doubts and recheckings, he finally leaves his computer in frustration. Given these kinds of contortions over a simple spelling, it's easy to see why OCD keeps people from moving forward.

CAN WE PREDICT WHEN OCD SYMPTOMS WILL APPEAR?

Some OCD patients cope with symptoms nearly everywhere they go, while others can predict their symptoms in just one or two situations. One person might be obsessed about avoiding silverware in restaurants, yet feel perfectly comfortable using forks and knives when eating at friends' homes. Another might hoard computers and other electronic equipment but give not a moment's thought to the idea of discarding newspapers, food containers, or other materials commonly associated with hoarding. A third OCD sufferer might "white-knuckle" her way through a day at school, avoiding embarrassing rituals around her friends, but experience an explosion of symptoms once she arrives at home.

OCD by the Numbers

Examples of such ruined lives are all around us. The medical community once thought that OCD affected only a handful of people, but with the vast improvement in definitions and diagnostic measures in recent decades, the incidence of OCD is now known to be quite extensive:

- Studies tell us that 6–9 million Americans, or 2–3 percent of the population, suffer from OCD.
- Those numbers translate to about one in forty adults and one in fifty school-aged children.

Given such statistics, most people probably know someone who is being challenged by OCD—but it's likely the person is suffering without treatment, is ashamed of the symptoms, and does not realize that he or she has a treatable disease.

In addition to its intense emotional impact, OCD takes a huge toll economically. One study ranks it among the top ten most burdensome medical and mental health conditions in the industrialized world. In 1990, OCD's direct costs to the U.S. economy were estimated at $2.1 billion, with indirect costs, such as low work productivity, adding over $6 billion to this amount. Further, OCD accounted for about 6 percent of the estimated cost of all psychiatric disorders. With diagnosis and treatment much more readily available since these tallies were done nearly two decades ago, you can imagine the real cost of OCD today.

The Therapist's View

Among mental health professionals in the United States, the accepted method for diagnosing OCD is based on the American Psychiatric Association's "official" definition of clinical OCD, published in the *Diagnostic and Statistical Manual of Mental Disorders, 4th Edition* (DSM-IV). This definition is technical, but it will give you a clear idea of the benchmarks a therapist would use in determining whether you have OCD. We've reprinted it here for your convenience.

Obsessive-Compulsive Disorder (Code 300.3)

A. Obsessions as defined by:

1. recurrent and persistent thoughts, impulses, or images that are experienced, at some time during the disturbance, as intrusive and inappropriate and that cause marked anxiety or distress.

2. the thoughts, impulses, or images are not simply excessive worries about real-life problems.

3. the person attempts to ignore or suppress such thoughts, impulses, or images, or to neutralize them with some other thought or action.

4. the person recognizes that the obsessional thoughts, impulses, or images are a product of his or her own mind (not imposed from without as in thought insertion).

Compulsions as defined by:

1. repetitive behaviors (e.g., hand washing, ordering, checking) or mental acts (e.g., praying, counting, repeating words silently) that the person feels driven to perform in response to an obsession, or according to rules that must be applied rigidly.

2. the behaviors or mental acts are aimed at preventing or reducing distress or preventing some dreaded event or situation; however, these behaviors or mental acts either are not connected in a realistic way with what they are designed to neutralize or are clearly excessive.

B. At some point during the course of the disorder, the person has recognized that the obsessions or compulsions are excessive or unreasonable. *Note:* This does not apply to children.

C. The obsessions or compulsions cause marked distress, are time consuming (take more than one hour a day), or significantly interfere with the person's normal routine, occupational (or academic) functioning, or usual social activities or relationships.

D. If another Axis I disorder [i.e., a separate clinical disorder; the examples listed include schizophrenia, Alzheimer's Disease, and drug addiction] is present, the content of the obsessions or compulsions is not restricted to it (e.g., preoccupation with food in the presence of an Eating Disorder; hair pulling in the presence of Trichotillomania; concern with appearance in the presence of Body Dysmorphic Disorder; preoccupation with drugs in the presence of a Substance Use Disorder; preoccupation with having a serious illness in the presence of Hypochondriasis; preoccupation with sexual urges or fantasies in the presence of a Paraphilia; or guilty ruminations in the presence of Major Depressive Disorder).

E. The disturbance is not due to the direct physiological effects of a substance (e.g., a drug of abuse, a medication) or a general medical condition.

OCD Is a Treatable Disease

Although OCD can ruin lives, what you need to know is that effective treatment is available. Treatment can help almost all OCD sufferers manage their disorder. One of the most satisfying aspects of my job as a clinician specializing in anxiety disorders, including OCD, is witnessing so many people getting so much better and often in a relatively short time span.

That said, several aspects of treating OCD can be profoundly frustrating. This disorder is hardly rare, yet few people with OCD understand that their symptoms are caused by a treatable condition. Consequently, they never seek help—or they wait, sometimes for decades, until their symptoms have damaged their lives and relationships.

PATIENTS WHO FEAR SUCCESS

For clinicians, one of the most exasperating situations in treating OCD is the patient who shows great progress in his treatment, then stops. Literally, some patients just stop treatment. It's because they fear success: Their OCD has been such a constant (though domineering and abusive) companion, they can't imagine living without it. They don't know what would replace the hours and hours they spend being preoccupied with their obsessions and compulsions, so success in conquering their OCD would leave a huge hole in their lives. This fear of success can defeat their treatment, and it happens more often than you might think. We do our best to incorporate some post-OCD support into their treatment. Our hope is that our patients will emerge with new goals and activities and be free of emotional dependence on their OCD rituals. We try to get them to a place where they are no longer afraid to leave their OCD behind.

It's also troubling that society still stigmatizes "mental" illness and treats it differently than "physical" illness. Indeed, this is another reason why so many people are reluctant to seek treatment for OCD. On top of all the anxiety they experience in living with the disorder, they're afraid of being labeled "crazy." Helping people to get over this hurdle is an additional goal of this book.

Unfortunately, some people with OCD have no access to clinicians with training and expertise in treating their condition. This is the case even in major metropolitan areas with more than one university medical center. Our patients and their families frequently tell us about their efforts to find a clinician and, in some cases, about the difficulty involved in getting a correct diagnosis or the complications that ensue when receiving treatment that was not appropriate for OCD. This book will provide you with some basic tools that will guide you through a self-help approach to dealing with OCD or that you can use in conjunction with working with a therapist.

If you have OCD, you can no more control the fact that you have it than you can control having high blood pressure—and, just like high blood pressure, OCD can be managed with the proper treatment. We hope this book empowers you to take charge of the disorder and go after the treatment that can make you feel better and give you back your life.

To the extent that she can be objective, Anne finds OCD to be an intriguing disease.* "With this disorder you can't trust your own senses, your thoughts run wild, and you can't stop thinking and doing things that you *know* are senseless," she said. "No matter how many times you tell yourself to stop, you can't. It's fascinating that the brain can work that way."

Fascinating, but not funny. There was nothing amusing about the hell that OCD created when she was in the throes of the disorder in her early to middle 20s. Getting out of the house was a monumental challenge every day. She would get up, make coffee, take a shower, and get dressed like any healthy person. But when it was time to leave the house she got stuck in a loop of recurring doubts—the obsessions—and performed long, involved checking rituals—the compulsions—in an attempt to ease the anxiety. And the loop repeated itself every night before she went to bed. The tormenting symptoms ate up hours each day.

For some reason, her OCD did not affect her very much at work, and she could hide the few symptoms that did emerge there. People in the office had no clue that she had OCD or any problem with anxiety. What some of Anne's co-workers did notice was that she was depressed. She was what the experts call "high functioning," even though she felt as though she was barely functioning at all.

Anne had graduated from the journalism school at Northwestern University and now held a very responsible job with a prestigious consulting firm. To the outside world, she was the picture of success. But in her private world, she lived a nightmare. At the time that she was at her worst, she found a book by Dr. Judith Rapoport, a leading authority on OCD and one of the first mental health professionals to devote her career to this disorder. In her book *The Boy Who Couldn't*

---

*Anne Coulter acted as a consultant for this book and her intimate knowledge of issues and feelings important to patients was enormously helpful. Her story and her identity are of course real. Many other stories and anecdotal examples also appear in the pages that follow and in those cases the reader should be aware that we have changed identifying features in order to protect privacy.

Stop Washing, Rapoport describes many of the patients she worked with: "They [OCD sufferers] might have found help earlier if they weren't so good at 'passing.' I know too many stories of public success and private hell; the ability to 'pass' now calls up my admiration and my alarm."

"Public success and private hell," Anne says, is the perfect description of her life when her OCD was strongest. The mere fact that someone's obsessions and compulsions are not visible does not mean the person is "fine." The brightest and most successful people—including children—can hide their OCD from the world and even those closest to them. Anne spent years keeping her symptoms a secret and trying unsuccessfully to just "stop" on her own.

But, she says, she was one of the lucky ones—lucky enough to find a social worker who identified her symptoms as OCD and referred her to a psychiatrist, who in turn was informed about the disorder, prescribed appropriate medication, and referred Anne to an anxiety treatment clinic for an intensive course of cognitive behavior therapy (CBT). That was a rare outcome back in 1990.

The medication helped her get through the CBT treatment program, but it was the CBT itself that gave Anne back her life. She still has OCD and always will, at least until a cure is discovered. The symptoms ebb and flow, particularly in times of high stress, but today, thanks to her treatment, they are manageable. And she knows she always can get a refresher course of treatment if she needs it. OCD is part of her, but it no longer rules her life.

Getting Help for OCD

Throughout this book, we will explore the path to recovery, beginning with the symptoms and causes of OCD. You will learn that there is no way to prevent OCD—*ever*—so if you didn't stop it from happening to you or a loved one, do not feel guilty!

You will learn enough about your OCD to know when to talk to a professional. The American Psychiatric Association recommends getting help when your symptoms cause significant discomfort or distress in your life, when they interfere with your ability to enjoy a normal work or home life, or if they cause you injury. You'll also learn how to find a therapist experienced in treating OCD and what to say when you meet with him or her. If you have a child who you think might have OCD, or someone else in your life exhibits the symptoms, you'll learn how to get help for them as well.

The prognosis for OCD is good once the disorder is treated. Neither medication nor CBT can completely "cure" OCD, but with proper treatment most people experience a significant decrease in symptoms. In short, people with OCD can learn how to manage the disorder so that it doesn't control their lives.

Frequently Asked Questions

Q: How likely is it that someone I know has OCD?
A: As noted above, studies indicate that 2–3 percent of American people—children as well as elderly, male and female—have OCD. That is, about one in fifty school-aged children and one in forty adults have the disorder. You may not observe people engaging in rituals, however, because OCD sufferers tend to be embarrassed by such symptoms and try to hide them.

Q: *I never heard of OCD until recently—is it a "new" disorder?*
A: Some forms of OCD were documented hundreds of years ago. Early religious texts mention symptoms that resemble scrupulosity, and several religious leaders of the 1600s and 1700s wrote about obsessive thoughts, advising readers not to fight their obsessions because doing so would only make them stronger.

Q: *My wife has an annoying habit of tapping her fingers on the table as she reads. She also bounces her right leg when she sits and talks to people. Can I tell her these habits are OCD symptoms, so she'll stop?*
A: You can tell your wife whatever you like, but her "nervous habits" don't indicate OCD. Such habits usually are mindless actions, whereas actual OCD compulsions, or rituals, are behaviors that are performed in order to ease anxiety caused by unwanted, intrusive obsessions.

Q: Do we know of any celebrities who have OCD?

A: Comedian Howie Mandel who, as of this writing, hosts the television show *Deal or No Deal*, has spoken many times about his OCD and contamination fears. (You'll notice that he doesn't shake hands either on the TV show or during interviews.) Marc Summers, who used to host a show on Nickelodeon, *Double Dare*, has done speaking engagements describing his OCD and how difficult it was to be covered in green slime as his hosting job required. He has also described the many hours he's spent making sure the fringe on his rugs was all lined up perfectly. And of course one of history's most famous OCD patients was tycoon Howard Hughes, whose symptoms were severe.

Q: How does OCD affect a person's intelligence?

A: It doesn't. People with OCD are as intelligent after their symptoms emerge as they were earlier in life. Sometimes, though, even smart people have very little insight into their OCD.

Q: If I don't have OCD, and don't know anyone with it, why should I care about it?

A: If you're a business owner, you'll be interested to know that OCD costs the U.S. economy more than $8 billion every year in missed work, treatment costs, insurance rates, and other direct and indirect costs. It accounts for about 6 percent of the cost of treating psychiatric disorders—and, as mentioned earlier, you probably *do* know someone with OCD. You just haven't observed their symptoms yet.

TWO

A Closer Look at the Most Common Obsessions and Compulsions

MOST PEOPLE WHO SUFFER from OCD experience both obsessions and compulsions. *Obsessions* are persistent, uncontrollable fears, worries, or doubts that a person finds intrusive, difficult to control, and disturbing. When they occur, they disrupt your train of thought and are extremely distracting. *Compulsions* are repetitive physical or mental actions, often called rituals, that you then perform in an effort to relieve the anxiety caused by the obsessions. Thus, the compulsions are an attempt to neutralize your anxiety-provoking obsessions—even though, over time, you realize that rituals do little to alleviate your discomfort. Instead, they begin to take over your life. For some people, OCD symptoms emerge gradually—during either their childhood or adult years—and worsen over time. For others, a specific event can trigger the sudden onset of symptoms.

Most people with OCD recognize, at least to some degree, that their thoughts and behaviors are unreasonable or excessive. Unfortunately, anxiety makes it quite difficult or impossible for them to break free of their time-consuming and exhausting rituals and mind-numbing obsessions. The problem is that the relief that comes from performing a ritual is only temporary. Compulsions actually end up reinforcing symptoms such that the more rituals you perform, the more intense your worrisome thoughts become, and the more difficult it is to resist engaging in compulsions in the future. The result is that the cycle of OCD behavior grows worse and worse, causing more and more distress, and taking up more and more time. This chapter provides a detailed overview of a wide range of obsessions and compulsions that are common to OCD.

Do You Need Professional Help?

If you're experiencing intrusive thoughts, performing unwanted repetitive behaviors, or both, then reading this chapter can help you decide whether those thoughts and behaviors might be related to OCD. If you find yourself engaging in obsessions and compulsions for more than an hour a day, if they significantly interfere with your normal activities, or if you find these experiences to be very distressing, you may want to meet with a mental health professional to find out whether your self-diagnosis is correct. If your OCD is causing you so much distress that you are becoming depressed and/or having thoughts of hurting yourself, or if you are using coping strategies such as alcohol or drugs to manage the anxiety, we strongly encourage you to contact a mental health professional.

Chapter 4 includes detailed information on how OCD is diagnosed. There you also will find checklists you can use to help determine whether you should seek professional help.

OCD Versus Other Compulsive Behaviors

One of the important distinctions we always make when educating people about the nature of OCD is that this disorder is very different from other types of compulsive behaviors they've heard of. Indeed, the terms "obsession" and "compulsion" are frequently misused.

There's No Such Thing as "Normal OCD"

One of the most fascinating things about obsessions and compulsions is that they can take virtually any form. Any troubling thought or repetitive behavior you might imagine can show up as an OCD symptom.

One client obsessed about the possibility that she would acquire her family members' unwanted attributes, such as being overweight or having a poor attitude. She compulsively pinched herself in an attempt to reduce these intrusive thoughts.

Another client tried to neutralize distressing thoughts related to intrusive sexual images involving her daughter and husband by repeating these color sequences out loud over and over: "red, silver, pink, and red" and "brown, black, brown, brown." She attempted to control this behavior in public by chewing gum and to hide her symptoms by feigning cellphone conversations, but she says that if she tries her distraction strategies without engaging in her rituals, her anxiety increases significantly until she eventually gives in and performs her color-sequence compulsion.

Yet another of our patients developed obsessions about contamination shortly after the birth of her first child. Her fears became so excessive that she would disinfect everything. Her family indulged her OCD until she started to spray Lysol on the family dog.

These bizarre thoughts and behaviors might be amusing to some people, especially if they don't know the deep anguish and shame they cause. When clients overcome such symptoms—especially when the behaviors seem bizarre, and they've been told by some uninformed professional that they cannot be helped—then their triumph over OCD is all the more gratifying.

Looking for Certainty

OCD is often described as "doubts running wild" or the "doubting disease." Doubt and uncertainty are part of human nature—we all struggle from time to time with life's unknowns. But for people with OCD, uncertainty causes uncontrollable anxiety.

The need to know something *"for sure"* takes on supreme importance for people with OCD. Yet their ability to *know* something that the rest of us take for granted—whether a door is locked or their hands are clean, for example—is broken. It's a cruel irony.

People with OCD perform compulsive rituals in an attempt to counteract obsessive fears. Many rituals follow logic—washing is intended to counteract germs, and checking a stove is intended to eliminate the possibility of a fire, for example. But other rituals make sense only to the person with OCD—repeating certain words to counteract "bad" thoughts or tapping the right and left thumbs the same number of times to make sure things are "even."

When someone first starts experiencing obsessive thoughts, performing a ritual may provide a feeling of relief or certainty for a short period. Checking two or three times to make sure the stove is off, for example, may initially give the person a sense of security. Inevitably, however, the obsessions keep returning, and easing the anxiety requires more and more counteracting rituals, performed for longer and longer periods of time. Soon that person may be checking the stove dozens of times or more. Eliminating doubt in life is impossible—and for people with OCD, there's always another "What if" question ("What if that burner is still on?") that has no answer.

A big part of the treatment for OCD is helping people learn to live with life's uncertainties. You'll find much more information on treatment in Chapters 6 and 7.

Common OCD Symptoms

The following list is based on our own and others' research, as well as on what we see in our clinical practice. These groupings of common symptoms are also generally accepted by OCD specialists.

- Contamination obsessions and cleaning compulsions
- Harm-related obsessions and checking compulsions

- Sexual and aggressive obsessions usually associated with avoidance-type compulsions
- Symmetry/ordering/perfectionism obsessions and compulsions
- Religious obsessions (scrupulosity)
- Hoarding-related obsessions and compulsions
- Other (symptoms that do not fit neatly into one of the more common groupings). Examples of other symptoms include reassurance-seeking and repeated questioning, both of which are particularly common in children.

While the vast differences among the various types of symptoms may make it hard to see them as being part of the same disorder, they all have two things in common: (1) The obsessive thoughts and compulsive behaviors feel uncontrollable and (2) the individuals involved desperately wish they could stop thinking what they're thinking and doing what they're doing.

Contamination Obsessions and Cleaning Compulsions

Obsessions about contamination may be the most common fear for people with OCD, and compulsive washing is undoubtedly the most familiar symptom—it's the one we usually see portrayed in movies and on television. But washing is just the tip of the iceberg for those with contamination obsessions.

Many people are familiar with the plight of Howard Hughes, the daring and flamboyant multimillionaire whose life unraveled completely because of his preoccupation with germs. The fear that started in childhood eventually led him to isolate himself from the world in dark rooms where windows and doors were sealed shut. Aides were required to hand him food and papers while wearing special protective gloves so that they wouldn't touch something Hughes had to touch. At the end of his life, Hughes was so incapacitated by his germ obsessions that he was unable to care for himself—he went unwashed, and his hair, beard, fingernails, and toenails grew to extremely unhealthy lengths.

OCD sufferers with contamination obsessions may fear becoming sick themselves, making others around them sick, or both. They may fear illness in general or specific diseases such as cancer, AIDS, and other sexually transmitted diseases, or even the flu. People with this form of OCD are plagued by troubling thoughts even when they're not performing cleaning and washing rituals. They agonize over the possibility that they accidentally touched something or someone and that germs might transfer to them. They worry that others might have touched something they have to touch and whether those people might be sick. They imagine germs and toxins "jumping" or "floating" through the air and onto them.

These are some of the symptoms most often associated with contamination obsessions and cleaning compulsions:

- Fear of body wastes or fluids, dirt, or germs
- Fear of environmental contaminants such as auto exhaust, smog, lead, or radiation
- Fear of anything sticky or greasy
- Fear of contact with animals (dead or alive) or with anyone or anything that appears dirty
- Fear of illness, hospitals, doctors or nurses, or even contamination associated with visiting an ill person or even viewing, from afar, a person who appears to be sick
- Excessive hand-washing, bathing, or disinfecting oneself or one's possessions
- Washing any item before bringing it into the house
- Using gloves, paper, or some other barrier instead of touching possibly contaminated objects or people directly

Sarah's story gives us a compelling picture of what it's like to live with contamination obsessions and compulsions. Hers is a classic example of sudden-onset OCD.

Sarah graduated first in her class at a prominent university, lived in Spain for several years, attended a top law school, and started working for a prestigious law firm in San Francisco. By all accounts, she was a happy and successful 28-year-old in the prime of her life.

One day she found a live mouse in her apartment. After she trapped it in a box an hour or so later, the mouse died. The fact that it died made her start thinking about contamination. If the mouse died, she thought, it must have had some sort of disease, and it must have spread that disease all over her apartment floor. Sarah suddenly felt extremely fearful and started scrubbing her floors with isopropyl alcohol and Lysol. Literally overnight, she found herself trapped in an unending loop of anxieties about germs and cleaning rituals.

Soon her mind started creating wider and wider circles of contamination. What if the mouse hadn't just been on the floor? What if it had run across the table? Then all the papers on the table would be contaminated, too. She started thinking in terms of "chains of contamination." If something she had touched was contaminated, then anything else she touched would also become contaminated. She had to keep track of what was contaminated and what wasn't or else clean everything to "be safe."

Within weeks, Sarah's anxiety about germs had spread far beyond the mouse situation. While walking down the street, she became afraid that the wind was blowing germs on her from garbage cans and trucks. Someone coughing near her conjured up images of germs flying at her, contaminating her body and her clothes. Getting to work took a long time because walking a block could take a half-hour. If she couldn't immediately identify spots on the sidewalk, she thought they were things that could contaminate her. She would circle around them, trying to figure out what they were or backtrack to see if she might have stepped on one. All the time she was trying to look normal in case she saw someone who knew her. People would stop and ask if they could help her find whatever she was looking for. By the time Sarah got to work every morning, she was drenched with sweat.

Somehow, she was able to keep up with her work at the law firm, but in her mind she was constantly tracking the day's contaminations. Every night when she got home, she went into full "decontamination mode." Here's how Sarah describes her rituals:

> Because I didn't want to have to wash the entire floor every night, I would step inside the door, take off my shoes, and put them in a corner. The bottoms of my feet were not contaminated because they had been inside my shoes, but the rest of my clothes were. I put them into the bag of contaminated clothes, but I had to be very careful putting them in so I wouldn't accidentally contaminate parts of the floor or furniture or the outside of the bag. (I didn't have a washer and dryer, and nothing could be worn twice without being washed, so my laundry bills were enormous.)
>
> Then I would carefully walk naked to the bathroom, making sure I touched nothing else along the way. Once in the shower, I started cleaning at the top of my body so that the contamination would wash down. Soap wasn't good enough—I used isopropyl alcohol to make sure I was killing the germs. If it was a particularly bad day, I would bring a bottle of Clorox into the shower with me and douse myself with bleach. A shower took at least an hour, sometimes more, and when I was finished I had to scrub the shower. Eventually, I had to go back to my shoes and wash the soles of them and the part of the floor they had been sitting on.

Her nightly rituals could last for six hours or more because if she made a "mistake"—touched something that she later decided was contaminated—she would have to start the entire decontamination process all over again. She went through cases of isopropyl alcohol and Lysol, and typically headed for bed as late as 2:00 or 3:00 in the morning, got up at 6:00 to go to work, and came home at night to repeat the exhausting rituals.

The mouse incident happened in October; by the following July, Sarah had quit her job and was mostly homebound because her OCD had become completely debilitating. Her parents flew to San Francisco and took her home to Chicago, where she was hospitalized by a prominent doctor who promised to "cure" her in three weeks with medication. She was still in the hospital two and a half years later.

OCD sufferers' definitions of what may be contaminated are virtually endless. Certain obsessions, like Sarah's, have some logic to them. A dead mouse, after all, could have a disease. Other common obsessions—saliva, blood, bodily secretions such as saliva or semen, pesticides, household cleaning products, lawn fertilizers, garbage cans, toilets, sewers, asbestos, lead paint, and spoiled food—also have some rational basis. These items *can* be dangerous if used inappropriately, but the OCD-related anxiety surrounding them tends to be greatly exaggerated and lacking in objectivity. Other fears may be less logical, such as a fear of certain odors or of anything sticky.

Some contamination obsessions have no connection whatsoever to anything logical. One of our clients was convinced that everyone with dark skin was contaminated. Other mental health professionals had chalked his fears up to racism, but extensive questioning revealed that he clearly was *not* a racist. He felt deep guilt about his obsessive fear of dark-skinned people because that fear was inconsistent with his beliefs, yet he couldn't control his obsessive thoughts or the washing rituals he performed both on his body and on things that came into contact with dark-skinned people in order to combat his anxiety.

Another case in which the contamination obsession had no rational connection to the washing compulsion is that of 14-year-old Max, who felt contaminated after being bullied at school. When his symptoms started, his only compulsion was to take a shower after being bullied; he reported that "cleansing" himself of the bullies' remarks relieved his anxiety. But over time, as the bullying continued, Max started avoiding the clothes that he wore on days he had been bullied because he thought they were contaminated. His avoidance of things he felt were contaminated spread to places (e.g., the living room, the dining room, the family cars) and objects (e.g., the blanket on the sofa he used when studying, his schoolbooks) that he alone perceived to be linked to the bullying experiences. His rituals expanded to include clearing his throat when he had a thought associated with bullying, as well as repeating activities (e.g., reading and rereading a sentence, getting dressed and undressed, or washing his hands multiple times) whenever he had a bullying-related thought.

Soon, Max refused to attend school, go on family outings, shower, or change his clothes.

Harm-Related Obsessions and Checking Compulsions

After contamination issues, checking may be the second most widespread OCD symptom. Checking very often becomes part of any OCD symptom—someone who washes compulsively may "check" to see if his hands are clean, and someone who has an obsessive need for symmetry may "check" to see if her books are lined up precisely—but here we're talking about rituals in which checking is the primary compulsion.

Checking is a normal part of life: From time to time, we all check to make sure we've done something. But most people are satisfied by checking once. And if they forget, they don't experience paralyzing anxiety or stop what they're doing to go back and check again. People with OCD don't forget, yet they go back to check over and over, maybe dozens of times, maybe hundreds of times. They not only feel compelled to check but usually feel they must perform the checking in a certain way. For example, the checking may take place internally, whereby the individual simply looks at something and tries to make a mental note, or it can involve an overt action, such as locking and relocking a door or flipping a light switch on and off repeatedly.

Checkers generally fear that harmful, negative, or embarrassing things might happen because they were "careless" or "made a mistake." They may worry about causing harm to themselves, to others, or to property. An intruder might break in, hurt loved ones, and steal possessions if they don't make sure the door is locked. The apartment building might burn down, killing some people and leaving others—including the OCD sufferer—homeless if they don't make sure the stove is off. The baby might die if they don't repeatedly make sure the car seat is buckled properly. These OCD sufferers feel a tremendous sense of responsibility and worry that such tragedies would be their fault.

In an effort to counteract their fears, people with checking compulsions try to control their environment by checking a wide range of items in an effort to keep things safe. As with other OCD symptoms, checkers are constantly trying to "be sure"—that the door is locked, the stove is off, the car seat is secure—so that no harm has been or will be caused by something they've done or not done. The persistent doubt inherent in OCD combines with the perceived likelihood of and responsibility for a catastrophe to create an unending loop of anxiety.

Common harming and checking symptoms include the following:

- Fear of harming others or yourself, either deliberately or by accident
- Excessively checking doors, windows, faucets, stoves, lights, or ashtrays
- Repeatedly going over your own words or thoughts to make sure they weren't offensive to anyone
- Repeatedly checking your own vital signs
- Repeatedly checking for hazards to adults or children

A common impetus for checking is the fear of having hit a pedestrian while driving in the car. People with this obsession go back over their routes again and again to make sure they haven't left an injured person lying in the road. A bump in the road or a pothole might trigger the checking; or there may be no incident at all, as when they see—out of the corner of their eye—a pedestrian sitting on a bench. For some checkers, hitting someone with the car and causing death or injury is the primary fear; for others, the fear revolves around being caught and punished for the crime of hit-and-run. Long after they've gotten out of their cars, they may listen to the radio and watch the local news to see if there's a report of a hit-and-run accident. Some OCD sufferers even call the police to see if anyone has reported this type of accident.

In other instances, people get stuck in unending loops of writing and rewriting things—from birthday cards to e-mails to shopping lists to reports at work. They obsess about the possibility that they misspelled or omitted a word, included a curse word, or made some other mistake and need to persistently recheck what they've written.

The types of things people feel compelled to check are virtually endless. As with other OCD symptoms, some compulsions have a basis in logic whereas others do not. We've had patients get stuck in loops of checking to make sure they haven't touched someone's crotch, that they don't "look homosexual," haven't sent a curse in an e-mail, accidentally allowed a pet animal to escape, and many other inexplicable thoughts.

ANNE COULTER'S CHECKING SYMPTOMS

When Anne's OCD symptoms first appeared, she was in her early 20s. Her rituals were very specific; most involved checking to make sure things were safe and secure, and the checking had to be performed in a certain way or it wouldn't "feel right" and she'd have to check all over again.

The kitchen was hardest to check because so many appliances generated heat and could cause fire if she wasn't "careful enough." She had to stand on a particular spot on the floor and start by checking the coffeemaker. That meant staring at the light to make sure it wasn't on, then repeating in her head "off, off, off" three times. Then she had to start at the coffeemaker's plug to be sure nothing was plugged in, and to silently repeat "nothing, nothing, nothing"—again, three times.

On her better days, Anne might check each appliance just a few times, but there were days when she checked each one dozens of times. If the toaster and coffee grinder were on the counter, she had to check them, too, in the same precise way.

Once everything on the counter "felt right," she could step over to another specific spot on the floor and check her gas stove from there. She had to stare at the switches for each of four burners and the oven, to make sure they all were in the "off" position. That meant looking at the word "off" on each switch, staring at the space in the middle of the "o," and silently repeating "off, off, off." Then she had to put her hand on each burner to make sure they all felt cool, over and over. The fact that she had performed the same rituals before going to bed the night before, and that she almost never used her stove before going to work, didn't matter.

Next, she had to stand in front of the back door, stare at the bottom lock to make sure it was in the locked position, and repeat in her head "locked, locked, locked." She went through the same ritual with the dead bolt, even though she could see the dead bolt was in place. She tried fooling herself by shutting her eyes and listening as she turned the lock, hoping that if she couldn't trust her eyes, maybe she could trust her hearing. It never worked—OCD made her doubt all of her senses.

And if she was distracted during her rituals by some random thought, or by a noise outside or the cat brushing up against her leg, she had to start all over again.

Those were just her kitchen rituals. She was compelled to do similar checking in every room of the house! When she finally was able to get "unstuck" and it felt as if things in the home were right, she could leave—but not before checking the front door lock, over and over and over.

Anne had checking rituals away from home, too. Walking down the street, she would think, "Are my keys really in my pocket?" She patted her pocket. A minute later she'd ask herself, "Are they still there?" and she'd pat again—until she reached her destination.

She often got stuck in an OCD loop in the car. Is the parking brake on? Is the sunroof closed? Are the windows up and the doors locked?

Before Anne knew anything about OCD, she thought she was losing her mind and it scared her. She remembers feeling like a freak. One of the worst parts, she says today, was the knowledge that her thoughts and actions were irrational. "If I had a dollar for every time I told myself to 'just stop it,'" she says, "I'd be wealthy beyond belief."

Sexual or Aggressive Obsessions

People with sexual or aggressive obsessions are particularly troubled by the upsetting nature of their thoughts and mental images, especially if they involve hurting other people. They may fear that they'll poison or stab someone, push someone in front of a speeding train, drown a baby, become a pedophile, give someone bad advice that leads to a catastrophe, engage in inappropriate or criminal sexual activity, fail to help someone in an imagined accident, and so on. Or they may have images of corpses or mutilated bodies stuck in their minds. Understandably, these thoughts cause deep distress. Moreover (and this complicates the situation even further), some of our patients have reported that family members and even mental health professionals have treated them as though they may act on their thoughts. (Mental health professionals have an ethical obligation to make sure that someone is not a danger to themselves or others and legally must report actual child abuse. This is why a professional will ask very careful questions in order to tease out whether these kinds of thoughts are OCD-related or an indication of some other disorder.)

Many individuals with sexual or aggressive obsessions think that simply having bad thoughts makes them bad people, that "normal" people don't have such gruesome or inappropriate thoughts, and that having these thoughts is the equivalent of actually carrying out the act. The belief that thinking it is the same as doing it is known as *thought-action fusion*. Of course, thoughts are simply products of the human imagination; they are not the same as actions. And the mere fact that a thought *feels* bad doesn't mean that it *is* bad or that you would *do* something bad. (For instance, writers like Stephen King conjure up all kinds of horrifying images, yet no one believes that he would act out his stories.)

Other OCD sufferers fear they'll harm themselves and go to great lengths to avoid handling sharp objects, walking near panes of glass, taking any kind of medication, or driving a car. They may worry excessively about acting on an undesired impulse, such as throwing themselves off a cliff or steering their cars into oncoming traffic.

Following are some common examples of sexual or aggressive obsessions and related compulsions:

- Obsessions about hurting yourself or others
- Recurring images of corpses or mutilated bodies

- Avoidance of objects, such as knives, scissors, and other sharp items that could cause injury
- Fears that you may have inappropriately touched a child when changing a diaper
- Fears about the possibility that you may be homosexual
- Fears that you may throw someone in front of a speeding train

One patient had intrusive thoughts and images about the possibility that she might kill young children by choking them. She feared she might impulsively grab their necks and strangle them before their parents could stop her. As a result, she avoided all children and sought constant reassurance from her husband—and even from her own child—that she had not strangled anyone.

Another of our patients had the morbid fear that he would hurt himself by impulsively poking out his eyes. He found this thought so terrifying that he refused to even touch anything that was sharp. His avoidance became so extreme that his wife had to cut his food and he would use only a spoon to eat.

Disturbing thoughts and images of a sexual nature are also extremely painful and humiliating for OCD sufferers. While having pleasurable fantasies is a normal part of being a sexual person, there is no enjoyment involved when the thoughts and images are repugnant and keep recurring. People with sexual obsessions may imagine having sex with members of their family, friends, strangers, or even animals. They may worry about having thoughts and feelings they consider to be unacceptable or immoral—a heterosexual person may obsess about the possibility of being homosexual or vice versa, or a married woman may obsess about being attracted to men other than her husband. They also may obsess about the possibility of sexually molesting someone—a man may have thoughts of raping women or an adult may have thoughts of molesting a child.

It's important to understand that the typical person with OCD would never follow through on his or her sexual obsessions and would not find any pleasure in the imagined behaviors. These sufferers believe that their thoughts are horrible and want to make them stop. And many fear that having the thoughts must mean they secretly want to act on them, which simply isn't true.

One client worried obsessively about appearing to be homosexual and constantly asked his wife if he "looked gay." Involving his wife in rituals placed significant stress on their relationship (indeed, this outcome is common in cases where people with OCD ensnare loved ones in their symptoms). He loved baseball but stopped watching games because the players' tight pants triggered sexual thoughts that he considered unacceptable. He also stopped wearing bright colors as well as certain pastel hues because he thought they could be construed as evidence of his sexual orientation; in short, he believed that specific colors might be perceived as "gay."

Perhaps the most devastating of the sexual obsessions involves intrusive thoughts about molesting a child. One of our patients was plagued by obsessions regarding whether she had picked up a child "right" or had done everything "right" in the process of changing a diaper; in other words, she was afraid she might have purposely touched the child's genitals with sexual intent. Of course, the difficulty here is that the client would have had to come in contact with the child's genitals in order to do a proper cleanup while changing a dirty diaper. During the moments when the anxiety attached to the obsessions was minimal, the client could rationally state that she had no sexual inclination toward the child and was simply doing the necessary cleanup or holding the child so he wouldn't fall. However, once her anxiety escalated, her fears and self-doubts became overwhelming.

As you can see from the foregoing examples, all of these obsessions have in common the theme of causing injury. The compulsions, though, fall into a variety of categories. Some people with sexual or aggressive obsessions will engage in checking, whereas others will ask for reassurance or avoid situations that trigger their harm-related fears.

Symmetry, Ordering, and Perfectionism Obsessions and Compulsions

Many OCD sufferers have a compulsive need to arrange things symmetrically or in some very particular order that makes sense only to them. They worry excessively about papers and books being aligned precisely, calculating numbers accurately, filling out forms correctly, or making their handwriting perfect. These people may spend hours arranging things "just so" and become very upset if anyone moves the items they've arranged. For some, the compulsions are intended to neutralize the fear that something "bad" may happen; for others, there is no feared consequence—they simply feel very anxious if things aren't "just right."

Consider the books in a bookcase, for example. There are any number of ways that someone with OCD might feel compelled to arrange them—by size (height or page count), color, subject, number (same number on each shelf), distance from the edge of the shelf, or some combination of these criteria. Virtually anything may be subject to symmetrical/ordering compulsions—the contents of desks, drawers, closets, and cupboards or the pictures on the wall or even how the clothing one wears is aligned. While most of us want clean clothes and a home where things are arranged so that we can find them easily, people with OCD take their symmetry and ordering compulsions to the extreme, becoming distressed whenever they are prevented from achieving their notion of what constitutes ideal symmetry or order.

A related symptom is the need to perform "evening-up" compulsions. Again, virtually anything is subject to this behavior. If a person bumps his left arm going through the doorway, he may feel the need to turn around, go through the door again, and bump his right arm. If he scratches one ear, he may have to scratch the other ear even though it doesn't itch. Shoelaces may have to be tied so they are exactly even.

Some individuals with OCD must have things done "perfectly." For example, their possessions must be placed in a particular manner. We have treated clients who would become enraged if a co-worker borrowed their stapler and didn't return it to precisely the right spot on their desk. Individuals with these rituals may spend excessive amounts of time adjusting items until they are precisely aligned, and the adjustments may be so minute that no one except the OCD sufferers themselves sees the difference. Students, whether in elementary school or college, may spend hours redoing their homework until it is perfect or simply procrastinate (i.e., avoid) because attempting to turn in something that is perfect is just too arduous and time consuming. In addition, they may reread excessively to ensure they have everything (literally) memorized so that they can achieve a 100 percent score on an exam. For some, the "just right" sensation is closely tied to perfectionism: It doesn't feel "just right" until it is perfect. As you will read in the example below, perfectionism is a theme that can permeate various forms of OCD. One of our more impressive experiences occurred during an evaluation of an OCD patient who, if he didn't state something perfectly or was interrupted in the process, would have to start all over again. When we finally added up all of the time spent evaluating him over the course of several days, the total came to seven hours. We were not surprised to find that his behavior had alienated his friends and family.

In clients with perfectionism, symmetry, or ordering obsessions and compulsions, the symptoms most often seen include the following:

- Keeping the home perfectly clean
- Keeping items such as clothing, knickknacks, kitchen utensils, and dishes in a specific order
- Keeping everything symmetrical and in order, from the fringe on a rug to one's own hair
- Avoiding perfectly arranged rooms because using them could make them disorderly
- Wearing only those clothes that are perfect or feel "just right"
- Repeating activities until they are done perfectly

Unlike those with other OCD symptoms, some of these sufferers do not have particular fears associated with their compulsive behavior. Whereas washers have anxiety about germs, for example, people who compulsively arrange things usually report simply that things "have to be this way" or have to feel "just right" or that things need to be perfect or at least perfect by their definition—otherwise, they feel acute anxiety.

While perfectionism, arranging, and evening up may sound like fairly harmless compulsions, these behaviors can be remarkably impairing. We've seen people in our clinic who are unable to accomplish *anything* because they spend so much time arranging and rearranging, evening up, or performing tasks in a "just so" way. One client of ours spent two hours arranging the items on his shelves before he could do a simple task. Another client was obsessed with putting her purse down in the "right way." She would lower it slowly, guiding it to precisely the right spot on the floor, and then put it down very gently. She repeated this action over and over until it felt just right. One of our school-age patients would go through the ritual of making sure all of his pencils were sharpened exactly the same way and were exactly the same length and could be perfectly lined up in his pencil case. It would take him hours of sharpening before he could sit down to actually begin his homework every night.

Avoidance is a very common OCD symptom: People simply try to stay away from things that trigger their onerous symptoms. Yet avoidance only heightens the disability that can accompany OCD, making it difficult or impossible to engage either in necessary activities, such as work, or in those activities they enjoy. Given that rituals can occupy hours, it's easy to appreciate just how disabling OCD can be if an activity most of us consider routine disrupts most of the day, every day, for months or even years.

Religious Obsessions

While stigma continues to surround OCD in general, some symptoms invoke deeper feelings of shame than others, particularly those that involve religious obsessions. Thought-action fusion—the belief that thinking it is the same as doing it (*"If I think I committed a sin, then I must have done it, or I might do it"*)—plays an especially strong role in these symptoms. You may recall our discussion of this belief in the section on sexual and aggressive obsessions. Everyone has intrusive thoughts, but OCD sufferers tend to believe that if they think it, then they could do it. And when the intrusive thoughts are about religion and the possibility of sin, many clients struggle because the issue of morality and what constitutes moral or ethical behavior is involved. People with these symptoms may be especially reluctant to seek treatment, out of fear of what people will think of them; in their minds, even thinking sinful thoughts is tantamount to having actually sinned and thereby being considered immoral by others.

Religious obsessions—often called *scrupulosity*—affect people of all faiths. Most people with this form of OCD worry about adhering in an exact way to their own religious traditions, but some are anxious about the nature of other religions. And while you might assume that everyone with this type of OCD is particularly devout, whatever their belief system, the truth is that even people who question whether God exists can suffer from scrupulosity. That said, people with particularly strict beliefs do tend to be more susceptible to religious obsessions, and their OCD seems to zero in on the concerns that plague them the most—fear of being condemned to hell or anxiety about selling their soul to the devil, for example.

Essentially, people suffering from scrupulosity try to control what they think, what they do, and even how they feel to make sure they're following the principles of their religion to the letter. They tend to worry about the following:

- Following religious rituals perfectly
- Having blasphemous thoughts or saying or hearing others say blasphemous things
- Having immoral/sinful thoughts or desires or being exposed to them
- Having committed immoral/sinful acts in the past
- Being punished by God for their thoughts, desires, or actions, many of which are normal aspects of life

People with scrupulosity often worry excessively about moral issues—whether they cheated someone, told a lie, or did the "wrong" thing. They may feel the need to pray repeatedly and/or pray in a certain way. They may feel the need to confess their perceived disobedience to a priest, rabbi, or pastor. Very often children with religious obsessions feel the need to confess to their parents about transgressions they believe they've committed.

As we mentioned earlier, the need to know something "for sure" is very important to people with OCD. One of the difficulties inherent in dealing with scrupulosity is the impossibility of achieving certainty when it comes to matters of a religious nature; after all, religion is based on faith, for which one of Merriam-Webster's definitions is "firm belief in something for which there is no proof." To complicate matters even further, much of what is related to religious beliefs is based on interpretation of the liturgy, creating even more uncertainty for OCD sufferers with scrupulosity obsessions, especially those who seek out numerous members of the clergy for their input.

One of our clients, a 16-year-old girl who had intrusive thoughts about God being mad at her if she didn't constantly follow the Golden Rule, prayed excessively in an effort to reduce her anxiety. Her definition of the "Golden Rule" consisted of dedicating her life to the well-being of others—clearly an excessive aim! She prayed every few minutes throughout the entire day.

Hoarding

"Hoarding" is defined as the compulsion to collect and save large quantities of things. This problem is seen in people with OCD, yet it's also a symptom of other psychiatric disorders. Most people who specialize in treating OCD regard hoarding as one of several "obsessive-compulsive spectrum disorders." (For more on these disorders, see Chapter 5.)

People who hoard have difficulty determining which things are truly necessary or useful. They're often heard saying things like, "I might need this in the future," "This is too good to throw away," and "This shouldn't go to waste." The obsession that most often drives hoarding behavior is the thought that if a particular item is thrown away it will be gone forever and that someday the person may need it or something connected to it. Rather than "risk" not having the item when it's needed, the person saves it. Many people who hoard seldom use or look at the items they save—they simply keep them "just in case." For others, the hoarded items are laden with great sentimental value and discarding them would be emotionally painful.

The most severe cases of hoarding often draw media attention. We've all seen news reports about people whose homes are filled literally from wall to wall and floor to ceiling with things that most people would describe as trash. The items may overflow from plastic bags, be contained in cardboard boxes, or spill from jumbled piles. The situation causes more than mere havoc; extreme hoarding can create health and fire hazards.

Hoarding symptoms most often seen include the following:

- Saving broken or useless items
- Excessively buying and keeping things—far more than you would reasonably expect to use in the near future
- Excessively saving newspapers, magazines, lists, and other items that contain information
- Being unable to throw things away because you might need them someday, or because they once were owned by a friend or family member
- "Collecting" items, including anything from toys to military paraphernalia to animals

Hoarding can cause extreme distress for family members, both emotionally and physically. They often feel they're living amidst chaos and have lost control of their surroundings. If they try to rearrange or clean out the clutter, they may incur the wrath of the person who suffers from hoarding symptoms. Family members, especially children, are often ashamed of the state of their home and embarrassed to have people see it. Hoarding can become a giant family secret that creates a zone of isolation. And, in the most severe cases, hoarding can make a home dangerous and virtually unlivable. In fact, we had a hoarding patient who lost his life in a house fire that resulted from excessive clutter.

The health risks are very real as well. While the majority of hoarders collect inanimate objects, our clients have included individuals who hoard animals. One person recently described by an animal sanctuary group had "collected" 800 cats who were living in squalor and were quite ill. The hoarder keeping the animals lived in similar conditions. Additional health risks associated with hoarding are incurred by the insects and vermin inhabiting the paper and clothing stacked in piles on the floor. A colleague of ours who is an expert on hoarding once described visiting a hoarder whose apartment walls were literally covered by cockroaches, to the point where it took him a moment to realize what was causing the walls to look like they were moving. We've even had patients who will hoard anything they have been in physical contact with, including uneaten food and bodily waste.

Items most commonly hoarded include newspapers and magazines, mail, books, empty boxes, old greeting cards, string, rubber bands, containers of all kinds, and lists. But OCD sufferers have been known to hoard almost anything. One woman who worried about things "going to waste" picked up items she found on the street. She would stop her car and fill it with anything she saw that might have some value, including trash, cans, old clothes or furniture placed by a Dumpster, and used newspapers and magazines. She collected enough junk to fill three trailers, one of which became so overloaded that it caught fire and burned to the ground.

But Is Hoarding a Symptom of OCD, or Something Else Entirely?

The experts are divided on this question. There is debate as to whether hoarding should be seen as an indicator of OCD, as an impulse control disorder on the OCD spectrum, or as a symptom of obsessive-compulsive personality disorder. (Again, see Chapter 5 for further discussion.)

While hoarding shares characteristics with other forms of OCD, it also differs in important ways. The compulsion to save things stems from the anxiety associated with getting rid of them, making it consistent with other OCD symptoms—an obsessive fear that leads to repetitive behavior. Yet, in contrast to those with other OCD symptoms,

people who hoard do not necessarily experience their fears or experience intrusive thoughts on a nearly constant basis. And whereas most
OCD sufferers experience more than one type of symptom—checking
and aggressive thoughts, for example—most hoarders do not experience others signs of OCD. In fact, OCD assessment research indicates
that symptoms related to hoarding tend to cluster together with little
overlap with other OCD symptoms.

Another reason why some mental health professionals believe that
hoarding may not be part of OCD is that medications effective in treating other OCD symptoms generally are not as effective in treating
people who hoard. On the other hand, cognitive behavior therapy appears to work with hoarders.

Given the strong anxiety involved in hoarding, we include the behavior as an OCD diagnosis. The urge to collect hoarded items that
many sufferers describe is functionally similar to an obsession, and
the hoarding behavior itself can be impairing and serve to reduce anxiety, much like other OCD symptoms.

Other Common Symptoms

A number of common OCD symptoms do not fall neatly into any
groupings. While they may seem very different from one another—
and from the other symptoms we've already covered—these compulsions are actually similar in that they are all intended to neutralize
the anxiety caused by a variety of obsessive thoughts.

- *Touching/tapping/rubbing.* Examples include the need to touch
  every parking meter while walking along the street, to always
  step through doorways with the same foot, to tap a pencil on
  the desk a certain number of times before beginning any task,
  and to rub one's hands against walls or other stimuli. There can
  be an overlap with symmetry behaviors in that some individuals with OCD have to touch something, such as a doorframe,
  with their left hand if they accidentally brushed against it with
  their right hand. A variation of this that's often seen in children

involves hopping: Some children with OCD have to hop a particular way or a specific number of times.

- *Counting/repeating.* Numbers, words and/or phrases, or even nonsense words or phrases may be repeated over and over, either out loud or silently, or they may be written and rewritten until a person has that "just right" feeling or until a specified number of repetitions are completed. Sometimes these rituals are related to a superstition—people perform them because they fear some consequence of not doing the rituals (e.g., "My mother will get sick").

- *Constant requests for reassurance.* Sometimes people with OCD feel a compulsive need to ask for reassurance to make sure they either understood something correctly (*"Are we supposed to answer the questions from Chapter 6 for tomorrow's homework?"*) or performed some task properly (*"Did I lock the front door when we left the house?"*). The person being asked for reassurance usually is a trusted figure—a spouse, parent, or teacher, for example—but sometimes complete strangers can be a source of reassurance as well. It's often important to differentiate whether this is a legitimate symptom of OCD or whether it is unrelated. Asking to have instructions repeated could be construed as OCD for the reasons described, but it is clearly not OCD if the individual has an undiagnosed hearing problem or refuses to wear his or her hearing aid! Note, too, that this compulsion, more than any other, involves the active participation of others and that family members may find themselves spending a great deal of time accommodating the OCD sufferer's repeated requests for reassurance. While continually reassuring someone with OCD may seem helpful, the act of reassurance actually reinforces the compulsive behavior. (For more on reassuring and accommodating people with OCD, see Chapter 10.)

- *Superstitions/special significances/lucky-unlucky things.* People may attach importance to virtually anything out of a belief that it is inherently "good" or "bad," and they may go to extreme lengths to avoid the "bad" things because of some feared consequence. They may obsess about dates (e.g., Friday the 13th), colors, clothing, or specific words or numbers, or they may feel the need to do things in a certain way (e.g., to always put on the left sock before the right sock). In some cases, the beliefs about what makes something good or bad are commonly held superstitions (e.g., the "bad" number 666 or the lucky number 7). In other cases, the significance is unique to the person with OCD. For one of our clients the number 2 had a negative connotation, yet she could not explain why 2 was "bad." For another, a bad thing had to be paired with a good thing, so if he thought about a bad number he had to immediately think about a good one.

- *Mental rituals.* Most of the compulsions we have described involve an observable behavior, such as washing or checking. Not all rituals involve a physical action, though. For some individuals with OCD, the compulsions take the form of mental rituals. These symptoms are, quite literally, all in one's head. As noted above, some people pair obsessions about a bad number with the compulsion of mentally reciting a good number. Mental rituals can also involve images or even nonsense syllables. But regardless of the form it takes, the mental activity is a ritual if its purpose is to neutralize anxiety. Examples of mental rituals would be repeating conversations in your mind, making mental maps of buildings or other places, memorizing meaningless information, or thinking numbers in certain sequences for no reason. There are some OCD sufferers who will tell us that they are "pure obsessionals." In other words, they don't think they are engaging in rituals. While this variation of OCD is possible, we have rarely if ever seen it occur. What we typically find is that the "pure obsessional" is actually engaging in mental rituals.

- *Avoidance.* Avoidance is a behavior that is most often associated with anxiety disorders other than obsessive-compulsive disorder. However, given the amount of distress that OCD can cause, it stands to reason that rather than spending hours and hours ritualizing, people find it easier simply to avoid anything that might trigger an obsession and the associated compulsion. Indeed, we have alluded to the role of avoidance in several of the descriptions of OCD symptoms noted earlier in this chapter. One extreme example of avoidance involved a patient with contamination obsessions. When she became contaminated, she would want to shower. However, it took twenty-three hours from the time she decided she needed to shower until the time she returned to her room after her shower was completed. It was far easier to avoid showering entirely than to engage in such a showering ordeal. We've also noted that avoidance is common among rituals associated with harming, sexual, and aggressive obsessions, but it can occur in virtually any form of OCD.

- *Compulsive slowness.* This OCD symptom is especially crippling because it can affect virtually every aspect of life and make completing almost any task extremely difficult. For some people, doing things slowly is related to the need to do things "just right," even if they cannot fully explain what that means. For others, operating at a slow speed is their way of ensuring that they do not accidentally lose something or harm someone through their actions. Someone who suffers from compulsive slowness might spend hours getting dressed each day, walk down the street at a snail's pace, or take weeks to choose the safest appliance for the kitchen. For still other OCD patients, slowness is an expression of their indecisiveness. When faced with a decision and the responsibility for that decision, they meticulously weigh the options. While this form of problem-solving can be very helpful, it takes the average person far less time than OCD sufferers. In many cases, it's because of their delay that someone else makes a decision or moves forward on a task, leaving the OCD sufferers feeling as though their concerns weren't given due consideration or regretting that, once again, a deadline was missed. For some OCD sufferers, indecisiveness is a result of their excessive concern over taking responsibility if their decision results in a negative outcome. For example, one of our patients agonized for months over the choice of the paint color for her dining room. She was afraid of being responsible for a "bad" decision if her family, friends, and neighbors didn't like the color. Compulsive slowness is often mistaken as a sign of other mental health problems, such as depression or even schizophrenia.

We had one client who was afraid that if she moved too quickly, she might slap, scratch, or otherwise hurt a loved one. She moved incredibly slowly in order to avoid coming into contact with—or even near—people and pets. If she did touch them, she would seek reassurance that she hadn't hurt them, or she would check the person or animal over and over again for cuts or marks.

JASON, A PERFECTIONIST AND A CHECKER

Twelve-year-old Jason had obsessions related to saying, writing, reading, and thinking about phrases "perfectly." His related compulsions included repeating phrases as well as rereading and rewriting until he felt "just right." He also had some checking behaviors (e.g., repeatedly checking doors and cabinets to make sure they were shut completely) and counting compulsions. In addition to his OCD symptoms, he felt depressed and hopeless, had trouble sleeping, and found it difficult to concentrate.

It all started at the beginning of seventh grade, when Jason—a straight-A student in his early years—began spending significant time rereading and rewriting assignments. Sometimes he would use up an entire class hour writing his name over and over because all the letters had to be "perfect" before he could move on. He also had extreme difficulty communicating with family members and others because of his need to repeat phrases over and over again until he said them "just right." For example, when saying "uh-huh," he would repeat the phrase up to a dozen times, using differing inflections.

Jason had played football for several years and enjoyed it, but he quit the team because he no longer could concentrate and perform during games. While standing on the sidelines he worried about having a "perfect" thought rather than paying attention to what was happening on the field.

For a time, Jason was able to keep his symptoms in check while at school, but they would erupt when he got home, causing him and his family great pain. His parents were extremely frustrated at not knowing how to help him when he was in obvious distress about obsessions or engaged in compulsions. They tried to comfort him during his "OCD episodes," but rather than feel better, he would get angry with them for interrupting his mental rituals.

Eventually, his OCD spiraled out of control to the point where he stopped attending public school and his parents had to turn to homebound schooling services. He not only withdrew from all social activities and avoided his friends after he left school but also resisted going to restaurants, malls, family gatherings, and church services because he worried about how he would handle his OCD thoughts in front of others.

When Doubts Run Wild

Everyone experiences doubt and uncertainty at some point. While these all-too-human feelings are no fun, for most of us they're only fleeting or temporary. But when they careen out of control and begin to intrude on everyday life and consume a great deal of time and energy, we have to believe that something more serious is going on.

Doubt is the fuel that keeps on feeding OCD, creating seemingly endless loops of obsessive thoughts followed by compulsive rituals. In our clinic, we've seen hundreds of clients with scores of different symptoms. While each of their individual experiences with OCD is unique, all of these experiences share two common traits: feelings of intense anxiety and the desire to make those feelings go away.

If you're looking for ways to alleviate your anxiety, the first step is to get a proper diagnosis.

Frequently Asked Questions

Q: *Do compulsive behaviors always indicate OCD?*
A: No, the disorders known as "impulse control disorders" also involve repetitive behaviors that are commonly, though not entirely accurately, termed compulsions. These include compulsive gambling, compulsive shopping, compulsive stealing, and drug addictions.

People with impulse control disorders are drawn to harmful activities. They may be troubled about these after the fact but, unlike OCD sufferers, they enjoy their compulsions while they are engaging in them. This is a confusing area even for some professionals. At the training workshops we've taught around the country, inevitably participants will ask about a patient they think has OCD. They will then describe someone who has a compulsive sexual behavior, for example. In this case, the behavior is positively reinforcing—the more rewarding the behavior is, the more the person wants to do it. By contrast, OCD patients *need* to perform their compulsions in order to ease their anxiety; they don't enjoy the hours they spend scrubbing, checking, tapping, counting, or other compulsions—the rituals are negatively reinforcing.

Not every compulsive behavior is a problem, either. Some people have rituals that don't interfere with their lives or cause them distress. We've all heard about professional athletes who have a pre-game ritual just as we may check to see if we turned off the coffeemaker before leaving the house. These rituals are benign. Unless the rituals spiral out of control causing interference and distress, they are not likely to meet criteria as OCD.

Q: *If a compulsion makes the OCD sufferer miserable, why doesn't she just stop doing it?*
A: Because doing the compulsive act relieves her irrational fear of the obsession. Checking door locks or stove dials for an hour before work each morning doesn't make sense to people who don't have

OCD—but people who have the disorder are easing their fears that if they *don't* check those things, the house may burn down or someone will break in and steal everything they own, ruining their families' lives.

Q: Does performing compulsions always ease anxiety?
A: For a very brief time, often at the onset of OCD, the compulsions may appear to relieve anxiety. Over time, they do not. If the OCD patient is a perfectionist and can't do the compulsive behavior absolutely perfectly or if he is in a hurry and can't check it for possible flaws, the compulsion actually could create anxiety, rather than alleviate it. Plus, as OCD symptoms take over a person's life, he comes to hate the disease and its hold on him, which creates more anxiety.

Q: Why did I develop my specific obsessions?
A: We think that most symptoms are related to the things that scare you the most, though sometimes those can be difficult to pinpoint. And it's not necessary to have had a traumatic or negative experience with that frightening idea in order for it to become an obsession; for example, you don't have to have been robbed or burglarized in order to be obsessed with locking your doors when you leave the house.

Q: I'm still confused by OCD and OCPD. What's the difference?
A: OCD is an anxiety disorder, whereas OCPD is a personality disorder. People with OCD are miserable with their symptoms—unwanted, intrusive thoughts and compulsive behaviors to ease the anxiety that those thoughts create—and desperately want to be rid of them, whereas people with OCPD will stubbornly hang on to their symptoms. In many cases, they like being perfectionists or inflexible and have no interest in changing, even if their symptoms eventually interfere in their lives. Also, people with OCPD do not have rituals. (See Chapter 5 for more information on this distinction.)

Q: If I check some items or activities two or three times, does that mean I have a "little bit of OCD"?

A: No—most people double-check certain things. Writers proofread their work, often more than once. Engineers check and recheck their calculations. Bank tellers count money two or three times before they hand it over to a customer. It's the way we do our jobs. Sometimes we may check more than once to see if we have pocketed our keys or turned off the coffeemaker. And we may even get annoyed about having to recheck things—but it doesn't really cause distress, take more than an hour a day, or interfere with our lives. Therefore, it's not OCD.

Q: I can't imagine living without the need to ease my anxiety, so I'm afraid that if I stop one compulsive behavior I'll just start up with another. Is there really help for me?

A: Yes—you certainly can triumph over your OCD! Years ago, psychiatrists and psychologists explored an idea they called "symptom substitution," which comes from Freudian and other psychoanalytically oriented therapies. However, while symptom substitution may be theoretically interesting, research has proven that it doesn't actually occur. Usually when someone is fearful that another symptom will appear, that symptom is already there—but because the main symptom is so overwhelming, the OCD sufferer pays less attention to the other one. With the development of research and our knowledge about which treatments work, clinicians are now treating OCD with CBT—and ERP—rather than with other forms of psychotherapy, which have proven less effective. CBT, or cognitive behavior therapy, is a process in which clients learn new, healthier thought patterns as replacements for the anxiety-causing thoughts of OCD; ERP, or exposure and response prevention, a form of CBT, teaches clients to stop responding to their obsessions with rituals by exposing them, little by little, to whatever they fear. So, if you now have more than one compulsion, you will have to eliminate all of them, one by one, with ERP. But there is no reason at all to believe that you will then substitute new rituals for the ones you just eliminated. You will read more about CBT and ERP throughout this book, particularly in Chapters 6 and 7.

THREE

The Biology of OCD: What You Need to Know

WHAT WE KNOW FOR CERTAIN, and what we want every person reading this to understand, is that *OCD is a treatable condition and for some people, it has a biological basis*. One of the earliest theories was that OCD is caused by guilt, but this was a time when psychoanalysts believed that OCD obsessions and compulsions were a Freudian defense—the patient's way of fighting urges to hurt his or her parents—and thus were rooted in some negative early experience. That belief never helped people understand OCD, nor did it result in an effective treatment. All it ever produced, really, were feelings of shame and remorse for the patients' families, who blamed themselves for "causing" the illness.

Those "old days" and old theories are over with now, and there are newer and more scientifically based explanations for what contributes to the development of OCD. By the time you finish reading this book, you'll understand that there are several explanations for how OCD develops—both biological and psychosocial—and all the myths you've heard will be laid to rest. You also will know much more about certain lifestyles and behaviors and how they contribute and relate to OCD.

It's always tempting, when we see someone behaving in an unusual way, to shrug it off as some "brain connection" gone awry. "Something doesn't connect in there," we might say.

But, in fact, what happens in OCD is very much like a disconnect inside the brain. The explanation of how it happens gets technical, so if you're the type of person who enjoys soaking up complicated, scientific details, you're going to love this chapter.

It Starts with the Nervous System

Our nervous system is made up of several components. Undoubtedly, the most important of these is the brain. Like other parts of our body, the brain is made up of cells, although in the brain and other parts of our nervous system the basic building block is the neuron, or nerve cell. Nerve cells are responsible for the way information is communicated both within the brain and between the brain and other parts of the body.

The brain itself is divided into sections, or lobes. When the brain is operating as it should, these sections are sending thousands of chemical messages to each other, every moment, at incredible speeds. The messages are instructions: They tell you when to eat, how to put one foot in front of the other, and when to turn the page in a book. They tell you how to breathe, talk, smile, kiss. They are responsible for your thoughts, your feelings, and your behaviors. All day long, these messages whiz by one another, like millions of tiny white lights crisscrossing inside your skull.

These millions of messages are carried along by chemical substances called *neurotransmitters*—liquid bridges that carry electrical impulses from one nerve cell to another. Have you ever soldered something? If you have, you know how the solder must be liquefied in order for it to connect two things. So picture two nerve cells in your brain, with the same sort of liquid bridge between them, enabling a message to zip across. That's what a neurotransmitter does.

Or, to picture it another way, think of a dish of water, and what happens when you put a few drops of dye or food coloring into the water. Very quickly, the dye migrates to all parts of the water. Messages between nerve cells travel in the same way, throughout the entire brain.

Researchers and clinicians who view OCD as a brain disorder, or a neurobiological condition, are very interested in what happens when certain messages are not delivered correctly. Somehow, communications break down between certain parts of the brain. We don't know what causes the neurotransmitters to stop doing their job properly, but we have some leads. These will be explored a bit later in the chapter.

Our experience at the Stress and Anxiety Disorders Clinic in Chicago is consistent with research that emphasizes the role of biological and/or psychosocial factors in the development of OCD. We see patterns within some families that demonstrate clear genetic origins of OCD, and we believe that some individuals inherit a genetic predisposition for OCD. A person could be living a tranquil, happy life, perhaps for decades, before OCD suddenly appears. It might be triggered by "strep" (a streptococcal infection) or by an event such as the one described in Chapter 2, when Sarah trapped the mouse in her apartment and her obsessions about contamination began taking over her life. Or, the OCD could show itself because of a mutant gene, with no influence from outside factors at all. Yet some people with a genetic predisposition never develop OCD, whereas others develop the disorder despite the absence of a family history or genetic link.

OCD and Your Brain

Many scientists consider OCD to be a brain disorder, and precisely *where* in the brain the breakdown happens can now be located. Using brain scanning or neuroimaging techniques such as positron emission transaxial tomography (PET) and functional magnetic resonance imaging (fMRI), researchers have found that in people with OCD, three specific sections of the brain function differently from the brains of people without the disorder. These three sections form a circuit, and each of the three "stops" on that circuit receives messages delivered by the aforementioned neurotransmitters continually, in an ever-repeating loop. Or at least that's how it's *supposed* to work when the neurotransmitters are functioning at their best and these three sections receive messages correctly.

A CAUTIONARY TALE

> A brief word to the wise: PET and fMRI are not the only methods that have been used to study the brain function of individuals with OCD. These techniques do, however, provide the strongest support for a brain-based model of OCD. It is also worth noting that not all studies consistently provide the same information. While it would be reassuring to think that the results of neurobiological studies form an exact science, they do not. And perhaps even more important, this is a growing area of research and new information is continuously being produced. What is true today may have evolved by tomorrow.

The most up-to-date neuroanatomical model of OCD involves both a direct and an indirect pathway including the cortico-striato-thalamic regions of the brain. This circuit begins with the orbitofrontal cortex, which is located in the front of the brain just above the eyes. The orbitofrontal cortex is crucial for decision-making as well as for our sensitivity to reward and punishment. If you think about how much difficulty some people with OCD have when it comes to making a decision such as to stop washing their hands, the relationship between the orbitofrontal cortex and OCD is understandable.

The second stop on the circuit is the striatum (sometimes referred to as the basal ganglia), which is located deeper in the brain. This area controls thoughts and sensations, and it may be implicated in "ancestral" behaviors such as grooming and checking. The striatum is also involved in executive function. Though not easy to define precisely, executive function typically includes making decisions, handling novel situations, troubleshooting or correcting errors, and overcoming the urge to respond in a habitual manner.

Inside the striatum is a small section called the caudate nucleus, the gatekeeper of our conscious behavior. In a brain that works normally, the caudate nucleus filters out weak and unnecessary thoughts and impulses, so that only the stronger, healthier ideas enter our awareness, ready for action or further thought. Serious thoughts, such as threats and other emergencies, are given top priority here. With regard to OCD, the caudate nucleus is thought to be involved with regulating worry. It also appears to serve as an information transfer point between the thalamus and orbitofrontal cortex.

The thalamus, the third stop on our brain circuit, is the shortstop that receives those high-priority messages from the caudate nucleus and whisks them on to the front area of the brain, including the orbital cortex. This action by the thalamus is a wake-up call to the front of the brain, a call to action: If a child runs in front of the car you're driving, or the phone rings late at night, it is the thalamus that tells you to slam on the brakes or wake up and answer the phone.

The cortico-striato-thalamic circuit is a beautifully orchestrated communication system. Unfortunately for people with OCD, the message delivery system malfunctions. The gate inside the caudate nucleus seems to jiggle loose and send more thoughts and sensations into the circuit than it should, including many that are inappropriate and would automatically be held back in a brain that's functioning normally. As a result, the thalamus becomes hyperactive and an incessant barrage of worry-related, intrusive thoughts begins to volley back and forth between the thalamus and orbitofrontal cortex. At that point, signals from the orbitofrontal cortex elevate the level of anxiety, leading to behaviors, or compulsions, that are meant to alleviate the problem. But, as you know, the compulsions fail to do their intended job.

If you've been diagnosed with OCD, you know what that experience is like: You feel overwhelmed. Your brain is telling you that you're late for work, yet you can't help but drive home again and check all the lights and all the stove burners, then clean all the knobs and cupboards, then clean yourself, then maybe check the burners again. You feel incredible distress at having to deal with all of these messages, so you consciously struggle to suppress the messages. But that doesn't work, either.

If you were to be given a PET scan during such an episode, the machine would indicate a jump in metabolic activity in your orbitofrontal cortex, the basal ganglia, and the caudate nucleus. Blood flow in these regions would also be increased. The inappropriate, persistent messages would crowd your brain, forcing their way into your awareness. Fighting to keep them suppressed would create even more anxiety.

Interestingly, researchers have found direct links between PET scan results and the severity of a patient's OCD symptoms. The more serious the obsessions and compulsions, the more dysfunction they find in this brain messaging circuit.

But there's good news as well: The relationship between biological action and OCD is just as clear *after* therapy has done its job. When effective treatment helps the person to calm and manage her symptoms, the chemical (metabolic) overactivity decreases as well. Treatment with medication and/or cognitive behavior therapy (CBT) affects the pattern of miscommunication within the brain circuit, allowing the brain's "instant messaging" system to begin working correctly.

Other neurological features besides the brain's messaging circuit are different as well. Magnetic resonance imaging (MRI) scans have shown that in people with OCD, a brain area called the globus pallidus (a part of the basal ganglia) is smaller than in other people tested, and the gray matter in a section important to brain networks, called the anterior cingulated gyrus, is increased. Children diagnosed with OCD have been found to have a larger thalamus than other children. And in adults with OCD, increased gray matter has been found in the left orbitfrontal cortex—an area responsible for some cognitive processes, such as decision-making. At least one study strongly suggests that such volume increases in gray matter density are due to the hyperfunctioning of the messaging circuit in the brains of people with OCD.

Serotonin and OCD

As scientists have worked over the years to discover what really causes OCD, they have considered a number of possible origins of this disorder. The most widely accepted of these was—and remains—the serotonergic theory.

Back in the late 1960s, before OCD was clearly identified, European doctors treated its symptoms with an antidepressant drug called clomipramine (which in the United States had the brand name of Anafranil). Clomipramine tamed some of the OCD symptoms because of its effect on two neurotransmitters, norepinephrine and serotonin.

Neurotransmitters such as norepinephrine and serotonin, you will recall, carry impulses between nerve cells (neurons) in the brain. Most of the time, our serotonin lives in little brain-rooms called vesicles, near the neurons' endings, where it stays until the neurons receive an impulse—some stimulus telling them to wake up and process a piece of information.

When that happens, the vesicles open their doors and release serotonin into gaps that separate the neurons. These gaps are called synaptic clefts, or synapses. Ideally, the serotonin flows across the nearest synaptic cleft and reaches specific serotonin receptors on the connecting neuron, much like climbers on Mt. Everest placing a ladder over a crevasse so they can safely cross it. Once the serotonin has bridged that synaptic gap, any remaining serotonin retreats back into the vesicle from whence it came, and waits for the next electrical nerve impulse to get it going again. That retreat of the serotonin is called "reuptake." The serotonin that has reached the adjacent neuron continues to be transmitted through the brain until its final destination is reached. As with all neurotransmitters, this is serotonin's mission in life: to enable the successful communication of information in the form of nerve impulses.

According to the serotonergic theory, in OCD the serotonin's timing is off. The problem is thought to lie in the reuptake process: Reuptake is premature, so the nerve impulse cannot execute its function the way it should. In other words, the serotonin is not in the synapse for a long enough period of time for the communication with the adjoining neuron to take place effectively. When this failed serotonin reuptake happens to many nerve cells at the same time, the brain malfunctions and OCD symptoms appear.

The serotonergic theory and the anatomical evidence described above provide the primary support for the idea that OCD is a biological disorder. But another finding is also relevant: When patients are treated with clomipramine for their OCD-related depression, their OCD symptoms diminish as well. Researchers already knew that clomipramine, or Anafranil, influenced serotonin by blocking premature reuptake in the brain, thereby making it easier for the serotonin to connect with receptors on the other side of the cleft.

Soon after the researchers noticed that Anafranil affected OCD-related depression, they found that the more Anafranil patients were given, the more their OCD symptoms improved. In the forty years since that discovery, other drugs that have a specific effect on serotonin have also been shown to relieve OCD symptoms. At the same time, researchers have discovered that drugs that act on other brain chemicals don't have the same effect. Owing to these clear findings, serotonin is now accepted as a key factor in managing OCD symptoms pharmacologically.

The drugs that have been most effective in treating OCD symptoms are those that affect serotonin. These drugs are called serotonin reuptake inhibitors, or SRIs. It's interesting to note, too, that although the neurons sensitive to serotonin's influence are found throughout the brain, those located in the frontal lobes and the basal ganglia are particularly susceptible.

Other Brain Chemicals That Affect OCD

Serotonin isn't the only neurotransmitter that has been implicated in the development of OCD symptoms. Dopamine is another one. An entirely different neurotransmitter found in the central nervous system, retina, and "sympathetic ganglia," dopamine helps regulate movement and emotions. When its levels are depleted, dopamine is believed to be a possible cause of Parkinson's disease and may be linked to the origins of OCD.

In addition, decreased levels of another chemical, N-acetyl-aspartate, which is a "neuronal marker," have been linked to more severe OCD symptoms. And choline, a substance derived from ammonia, may play a role in pediatric OCD. All of these chemicals need further study: Do neurotransmitters and other chemicals influence OCD symptoms, or do the symptoms change the brain? Which came first—an imbalance of chemicals in the brain or the disorder itself? And why does OCD usually emerge during a person's late teens or early 20s? Does it have something to do with the quantity and activity of such chemicals during those years? Or does the onset of OCD have more to do with the stress of growing up, along with the surges of brain chemicals, hormones, and other substances during that difficult time? Answering these and other questions, especially in regard to the brain chemicals we've already linked to OCD, will get us closer to the elusive cure; indeed, doing so is the focus of much ongoing research.

We should stress, too, that even when several contributing factors exist in your life, OCD will *not* develop unless your brain chemistry is set up for it. A lot of people who experience abuse or other childhood traumas or a series of stressful events never develop OCD.

It's a Family Affair

As clinicians treating OCD, we have often asked about other members of a family and whether they suffer from OCD or other mental health problems. In response, we've sometimes heard about a blood relative who is believed to have OCD—but, since gene mapping isn't yet commonly done, there has been relatively little definitive information to back up our clinical hunches. In 2003, however, scientists were finally able to confirm that OCD can have a hereditary component. In a collaborative study funded by the National Institutes of Health, researchers hit the scientific jackpot when they discovered not only a mutated serotonin transporter gene called hSERT in unrelated families with OCD but also, in some of the test subjects, a second OCD-related gene mutation. That second irregularity was linked to boosts in chemical brain activity as well as to severe symptoms.

This landmark study was the evidence we needed to confirm what we'd believed for years, that the link between OCD and heredity is real. The initial genetics project was followed in 2007 by a study conducted at Duke University Medical Center. Researchers found that genetically altered mice lacking the SAPAP3 gene spent more than three times as much time grooming themselves as did those with the gene. And in another compelling study, identical twins proved to be more than twice as likely to have OCD than fraternal twins, even if they were raised apart. Scientists also have observed, in many studies, the likelihood that children have about a one-in-four chance of being diagnosed with OCD if a close relative—that is, a parent or sibling—has the disorder.

A different study, one performed at Johns Hopkins University, showed half a dozen spots in the human genome that could be connected to OCD. More than 200 families were involved in this study, all had at least two siblings who had been diagnosed with OCD, and investigators found markers at six sites on five chromosomes that appeared more frequently than in families without OCD, or even in members of their own families who hadn't been diagnosed with OCD.

Yet another finding connecting genetics and OCD—in this case, from two separate studies—involves the isolation of a gene that regulates glutamate, a brain chemical that stimulates signals among neurons. When the brain experiences an overload of glutamate, it sends too many signals. (Aside from its implications for OCD, which strikes boys and girls at about the same rate, the glutamate gene seems to interact with a gene that has been implicated in the development of Tourette's syndrome. For more on the Tourette's/OCD connection, see Chapter 5.)

When all the genetic studies are collected and reviewed, it seems that even in a hereditary and biological sense, OCD makes its first appearances at different "points of entry" in the brain. For this reason, scientists sometimes refer to OCD as a "complex" genetic disorder, or they discuss it in terms of "segregation" in the brain—whereby different genes act together to produce one trait, or several sites on one gene together produce a tendency or disorder. In short, research has yet to pinpoint a single gene that "causes" OCD.

Other disorders related to OCD also appear to have hereditary qualities. We'll learn more about these "obsessive-compulsive spectrum disorders" in Chapter 5, but it's worth mentioning here that tic disorders, compulsive behaviors such as pathological skin-picking and nail-biting, and other anxiety disorders are likewise found more frequently among relatives than in the general population.

We have much to learn about OCD, and how and why it clusters in families. Genetics can make a profound contribution to the development of OCD—that much is certain. It's worth keeping in mind, though, that the presence of a genetic predisposition for an illness does not necessarily mean that the illness will develop. (Geneticists refer to this distinction in terms of genotype versus phenotype.) Indeed, there are other conditions—such as environmental factors or learning experiences—that can also be causal. So, trying to tease out the root cause of OCD can be frustrating, since all of these factors make their own unique contribution to the development of the disorder. Narrowing our investigations to identify which gene or genes are responsible, and which genetic, biological, or environmental characteristics create the possibility for OCD-related mutations to occur in genes in the first place, will occupy genetic researchers for a long time to come.

Factors That Contribute to OCD Development

When patients come into our clinic, we often discover a long list of biological, environmental, and medical factors in their backgrounds, all of which may have contributed to the development of their OCD symptoms. We also typically find that OCD occurs in concert with other disorders rather than in a vacuum. While this chapter has stressed the neurobiology and genetics of OCD, bear in mind that these biological models may be applicable in somewhat different ways in cases where OCD occurs in combination with other psychiatric conditions such as depression or substance abuse. (You'll find out more about dual diagnosis—comorbidity—in Chapter 5.)

In still other cases, a person's genetic or biological vulnerability to OCD may be triggered by a *combination* of biological and environmental factors crucial to the onset of OCD. Yet despite the variety of biological explanations for the disorder, there is no definitive medical test that can be used for diagnostic purposes. Our technology has not yet reached that level of sophistication. ·

Here are some of the factors most frequently seen in OCD development:

- *Substance abuse.* We know that some drugs, such as cocaine, affect the ability of certain neurotransmitters, such as serotonin and dopamine, to function effectively; however, we are not certain as to how the substance abuse itself triggers or enables OCD symptoms. A 1993 study performed at Johns Hopkins University did show an increased risk of OCD among adults who used cocaine and marijuana.

- *Stress-induced OCD symptoms.* Most researchers and clinicians would agree that stress can aggravate OCD symptoms. Indeed, excessive stress rooted in the problems of daily living—job pressures, finances, fatigue, illness, relationships, even premenstrual hormone shifts—is known to affect OCD symptoms. More specific studies of the stress of pregnancy and the post-partum period in relation to OCD, however, have found no clear connection, although more research in this area is needed. (Interestingly, in "normal" couples who participated in a research study focusing on the pregnancy and post-partum period, both husband and wife experienced a surprising increase in the number of intrusive, harm-related thoughts pertaining to their child.) Extremely stressful events, such as fighting in a war, can also trigger obsessions. Alternatively, the trauma may be relatively minor, as when Sarah caught the mouse and her contamination fears soon took over her life.

- *Habits and learning.* The obsessions associated with OCD—which, remember, are thoughts that cause intense anxiety and fear—can be suggested by any number of influences that we're exposed to every day. Some people develop fears of worldwide threats, such as AIDS or bird flu, while others adopt fears suggested by their families. An example of the latter would be a person who grew up during the Great Depression, or with parents from that era, who begins to engage in hoarding behaviors. Compulsions appear to be more closely associated with habits and upbringing than are obsessions. A child who has a genetic tendency toward OCD and whose parents expect perfection might develop symptoms that reflect this expectation, such as constant checking, redoing homework, and evening-up. Similar perfectionist compulsions are also seen in people with OCD who were raised in a chaotic environment.

Every day, we learn more about these kinds of associations, and every new piece of information builds on what we already know. But we need to gain even more understanding of OCD's genetic causes and environmental and biological influences, and learn more about its relationships to other conditions. The greater our knowledge regarding the ways in which various factors contribute to the development of OCD, the more effectively we will be able to diagnose and treat this disorder.

Frequently Asked Questions

Q: What's the difference between the causes of OCD and the things that contribute to it?
A: One theory is that OCD is caused by a chemical imbalance in the brain whereby neurotransmitters, most often serotonin, don't relay information properly and create a biologically based anxiety disorder. This imbalance may be genetic, or there may be some other explanation for why it has occurred. Contributing factors, on the other hand, are "triggers" such as overwhelming stress or a traumatic event (a family reunion, for instance, or seeing a dead mouse) that might bring on OCD symptoms.

Q: Are symptoms inherited, too?
A: No, there is no evidence that a parent and child with OCD will develop the same symptoms. For example, a mother with contamination issues may have a daughter with harming obsessions. Further, the fact that a parent has OCD doesn't guarantee that the child will inherit it. The child may develop a different anxiety disorder, or he may not have any problem with anxiety disorders whatsoever. However, it's normal for all kids to copy their parents' behaviors. A son's OCD symptoms might resemble his father's simply because he has learned the father's habits.

Q: If I have OCD and see my kid copying my rituals, how worried should I be?
A: In addition to copying parents' behaviors, children develop rituals as a "normal" part of growing up. Unless your children's rituals grow to the point where they begin to interfering in their lives, don't worry. If the rituals continue to grow, talk to an expert and get a diagnosis.

Q: Is a nervous or timid person more likely to develop OCD?
A: It's true that a person with little self-confidence might dwell on troubling thoughts and become anxious. But whether that anxiety develops into OCD depends on the brain chemistry specific to that person.

Q: Is there a single "OCD gene"?
A: Not exactly. But in a 2003 study by Norio Ozaki, M.D., of the National Institutes of Health, DNA samples did show a link between some neuropsychiatric disorders, including OCD, and a rare mutant gene. In addition, more severe symptoms were found in cases where the same gene had a second mutation.

Q: How "inherited" is OCD?
A: About 25 percent of people diagnosed with OCD have a family member also diagnosed with the disorder.

FOUR

A Step-by-Step Guide to Getting a Diagnosis

NOW THAT YOU recognize your behavior as possibly symptomatic of OCD, you need an accurate diagnosis. This chapter will tell you

- why a good diagnosis is essential,
- what you should do next,
- whom you should talk to,
- how to go about getting diagnosed,
- how long a good diagnosis should take, and
- what to expect along the way.

If you have or think you have OCD, the symptoms we will be describing are probably very familiar to you, and you most likely know firsthand the distress that struggling with obsessions, fears, doubts, and never-ending compulsions causes. Anxiety is your constant companion, bringing with it the checking, counting, repeating, cleaning, and touching behaviors that ultimately have taken over your life. If you suspect that a loved one has OCD, you now have more insight into what that person suffers, all day long, every day.

Still, OCD is difficult to diagnose because so many symptoms resemble ordinary behavior; we all straighten pictures on the wall and double-check door locks from time to time. This chapter will give you tools for self-assessment; many therapists, in fact, encourage prospective clients to examine their own behaviors before their initial appointment. However, if you do try to evaluate yourself, it's essential that you follow up with a professional.

As you already know, the extreme behaviors associated with OCD not only affect the person suffering from the disorder but also can intrude on relationships, which may then begin to erode. Concentrating on work or studies becomes impossible. Even getting *to* work or school is impossible when a person feels compelled to shower for hours, or scrub and disinfect entire rooms every day.

Are Your Symptoms Really OCD?

First, let's acknowledge that anyone can have a few symptoms that resemble OCD. In our clinic several years ago, we put together a self-report questionnaire that listed OCD symptoms. When we used it as a screening instrument in a study we were conducting in a primary-care medical practice, over 30 percent of the patients indicated that they had OCD. Yet the prevalence of OCD in the general population is only about 2 percent. Clearly people will overdiagnose themselves.

You may be curious as to why so many of these individuals reported that they believed they had OCD. If you ask people whether they fear being contaminated, most will respond "Yes." And if you ask what they would do if they thought they were contaminated, many people will understandably state that they would wash their hands or use a disinfectant or an antibacterial product—a reasonable reaction, especially during flu season. Similarly, many of us will check to see whether we have taken our keys, turned off the coffeemaker, and so forth. As you will read below, such thoughts and actions can be considered normal; whether a given behavior is instead OCD-related is a matter of both quantity and quality.

There are a lot of people whose symptoms are subclinical—meaning that they don't necessarily have a condition that needs to be treated. Only a professional who is experienced in evaluating and diagnosing OCD will be able to tell you definitively if you have OCD. However, if you are honest with yourself, you should be able to determine not only whether your symptoms are interfering with your life and/or causing you distress but also whether it's time to do something about it.

Many patients come to our clinic because they have been referred to us by a physician or a social worker or their therapist. However, we also have a lot of patients who simply took a hard look at their symptoms and behaviors, realized they needed help, and came to us on their own. A bit later in this chapter, you will see a questionnaire that you can take if you would rather do your own screening first, before seeing a professional. Neither approach is "better" than the other. Indeed, merely by reading this book you've taken an important first step toward finding out whether you or someone you love has OCD.

Many people who suffer from this disorder are very secretive about their condition because they recognize that what they are doing is different from the behaviors of other people and they fear they will be regarded as "crazy." But remember what we said earlier: People with OCD are not crazy, they simply have an anxiety disorder that is disrupting their lives. What's important is that they take the *next* step and get an accurate diagnosis now, because they're not going to get better until they do.

JESSIE'S DIAGNOSIS STORY

The path that brought Jessie to wellness is full of drama and heartbreak. The daughter of an alcoholic, abusive policeman, Jessie remembers, as a little girl, putting down towels in front of her as she slowly made her way from the bathtub to her bed, so she wouldn't get "dirty" after her bath.

As a teenager, she was terrified of roaches and flies. "I cleaned and scrubbed, wherever I had seen one crawl," she says. "I exhausted myself, performing this cleaning ritual." She married at 17 and had a daughter, whom she remembers bathing over and over, all evening long, until the bar of soap was just a sliver and the water had long ago grown cold.

If she dropped the soap, she had to start all over again. "That's what my girl remembers about her childhood," says Jessie, now in her 50s. "She remembers that I forced her to be cold. When I finally let her go to bed, I thought the blanket was dirty so I wouldn't give it to her."

Over the years, each of Jessie's OCD episodes were triggered by some traumatic event, such as her mother's death; it would appear for a few months, then subside until something upset her again. The theme always involved cleaning. A simple trip to the supermarket would mean an entire evening of scrubbing: The groceries, even the canned goods, had to be cleaned before she could put them away, the car had to be thoroughly cleaned because she had touched it with "dirty" hands, and then she had to bathe herself and her children, often into the early morning hours. If she or her children even touched a wall on the way to their beds, the bathing started again.

Jessie sought therapy several times. At one point, she checked herself into a "codependency treatment center" for three weeks, but while she learned a lot, her OCD went undiagnosed. Although most of the therapists and staff there recognized that Jessie was depressed, they didn't ask the questions that would have revealed Jessie's OCD.

Finally, just three years ago, Jessie's psychiatrist recognized her OCD symptoms and referred her to a clinic in Florida. After suffering with OCD symptoms for decades, Jessie had an accurate diagnosis and the door opened to what she describes as "extreme and difficult" outpatient treatment.

"Now, I am free," she says. "Please have hope, those of you who have OCD and want to get over it. You must go through more than you can imagine to do this, but it is worth it." Jessie still suffers from major depression, and she aches for her daughter, recently diagnosed with OCD. "Yet, I live my life better now without OCD," she says. "I am very blessed."

Evaluating Yourself for OCD

For most people with OCD who set out to evaluate themselves, the attempt at self-diagnosis occurs fairly early in the assessment process—in fact, it may be what has prompted you to read this book. We have numerous patients whose first step toward getting well was a self-evaluation. In fact, many people who are self-referred to our clinic searched the Internet for information about their symptoms and gave themselves a preliminary OCD diagnosis after recognizing their behaviors based on online information or assessment tools.

Self-assessment is a valid (and, some might say, necessary) first step toward a clinical diagnosis of your OCD—as long as you realize that *your diagnosis could be wrong.* I cannot emphasize strongly enough that, even if you diagnose your own OCD, it is *extremely important* to follow up by seeing an experienced professional.

As helpful as the information available on the Internet or in books may be, we've had many people come into the clinic and tell us they have panic disorder, for instance, when in actuality they have social anxiety disorder. Others will say they have a germ phobia when they really have OCD. And hoarders will come in and tell us that they don't understand why their families are so upset over their "collections"—which, it turns out, are occupying almost every square inch of space in their homes. Just as some people may overdiagnose themselves as having OCD, others may misdiagnose their problem. Part of a clinician's job, then, is to educate patients both about why the clinician has a different perspective on their self-diagnosis and about the details of the disorder and its treatment.

As we mentioned earlier, everyone experiences inappropriate thoughts or impulses from time to time. It is the rare person who honestly can say he or she has never straightened a picture frame before feeling comfortable leaving a room, or had an inappropriate sexual fantasy, or checked more than once to be sure they had locked a door or had their keys.

But these are normal thoughts that we shrug off. We indulge in our harmless, momentary, odd behaviors, calling them superstitions or quirks, and—most important—we don't spend more than a few seconds thinking about them or allow them to disrupt our lives.

In fact, it's often when the person's quality of life has taken a downturn that he or she seeks help and the OCD is finally diagnosed. Other times, family or co-workers who care about the person who is suffering let that person know they see how distressed the person is and that they want him or her to get the help they need. This process, in which seemingly harmless symptoms deteriorate into a clinical disorder, can happen in a few weeks or over a decade. In fact, a study funded by the National Institute of Mental Health and published in the February 2007 issue of *American Journal of Psychiatry* found that about half of adults with anxiety disorders, including OCD (along with panic disorder, post-traumatic stress disorder, generalized anxiety disorder, and various phobias), had displayed symptoms of some psychiatric illness before their 15th birthday.

There are categories of beliefs to which people with OCD typically are vulnerable. A group of expert researchers and clinical scientists known as the Obsessive-Compulsive Cognitions Working Group has identified six beliefs or appraisals that are common to individuals with OCD:

- *Overestimating the importance of thoughts.* Many individuals suffering from OCD believe that thinking something is just as bad as doing it. They fail to differentiate between thoughts and action. Further, they believe that any thought they have, especially one that triggers a negative reaction, must be important and is worthy of attention.

- *Beliefs about one's ability to control thoughts.* This appraisal involves OCD sufferers' ability to dismiss intrusive thoughts. In other words, they may hold beliefs about how much control they should and can have over their thoughts. Someone with OCD might believe, for example, that he should be able to not think about checking the coffeemaker. (As a challenge, try to not think about whether your own coffeemaker is on!)

- *Inflated responsibility.* Individuals with OCD may incorrectly gauge the degree to which they are responsible for their intrusive thoughts as well as for the catastrophic outcomes associated with the thoughts. For example, they may believe that if they have any influence at all over the occurrence of an event, they are completely responsible for preventing that event from happening. In this context, errors of omission are just as bad as errors of commission.

- *Intolerance of uncertainty.* Those suffering from OCD often experience difficulty making decisions or have to be absolutely sure before they can commit to a decision. A situation that is ambiguous creates undue, intolerable anxiety.

- *Overestimation of threat.* This belief domain comprises probability and severity errors. Specifically, people with OCD may incorrectly believe that it is very likely something disastrous will happen and that the consequences will be extreme.

- *Perfectionism.* For many people with OCD, there is a great need for everything to be perfect. Books may need to be perfectly aligned, every hair must be in place, or a score of less than 100 percent is akin to failing.

As you become more and more aware of your obsessions, do you recognize any of these belief domains appearing? You may find that your thoughts and beliefs are typically directed toward one of these areas or, alternatively, that more than one area fuels your beliefs. Either way, once you have determined what your pattern is, you may be able to look at what you're thinking more objectively and evaluate what it is that you're saying to yourself.

But because OCD shows itself in private obsessions, not to mention behaviors that virtually everyone has performed once or twice, it can be an extremely difficult disorder to diagnose—especially since most people with OCD are initially reticent to talk about their obsessions and rituals. OCD isn't like high cholesterol, which can be detected with a simple blood test. A doctor can't hear OCD through a stethoscope, see it on a blood pressure dial, or weigh it on a scale. This is what makes OCD difficult to diagnose, and why so many people live with its symptoms for years before they receive a diagnosis—and, finally, relief.

Thus you must persist. Without a good diagnosis, your symptoms won't be treated, and they won't go away. A clear case formulation—one that details exactly what form your disorder is taking, and what needs to happen in order to resolve it—is the first step toward putting together a comprehensive treatment plan. It's a kind of road map. As treatment progresses, you may take some detours or alternative routes. But at least you've found a place to start, which is necessary before you can get better.

We mainly see two types of patients—those who want to know everything they can about their OCD and confront it head-on, and those who want to hide from it. Many of those in the first group are the same ones who try to diagnose themselves before they see a doctor. If that sounds like you, take a close look at the questionnaire we've included in the Appendix at the end of this book. This questionnaire is a self-report version of the Yale-Brown Obsessive-Compulsive Scale (YBOCS). It's one of the most popular OCD evaluation tools and, indeed, the one we use in our clinic. Designed to help mental health professionals ascertain whether a person's anxiety symptoms might actually signal OCD, the YBOCS also can serve as a handy, straightforward self-evaluation checklist if you suspect OCD in yourself or someone you know.

Keep in mind that a high score on this questionnaire does not necessarily mean you have OCD. Only an evaluation by a mental health professional can give you that firm diagnosis. Just answer the questions as honestly and accurately as you can, and if the answers point to possible OCD, you should make an appointment to talk with a professional about your symptoms and what they might mean—and take your YBOCS answers with you to that first appointment.

JONATHAN'S DIAGNOSIS STORY

As a college student, Jonathan's harming obsessions so frightened him that he dreaded coming home for visits. "The first was at Thanksgiving, 1979," he says. "I had these horrifying fears that something was wrong, something bad was going to happen." Within a day, his anxiety became a fear that he would stab someone. He sought help from the counseling service at the university, but, he says, "they didn't know what I was talking about." No one seemed able to help Jonathan with his obsessions and he didn't share his fears with anyone he knew, not even his wife.

The obsession always was triggered by a big family event. "I'd think, 'Oh, no, I hope I don't obsess about stabbing people during the party'." He began avoiding anything that suggested death: He refused to drive past funeral homes or to watch movies that included people getting stabbed. For fourteen years Jonathan went undiagnosed, living as normally as possible. "It's as if I would go on a two-week OCD binge from time to time," he says. "For a couple of weeks I would be crippled by my obsessions; I couldn't get the images of stabbing people out of my mind. Then, after two weeks, the obsessions would float away and I'd be fine again for a while."

Meanwhile, Jonathan developed compulsive behaviors, especially checking rituals at bedtime—checking doors, checking the stove, checking that the kitchen knives were safely put away, locking doors, checking locks again. These rituals weren't terribly time-consuming, but he had to do them. It wasn't until his daughter was born in 1993 that he knew he had to get help. "I fell apart," he remembers. "I couldn't stop worrying—What if I stabbed her in crib?"

He made an appointment with a psychiatrist who said, "I've heard of this—I think you might have OCD." She referred him to another clinician who led a support group of OCD patients, an experience Jonathan describes as an epiphany. "I thought, 'My God, there are people just like me.'" For the rest of the year, Jonathan researched OCD and talked to other doctors, searching for the best treatment possible. He settled on an outpatient program.

After so many years of keeping his disorder a secret, Jonathan's outcome is a happy one: Because he finally received an accurate diagnosis, it took just three sessions with the OCD program before he had all the tools he needed to manage his obsessions and compulsions. Having grasped the basic principles for treating his OCD, he could now work with his therapist over the next few months in an aggressive program of exposure and response prevention (ERP) to resolve his symptoms and move on with his life.

Now . . . Get a Diagnosis

Most of our patients with OCD symptoms know something is "wrong" before they come to our clinic. Because you're reading this book, you have a head start: Many patients with OCD don't mention all of their symptoms when they first see a doctor—in some cases, because they don't realize that some of their behaviors *are* symptoms and, in others, because they are so fearful of what their symptoms may mean. For example, someone who experiences intrusive thoughts about inappropriately touching a child may fear that he is a pedophile. That thought is understandably distressing.

We learned from Jonathan's story that he kept his OCD symptoms a secret for years, even from his own wife, because his harming obsessions were so upsetting. But, undoubtedly, he was also concerned that if he told others, they might think he was capable of stabbing someone—even his own child. Among our patients we see a lot of secrecy, which points to another real obstacle to an accurate OCD diagnosis—concern over the consequences of disclosing the content of obsessions.

It's difficult to measure, but we think embarrassment stands out as one of the biggest barriers to effective treatment. You may have felt this about your own symptoms; indeed, many people are ashamed of their obsessions and compulsions, and they spend months or years trying to keep them hidden from their families, friends, colleagues, and even their doctors. In fact, convincing readers to move past the stigma and get help for their problem was one of our chief motivations for writing this book.

Just remember: OCD is an anxiety disorder and it is treatable. It doesn't mean you are crazy or that you will act on your intrusive thoughts no matter how extreme they may seem to be. By definition, what differentiates OCD from other psychiatric conditions is that people with OCD are distressed by their obsessions. The technical term is that their obsessions are "ego-dystonic." What's crucial is that you receive an accurate diagnosis; once you do that, your OCD will be as treatable as a broken leg.

There's nothing mysterious about getting a good diagnosis. Below you'll find some questions and answers to serve as your guide.

Whom Should I Call?

There is no "right" way to find a trained professional for your OCD diagnosis. If you have a family doctor, she can refer you to a specialist. Or, you can call a psychiatrist or other mental health professional.

We have personally seen many patients whose first call was to an OCD-related organization, such as the Association of Behavioral and Cognitive Therapies, the Anxiety Disorders Association of America, or the Obsessive Compulsive Foundation. Many specialized professional organizations such as these have listings of professionals with expertise in treating OCD. Other patients simply "Google" OCD and their city, and find clinics and clinicians that way.

Chapter 12 of this book provides a lengthy (though by no means complete) list of resources that will give you a host of options for finding the right doctor for you. One factor to keep in mind is your personal health insurance: Some insurance companies require that the primary-care physician make the referral in order for treatment to be covered, others insist on authorizing the treatment themselves, and still others require that you see a professional covered by your plan. Read your policy carefully or call your insurance company before you make an appointment.

How Quickly Can I Get a Diagnosis?

A clinician who's experienced in diagnosing and treating OCD might be able to get a reasonably accurate picture in as little as fifteen minutes. Indeed, someone experienced in treating anxiety disorders knows *exactly* what questions to ask—and this is the strongest rationale we can give for seeing a specialist. Bear in mind, however, that a more thorough evaluation, including a case formulation, will take at least one hour.

Many OCD specialists also use some form of structured clinical interview, which helps to clarify the full range of diagnostic possibilities, although this is likelier to be the case at teaching hospitals and specialty anxiety clinics than in other more general mental health settings. The use of a structured, diagnostic clinical interview as part of the evaluation is extremely helpful in speeding up the diagnostic process, but it may mean that the initial evaluation takes longer than an hour.

Despite the popularity of OCD as a topic of movies and television programs, we still run into mental health professionals who have very little experience with diagnosing anxiety disorders. The majority of such professionals, including psychiatrists, psychologists, social workers, and counselors, have very limited training in systematically diagnosing and treating anxiety orders in general and OCD in particular. If you think you have OCD based on some of the information we're providing in this book, and you see a clinician who instead focuses on something like a comorbid depression—that is, depression that coexists alongside OCD (see Chapter 5)—this is someone who most likely hasn't had a great deal of experience treating OCD or doesn't recognize what it is.

What Should I Ask the Clinician?

When people call our clinic, we ask them to provide us with some background as to what they think is going on. If they suspect they are suffering from OCD because they have taken the YBOCS or have read material about OCD, that's helpful for us to know. Sometimes, the information that people have read is extremely beneficial; at other times, we need to be prepared to correct some of the misinformation that, unfortunately, is also available.

Beyond that, patients need to ask the following questions:

- How long have the professional staff been treating OCD? (Obviously, longer is better. Our own staff have anywhere from two to almost twenty years of experience.)

- What background and training do the staff have? (Training resulting from having completed a specialized post-doctoral fellowship in anxiety disorders would be ideal. However, field placements, internships, and rotations in anxiety and OCD treatment are more likely. Some mental health professionals receive training through Behavior Therapy Institutes offered by the Obsessive Compulsive Foundation. But, above all, what you need to find out is whether the professionals received supervised training rather than simply having taken a class or workshop that didn't involve supervision.)

- Do the staff use cognitive behavior therapy in treating OCD? (*Best answer: Yes.*)

- Do the staff use exposure and response prevention in treating OCD? (ERP is discussed in detail in Chapters 6 and 7.) (*Best answer: Yes.*)

- Do the staff use medications in treating OCD? (Medications as a form of treatment are generally available through psychiatrists. However, not all patients want to take medication, so this will be an individual decision. Your therapist and psychiatrist should be able to work collaboratively, with one providing ERP and the other providing medication management.)

A word of caution: If you plan on contacting a clinic rather than an individual practitioner, your initial call may be taken by a receptionist or intake worker who is not a clinician. And this person may not have the answers to your questions. It is perfectly reasonable to ask to have your call returned by one of the professional staff who treats OCD *before* you agree to be seen for an evaluation. If coming in for an evaluation means you will have to travel a considerable distance, keep in mind that most of us who work in this specialty area know the other people who are specialists and, whenever possible, would be happy to help you find someone with the necessary expertise who is closer to your community.

What Else Can I Expect Along the Way to an Accurate Diagnosis?

1. You should expect that the clinician you are seeing is open to being asked about his or her training and experience, without getting defensive.

2. You should expect that the clinician will *not* describe himself or herself as "eclectic" or "integrative" or "prescriptive." Those adjectives all mean the clinician does not primarily use CBT and ERP (a form of CBT), which is the therapy of choice for treating OCD.

3. For treatment programs such as the one we provide at our clinic, you should expect to fill out a packet of medical and personal forms prior to scheduling an appointment.

4. You should expect to make the call to schedule the appointment yourself; most professionals want to speak with the patient and not a family member. This is particularly true in the case of OCD, as the family may be more eager than the person with OCD to get the person treated.

5. You shouldn't be surprised if the person conducting the evaluation or diagnostic interview is not the clinician you will see for therapy. At some clinics, the initial interview is conducted by an intake clinician; alternatively, that role may rotate among the staff. The results of the evaluation are then discussed among the staff in a team meeting, at which point you are assigned to a clinician. The decision as to which clinician this will be may depend on whether you need medication and ERP or just ERP, how often you need to be seen, when you and a staff person are available to meet, and so on.

6. If you want to meet with a doctor who has a national reputation, expect to be put on a waiting list or to be told that the doctor isn't accepting new patients. The more renowned the doctor, the more likely his or her caseload will be full. If that doctor wants to refer you to another clinician in his group, ask if the new doctor is trained in CBT and ERP. At our clinic, all of the staff are CBT-trained and experienced. They wouldn't be working here if they weren't.

7. You should expect to be treated with respect, even by receptionists and other support staff.

8. You should expect to be brief in those first phone calls; it's your responsibility to keep the conversation reasonably short and to the point, and to not monopolize staff time. We are happy to do what we can to educate and be compassionate, and we realize that this may be the first time you are talking to someone who really understands what you are saying. However, we have busy schedules and may need to end a phone call sooner than you would like.

9. You should expect that a clinician will never be surprised to hear about extreme symptoms—if the clinician is surprised, their reaction may indicate a lack of experience. I can't tell you how many times a patient has asked me, "Isn't this the weirdest thing you've ever heard?" My response is generally, "You're not even close."

10. If you are contacting a university teaching hospital, do not be surprised if you are scheduled to see a trainee. This does not mean you are getting second-rate care. Many of us who are faculty members at teaching hospitals are responsible for training and closely supervising psychiatry residents and psychology interns. It is reasonable to ask who is providing the supervision if you are seeing a trainee.

SARAH'S DIAGNOSIS STORY

Sarah, whose story you first read in Chapter 2, lost years of normal living because she initially didn't receive an accurate diagnosis. Looking back on the years when her OCD went untreated, Sarah now believes her illness was, in her words, "very, very severe."

Sarah's OCD, you may recall, was triggered when she saw a mouse in her apartment. Almost immediately after she caught the creature, her contamination obsessions began.

Sarah was no stranger to therapy; her grandfather had studied with Freud and she had undergone analysis in college. She was living in San Francisco and had recently graduated from law school and launched her own practice. "But here was my life," she says. "I got up at 6:00 A.M. because there was extra cleaning to do. It took me an hour to get to work because I had to retrace my steps; I was afraid of stepping on blood. When I got home, I had to clean; I went through gallons of cleaning products."

Back in her hometown of Chicago, Sarah's sister and parents were doing all the research they could, but in the 1980s, she says, "Nobody was talking about OCD. We thought I had a phobia of germs."

As her OCD symptoms progressed, she couldn't leave her apartment or care for herself. She found a doctor at Stanford who was treating phobias, but she was too sick to get to his office. Finally, her parents had to travel from Chicago and take her home with them. Still, it would be a long time before Sarah found the help she needed.

She took a long detour after reading a story in the newspaper about a high-profile Chicago businessman who was successfully treated for depression. She called that man's doctor and was told, "I'll cure you with drugs within three weeks."

"I was suicidal by then," Sarah recalls, "and I was ready to try anything." She was admitted to the hospital for drug therapy and given antidepressants. Still, no one was using the term "OCD."

Sarah's "three weeks" of hospitalization became an astounding twenty months, during which time she gained eighty pounds, "and the drugs didn't help me at all." Then, out of the blue, her sister in Washington, D.C., met someone at a brunch whose sister had been diagnosed with OCD. That woman had been treated by Edna B. Foa, Ph.D., a psychologist who was pioneering the treatment of OCD at Eastern Pennsylvania Psychiatric Institute. Dr. Foa was using a method called "exposure and response prevention" (which, as noted above, you will learn more about in Chapters 6 and 7), and Sarah's sisters flew with her to Philadelphia to meet with Dr. Foa. (Dr. Foa is now a professor of Clinical Psychology in the Department of Psychiatry at the University of Pennsylvania.)

Sarah began her intensive treatment with Dr. Foa the following month, and after just three weeks, she says, "I was functional again—after three years of being almost completely disabled!"

"But if all you have is a hammer, then every problem is a nail," she adds. "If the doctors didn't know what OCD was, they based their diagnosis on what they knew. If they didn't know how to treat OCD, they used the only tools they knew. One was analysis, and the other was medications. Only when we went to see Dr. Foa, who had worked with OCD and recognized my symptoms pretty quickly, did I get the help I needed."

Once she was being treated by an OCD specialist, Sarah's turn-around was dramatic. "You don't often find that kind of intense drama now, either in how sick I was, or how quickly I turned it around. But I was able to do that because, at long last, I was given the correct treatment. It happened because I was in *that* program and I was ready to get better. And the fact that I'm married now, with a child, is just a miracle."

Refining the Assessment

We've known since the early 1990s that, in most instances, both obsessions and compulsions are present in a person with OCD. Even thirty years ago, when very few studies had been done on the disorder, we were learning that almost all people with OCD reported both obsessions and compulsions, and that most compulsions were performed for the explicit purpose of relieving anxiety caused by the obsessions. It's that active–reactive relationship between obsessions and compulsions that so often leads to a diagnosis of OCD.

We also can tell you that, while your obsessions generally can be categorized by known "themes"—contamination, aggression, symmetry/order, religion/morality, hoarding/saving, sexual, somatic, and miscellaneous (e.g., saying that certain things will hurt someone)—the variations on those themes are endless. You might even experience a number of *different* obsessions over the years, followed by different compulsions. But the OCD itself will remain OCD: All of your obsessions will be intrusive and unwanted, and they will cause you pain.

Once researchers knew about that solid relationship between obsessions and compulsions, they were able to isolate three important characteristics of clinical obsessions that set them apart from other types of repetitive thinking:

1. Clinical obsessions are unwelcome thoughts. They intrude at inconvenient times and sometimes (but not always) are triggered by something the person sees or hears.

2. The obsessions themselves are in direct conflict with the individual's personality, values, morals, and expectations. You may recall that we previously referred to obsessions as being "ego-dystonic." An example is a religious person's fear that he never will enjoy a positive relationship with God or guilt over immoral images that intrude into his mind. Or, a contamination obsession might develop in a person who keeps a clean house and maintains good personal hygiene under normal circumstances.

3. The last characteristic is neutralization. Obsessions, as we've noted, are unpleasant, if not repugnant. In an effort to decrease or neutralize the anxiety that they cause, the OCD sufferer engages in some mental or behavioral ritual. This is how compulsions develop: Compulsions are an attempt to fight the intrusive thoughts.

OCD and Comorbid Conditions

Another important insight we've gained in the past ten years is that people diagnosed with OCD are at higher-than-normal risk for additional psychiatric illnesses. Most prominent among OCD patients is the co-diagnosis, or *comorbidity*, of major depressive disorder (MDD). In short, it's very common for people with OCD to also experience clinical depression—and this is another reason why it's so important that you get an accurate diagnosis, *even if you're already being treated for depression!* While the medications that are frequently used to treat depression may be the same as for treating OCD, the CBT treatment for depression is *not* the same as the CBT treatment for OCD, and without a comprehensive diagnosis, your OCD symptoms won't get treated.

One study found that for most people, the OCD occurred before the depression, leading the researchers to conclude that the MDD developed as a response to the dysfunction caused by OCD. Additional studies have shown that OCD is often complicated by the presence of other anxiety disorders. In fact, where anxiety disorders are concerned, comorbidity is more the rule than the exception. There is also a group of diagnoses referred to as "obsessive-compulsive spectrum disorders," which we discuss more fully in Chapter 5. Taken together, the studies and new information regarding OCD and co-morbidity underscore the need for an early and accurate OCD diagnosis, so that accompanying and debilitating illnesses don't have a chance to develop. If you do have other, comorbid conditions, don't give up hope. This simply means that treatment may be more complicated or take a bit longer. The important point to remember is that if you diagnose and treat your OCD before the other disorders appear, chances are much better that you won't experience them.

ANNE COULTER'S DIAGNOSIS STORY

Anne is one of the fortunate few who received an accurate diagnosis and appropriate treatment the first time she saw a psychiatrist. Only a short time before, she had revealed her secret—that she experienced uncontrollable thoughts and performed checking rituals that used up hours each day—to a social worker, who then said, "What you're describing sounds like obsessive-compulsive disorder. Have you heard of it?"

She had, but this was the late 1980s when OCD was barely on the public's radar screen, and those who had heard of it (including Anne) knew only about repetitive hand-washing. "I didn't have that symptom," Anne says today, "so it never occurred to me that OCD was the problem. I just thought I was losing my mind."

At that point, she'd already been seeing the therapist for about a year. She had sought help for depression, which, unbeknownst to her, was related to the OCD. But for a long time she was too embarrassed to talk about the thoughts that raced through her mind and the compulsions that consumed her. She thought she should be able to control them. In hindsight, she saw that by hiding these symptoms from the therapist, she had wasted valuable time that she could otherwise have invested in getting the right treatment.

When Anne began her therapy, she was 26 years old. Her first checking symptoms had appeared several years earlier; gradually, the list of things that "needed" constant checking grew longer and the checking rituals grew more elaborate and time-consuming. She also experienced some obsessive thoughts that plagued her but had no associated compulsions. The anxiety generated by all these symptoms was exhausting, and keeping such an enormous secret heaped on even more stress and fatigue. She was desperate for relief.

The social worker referred Anne to a psychiatrist experienced in treating people with OCD. During her first appointment, the doctor used the YBOCS test to aid in making a diagnosis. "Depending on your perspective," Anne says, "I either passed with flying colors or flunked miserably!" The YBOCS showed that she did, indeed, have OCD. The doctor prescribed Prozac—then one of the few available medications approved for treating the disorder. In addition, Anne was very fortunate to live near a university clinic that specialized in treating OCD.

After learning that her condition had a name and a biobehavioral cause, and that effective treatment was available, Anne had hope that relief was possible. She read everything she could about OCD, though in those days there were few resources. Dr. Judith Rapoport's book *The Boy Who Couldn't Stop Washing* was, in her words, "a godsend. It was full of stories just like mine! Knowing that so many other people suffered from the same disorder was profoundly comforting to me— I wasn't 'going crazy' after all."

After the OCD Diagnosis

Once your OCD is diagnosed, treatment can begin. You should expect to meet with and get feedback from the clinician who completed your evaluation. Alternatively, if the policy of the clinic where you were seen is to have a team meeting, the person who conducted the evaluation will inform the team, the clinician providing the actual treatment will be assigned, and that clinician will conduct the feedback session.

Regardless of who leads this next meeting, you should expect at least a portion of the session to be devoted to summarizing the content of the evaluation and providing psychoeducation about OCD in general and your symptoms and comorbid conditions in particular. At this point, the clinician will be able to provide a case formulation that will take the causal factors underlying your OCD into account and highlight how other, maintenance factors allow your OCD to thrive. He or she will also be able to outline a general treatment plan and subsequently work with you to refine that plan. And then the hard work begins.

Frequently Asked Questions

Q: I think I might have OCD, but I just had a full physical checkup for my job and it didn't suggest anything about OCD. Am I in the clear?

A: A physical exam won't lead to an OCD diagnosis—though it's possible the person giving the exam might spot some physical *results* of OCD rituals, such as bald spots if you have trichotillomania, or rough, raw-looking hands if you've been scrubbing them too much. Rather, an OCD diagnosis is based on a professional's assessment of possible obsessions and compulsions. In the majority of cases, people have to tell their healthcare provider about their symptoms. Most primary-care physicians have very little experience with OCD.

Q: I'm afraid of being diagnosed with OCD, even though I hate my symptoms. What's up with that?

A: There can be a lot of reasons for your reticence. One of the key features of OCD is that sufferers *know* that their obsessions do not reflect the way most people think. As the obsessions become more intrusive and frequent and the rituals begin to take up more and more time, many people with OCD begin to think there is something wrong with them. Having a professional confirm that you have a psychiatric diagnosis may cement your belief that "I'm crazy." But as we keep pointing out, having OCD doesn't mean you're crazy—it means you have an anxiety disorder.

Q: My sister is a 23-year-old ballerina. Before each performance, she has to sniff her "blankie"—her baby blanket—and sing a song she loved as a baby. Does she have OCD?

A: Your sister may have some problems with anxiety, but she probably doesn't have OCD because her symptoms don't interfere significantly with her life and she doesn't seem to have unwanted thoughts.

Brief pre-performance rituals are not uncommon in show business (and in professional sports), but they are not necessarily OCD rituals. If your sister's "stage jitters" really did interfere with her performance, she would benefit from talking with a professional who could teach her how to better deal with them.

Q: *I want help now; I don't want to spend time reading books and thinking about this. Give me some resources for getting help fast.*
A: You can do a quick search for a clinician in your area on these websites: www.ocfoundation.org (Obsessive Compulsive Foundation), www.abct.org (Association for Behavioral and Cognitive Therapies), and www.adaa.org (Anxiety Disorders Association of America).

Q: *How will a therapist know that my symptoms are OCD instead of some other anxiety-related disorder?*
A: Clinicians who are trained and experienced in working with OCD can distinguish it from such conditions as addictive disorders, panic disorder, generalized anxiety disorder, post-traumatic stress disorder, and depression. You need to ask questions in your initial meeting to establish that your therapist does indeed treat OCD—and that he or she uses CBT and ERP as the treatment of choice.

Q: *I don't know whether I have OCD or phobias. What's the difference?*
A: OCD is defined by its obsessions and compulsions—rituals you perform in an attempt to relieve the anxiety caused by your obsessions. With phobias, however, there are no rituals; your response to things that generate fear, such as spiders or high places, is simply to avoid the source of your fear. Frankly, we have patients who, when they initially called us, said that because they were spending long hours scrubbing and sterilizing, over and over, they believed they had a "germ phobia." It sends up a red flag and usually we have to explain to the callers that, because of their cleansing rituals, they don't have a phobia—they have OCD.

FIVE

If It Isn't OCD: Understanding Related Disorders, Comorbidity, and the Obsessive-Compulsive Spectrum

AS WE DISCUSSED in the previous chapter, OCD symptoms don't go away on their own. For most people, seeing a clinician who can confirm that they do, in fact, have OCD is an important first step and, for many, seeing a therapist who is skilled in treating OCD will put them on the path to recovery.

But if you're like most OCD patients, your OCD won't let you off the hook with just one diagnosis. That's because OCD rarely works alone. Chances are, you also experience symptoms of other anxiety disorders, depression, or substance abuse—conditions that practitioners call "comorbid disorders" because they exist alongside OCD.

And they are not rare occurrences: Comorbidity is the rule, not the exception. On the other hand, your OCD might appear to be very different from the obsessions and compulsions usually associated with OCD. There are a number of conditions considered to be technically (and biologically) related to OCD. These conditions are referred to as "obsessive-compulsive spectrum disorders" and they include Tourette's syndrome (TS), hoarding, skin-picking, body dysmorphic disorder (BDD), and trichotillomania (also called "trich," pronounced like "trick," or "TM" for short). Depending on what you read, this list can be even more extensive; we will discuss later why we have included only these conditions.

This chapter will also inform you about comorbid and spectrum disorders and how they relate to your OCD—and, most important, why you need to get help for them. As with OCD, the symptoms of these disorders generally won't go away until you do something to intervene. That may mean using this book to help yourself or seeing a professional in order to get an accurate diagnosis and treatment. You can't afford to take any shortcuts! It really is vitally important that you seek out a professional if you are so depressed that you are contemplating hurting yourself, if you have been self-medicating with alcohol or drugs as a means of trying to cope with your OCD, or if the prospect of attempting to manage your condition on your own is overwhelming. A mental health practitioner can be of invaluable help if your attempts at self-help have been stalled or you aren't getting the results you would like on your own.

Comorbid Conditions

Which comes first—OCD or comorbid conditions? Can a person's OCD symptoms cause his depression, alcohol abuse, or another one of the anxiety disorders? Or would an already-existing comorbid disorder make it easier for OCD to rear up? These are the kinds of questions that can keep scientists busy for years, and precise answers are yet to be found. What's most important for you or your loved one to understand is simple, however: According to one prevalence study drawn from the general population, nearly half of all individuals with OCD have a comorbid anxiety disorder and 27 percent have been diagnosed with major depression.

What clinicians *have* learned is that comorbid conditions can complicate both your diagnosis and your treatment. They can camouflage what's really happening and can lead to a misdiagnosis of your OCD. For that reason, it's important that you learn about the conditions that occur comorbidly with OCD and pay close attention to your own symptoms so you can report them accurately to your therapist.

The most common OCD comorbid conditions are detailed in the subsections below.

Depression

Depression is the most common comorbid condition among OCD patients, affecting 27 percent of those already diagnosed with OCD. Unlike most of the other comorbid conditions, depression often is secondary to the OCD rather than distinct from it—meaning that the depression developed as a result of OCD itself.

Patients often become depressed over the ways in which OCD has disrupted and ravaged their lives. If you believe you have OCD, you should watch for these symptoms of depression:

- Loss of interest in daily activities
- Feeling sad much of the time
- Crying for no obvious reason
- Problems with sleeping, concentrating, or making decisions
- Unplanned weight gain or loss
- Feeling fatigued, worthless, and irritable
- Thoughts of suicide

With some comorbid conditions, the therapist finds it easiest to treat the comorbidity first, so that treating the OCD will be less complicated. This is particularly true in the case of depression: If the depression is severe, and especially if the clinician believes there might be a suicide risk, then obviously it's in the patient's best interest to get the depression under control first. If you have been experiencing thoughts of harming yourself or you have been thinking about suicide, it is especially important that you seek out help. Or, if you are already seeing a mental health professional, tell him or her about these thoughts. Because OCD is associated with harm-related obsessions, it is especially important to talk to your therapist so that he or she can assess whether you are at risk.

But even if the depression is less serious, it should still be be treated first because moderate depression can affect the outcome of OCD treatment. It can influence a person's motivation level and hope for the future. However, it's a balancing act. For some of our patients, the depression improves once they start making progress with their OCD. Regardless of which condition is treated first, the treatment of choice is cognitive behavior therapy, often in conjunction with medication.

Panic Disorder

Almost everyone has experienced at least one panic attack. During such an attack, an intense fear washes over you for no apparent reason. The symptoms are as follows:

- Difficulty breathing, shortness of breath, or feeling "air hungry"
- Dizziness or lightheadedness or feeling faint
- Chest pain, discomfort, or tightness
- Tingling or numbness in the extremities
- A fast heartbeat or feeling like your heart is pounding
- Fear that you are dying, losing control, or "going crazy"

The fear of losing control, in itself, can bring on even deeper fear as well as repeated panic attacks, which are the cornerstone of panic disorder. If you experience frequent panic attacks, you should be aware that the primary symptom of panic disorder is the ongoing fear of the symptoms you are experiencing and of having more panic attacks.

Women are twice as likely as men to have panic disorder, and it's possible that a genetic link exists. Yet no specific biological cause has been found. In many cases the attacks do seem to follow or accompany stressful events, however.

In our clinic, we've seen patients who become so fearful of having a panic attack that they begin to avoid situations that they associate with their panic attacks. When both panic and avoidance occur, the resulting condition is termed "panic disorder with agoraphobia" (as distinct from "panic disorder without agoraphobia"). For example, if the panic attack happened while a person was exercising, she might stop working out; if it occurred in a school setting, she might develop a fear of the classroom and stop attending school. And when we see this avoidance in someone who happens to have OCD, then we have to ask, Are the panic and avoidance related to the OCD symptoms? In other words, are the person's obsessional fears triggering the panic, or have her rituals become associated with the panic as a means of preventing the attacks? In some cases, such as the foregoing one, the panic attacks are intertwined with rather than distinct from the OCD. In others—as when, for example, someone with OCD is avoiding driving because he fears that he is going to panic and that the panic will cause him to lose control of the car and cause an accident—the panic disorder with agoraphobia is comorbid with the OCD.

JODI'S PANIC ATTACKS

After twelve years of teaching 8-year-olds, Jodi thought she could handle anything—except the terrifying experience of joining friends on a getaway.

Jodi and her friends had gone to college together. That's when Jodi's feelings of panic had started; they felt like big rubber balls welling up from deep inside her, choking her breath and making her heart beat so hard she thought it might jump out of her chest and fall onto the floor, and then she would die. It happened whenever she felt trapped and unable to leave—as was the case when she had to wait for what seemed like forever in order to return a sweater she had bought, and when she walked into the doctor's office and found out that her doctor was running late for her appointment.

Sometimes she coasted along for quite some time, enjoying her life between panic attacks. Then another one would hit her, and the attacks would be with her every day for weeks, lobbing suffocating, paralyzing assaults against her body.

Now, going on vacation with her friends, she would have to try to time her arrival at the inn so there wouldn't be a line of guests waiting to check in. Her friends had always teased her good-naturedly about her attacks—but then, they didn't have to live with the fear that one would come out of the blue and play havoc with their lives.

Lately, though, the panic disorder—that's what the doctor called it—was getting her down. Just knowing a panic attack could erupt at any time was making her depressed. She kept thinking that, with a bit of luck, she might be able to ward off an attack and had begun a strange ritual in the kitchen every morning: She couldn't sit down to breakfast until she knew "for sure" that she had closed the milk carton, put away the sugar, and cleaned just the right number of blueberries for her cereal. And she couldn't know those things for sure until she had checked them, five or six times. Once she completed her "lucky" ritual, she felt reassured that she just might be able to keep the panic attacks at bay.

Jodi didn't tell the doctor about her superstitious ritual because she didn't see its significance. Had she mentioned it, the doctor probably would have referred her to someone who specializes in OCD, because he would have recognized that she was exhibiting OCD symptoms with a comorbid panic disorder. The more panic attacks she experienced—at the library, in the bank, wherever she was stuck waiting—the less control she felt that she had. At home, though, at the breakfast table, she had perfect control.

It would be two more years before Jodi got help for her anxiety. One morning, a friend stopped in for coffee, unannounced. She saw Jodi's blueberries, all lined up and waiting to join the cereal, and she asked Jodi what was going on. Jodi, a bit red-faced, explained that it was a superstition and seemed to be helping her prevent her panic attacks. When the friend asked whether there were other things that helped her to stay calmer, Jodi thought for a while and then told her that maybe there were. In fact, she realized that she was giving herself more time to get out of the house because she had to check that she had her keys and that the lights and appliances were turned off. She also told her friend that when she was doing her chores around the house, if she got distracted by answering the phone, she had to start all of her cleaning over; otherwise, she might feel anxious.

With cognitive behavior therapy, Jodi remembered that she had always been afraid of feeling trapped. When playing hide-and-seek, for example, she would never hide in the back of a closet or anywhere else she felt she couldn't escape from. She was afraid that she might get stuck and suffocate. No one took her seriously back then; instead, people would tell her horror stories about people being trapped in mine shafts and dying and thought her reaction was funny.

Jodi's therapist worked with her over the next few months, even taking her on outings so she could practice waiting in line at a restaurant, dealing with the crowd at a movie opening, or going shopping on the worst possible day of the year—the day after Thanksgiving. Jodi mastered all of those situations, practicing whenever she saw an opportunity. Today she thinks nothing of driving to her own getaway and dealing with check-in lines and airport security, or going to a spa where she can happily sit in a small steam room that previously would have made her feel trapped and unable to breathe.

In addition to overcoming her panic, Jodi realized that her "superstitions" were, in fact, just that. Her rituals hadn't prevented her from panicking but, instead, had just added another layer of problems. Her therapist had her test out her beliefs by asking, Was her chance of having a panic attack any better or any worse if she didn't complete a ritual? What Jodi quickly realized was that she didn't have control over her panic. The only thing that helped her was to become less fearful of her symptoms—and the only thing her rituals did was consume her time.

Obsessive-Compulsive Personality Disorder

Rules are rules! That's the refrain you're likely to hear often from someone with obsessive-compulsive personality disorder (OCPD). About 16 million adults in the United States, or almost 8 percent of the population, are estimated to be suffering with OCPD; it's one of the most prevalent personality disorders we know.

OCPD is marked by rigid devotion to rules and regulations, and a serious need for order and personal control. People living with OCPD don't delegate tasks; such perfectionists will do all the work themselves to see that it's done right—and while their perfectionism might be admired from afar, it's difficult to work alongside. So, people with OCPD often find themselves without social connections.

Obsessive-compulsive personality disorder is fundamentally different from OCD, panic disorder, and any of the other comorbid conditions noted. This condition is a personality disorder and, as such, is viewed as secondary to other, more acute conditions when clinicians make diagnoses. What this means is that OCPD, or any personality disorder, doesn't disrupt a person's life in quite the same way as more acutely occurring conditions. It's more like a low-grade infection: You may not feel great, but you're not sick enough to take the day off of work or school. On the contrary, people with a personality disorder tend to think they are fine; it's other people who have the problem. For the person with OCPD, abiding by the rules makes sense—it's the way life "should" be, despite the inconveniences and disruptions that this rigid adherence to rules causes in other people's lives.

If you think you have OCPD, you may have several of these symptoms:

- Inappropriate concern with lists, rules, and details
- Over-the-top devotion to work
- Miserliness
- Refusal to throw things away
- Rigid, judgmental attitudes about the morals of others
- Unwillingness to delegate work
- Feeling out of kilter or becoming upset when rules or routines are disrupted

These characteristics don't disappear with treatment; but, in fact, it may not be practical for all of them to disappear. No one would want to hire an architect who wasn't attentive to details and to the rules involving design and engineering. What treatment *will* do is help the person become, shall we say, more mellow. He will still value thrift, hard work, and strong moral values, but he will be less rigid, more flexible, and capable of compromise.

As with OCD, the treatment of choice for people with OCPD is cognitive behavior therapy, which teaches the patient to relinquish control and accept change and uncertainty in his life. Clinicians sometimes will prescribe medications as well, especially if the patient is suffering from depression. (Medications are typically not effective for treating most personality disorders.) Interestingly, once the patient is diagnosed and begins treatment, his OCPD tendencies actually can work in his favor for a faster, more complete recovery, inasmuch as his self-control won't allow him to skip his meds or stop treatment!

Social Anxiety Disorder

Everyone gets the "jitters" when they perform certain tasks. Public speaking, or giving a presentation to colleagues, gives most people "butterflies" in their stomachs. Asking someone out on a date or confessing something to your partner are situations that would make anyone nervous.

For some people, however, being in a position where others might judge them is downright terrifying. They may feel extreme anxiety performing even the simplest of tasks—eating with co-workers, or giving someone directions—because they fear they will humiliate themselves. If this sounds familiar, you may have social anxiety disorder (SAD). Symptoms include the following:

- SAD manifests as an intense, persistent, and chronic fear of being watched and judged by others and of doing something embarrassing.
- This fear is so intense that it often interferes with school, work, and normal friendships.
- SAD can be limited to one type of situation, such as eating with others or giving a speech, or it can be so broad as to cause anxiety around all other people, including even family members.

- The most bothersome physical symptoms include blushing, profuse sweating, and trembling—symptoms that others may notice.
- SAD is often accompanied by other anxiety disorders or by depression.
- Some people with SAD turn to substance abuse in their attempts to tame their anxiety with alcohol or drugs.

The hallmark of SAD is the fear of embarrassment, humiliation, or disapproval. As with many other anxiety disorders, people either avoid situations or "white-knuckle" their way through situations that trigger these fears. Sometimes, the anxiety is so great that the SAD sufferer may experience a panic attack. One of the differences between panic disorder and SAD is that the symptoms of the former are a source of fear whereas those of the latter are cause for embarrassment. Another is that individuals suffering from panic with agoraphobia want to have other people around since they are a source of help, whereas those suffering from SAD would prefer to be alone since having others around, should they become anxious, would potentially mean that this "audience" might ridicule them.

Experts estimate that up to 13 percent of the population meet the diagnostic criteria for SAD at some point in their lifetime, making this the most prevalent mental health disorder in the United States. The anxiety that people experience when giving a speech or going on a first date is expected—it doesn't interfere with their lives or make them miserable. But if you are like those people whose social fears interfere with their work lives or social relationships, then you might want to talk with someone. A clinician will look for an ongoing fear of social situations in which you think you might be embarrassed, as well as for a high level of anticipatory anxiety over those situations. Like panic disorder, social anxiety disorder can lead to depression and substance abuse, so if you recognize that persistent feeling of fear, you might want to do something about it.

An accurate and complete diagnosis is especially crucial when social anxiety disorder is layered onto OCD. Are you afraid of shaking someone's hand, for instance, because you are afraid of contamination, or because you think the other person will laugh at your fear of contamination? The answer to this question could impact your treatment and, ultimately, your recovery.

An example presented itself at our clinic. We were running a group for several of our patients with OCD and invited a new person, Jim, into the group. Jim staunchly refused to participate. We had anticipated that he might not want to join, but our explanation was different from Jim's actual reason. We knew that because of his OCD, he had difficulty sitting on some pieces of furniture. If the furniture appeared stained or less than immaculate, he feared becoming contaminated. Naturally, we assumed this was what was holding him back from joining the group. What we learned several weeks later, however, was that he was fearful of the group—but not because of contamination. The idea of having to introduce himself to a group of strangers and become the center of attention, even for thirty seconds, was terrifying for him. It was his SAD that was the obstacle.

If you have social anxiety disorder, you'll find that cognitive behavior therapy is the most effective treatment because it shows you that your own thoughts, not other people or situations, will determine your actions. Exposure therapy and medication might also be part of your treatment plan. (For more on treatments, see Chapters 6 and 7.)

Generalized Anxiety Disorder

This disorder is exactly what the name implies. If you suffer from generalized anxiety disorder (GAD), you probably feel anxious or worried most of the time, without reason, to the point where your excessive worrying affects your home and work life. Like most people, GAD sufferers view their physical symptoms as signs of "stress"; but then, most people with such symptoms would make an appointment to see their primary-care physician rather than a mental health professional. It's for this reason that in anxiety specialty clinics such as ours, it's fairly unusual to see someone who has a primary diagnosis of GAD. Some of the symptoms of GAD are as follows:

- Restlessness, startles easily, can't seem to relax
- Excessive concern about health issues, money, and family and work problems
- Difficulty concentrating
- Fatigue
- Irritability
- Impatience
- Muscle tension
- Sleep problems
- Stomachaches and diarrhea
- Headaches

People who experience a constant feeling that "something bad is going to happen" or are always focusing on the "What ifs . . ." may have GAD. Even when they aren't in a state of high nervousness, they feel anxious and uncomfortable. It's a fairly safe bet that the person you see who is constantly fidgeting has GAD. Unlike several of the other anxiety disorders, GAD can develop at any stage of life, including late in life.

Like OCD, GAD develops around specific thought patterns—obsessions in OCD, worries in GAD—so it almost seems logical that they would appear together in the same person. Indeed, it is sometimes hard to tell whether someone is suffering from GAD or OCD. One big difference is that GAD sufferers do not have rituals. Among many of our patients, their OCD masks their GAD. In fact, we can have a difficult time identifying the worries related to GAD until the obsessions are under better control.

GAD is diagnosed according to strict criteria, according to the fourth edition of the *Diagnostic and Statistical Manual of Mental Disorders*; in fact, we have used the DSM-IV's criteria and symptoms lists for all of the anxiety disorders in this section. One of the chief diagnostic measures for GAD is excessive anxiety and worry every day for at least six months. GAD, like the other anxiety disorders, is treatable. Cognitive behavior therapy can help you replace your negative, unhealthy worries with more realistic appraisals of the situations that you find so worrisome. Some psychiatrists also prescribe antianxiety medications or antidepressants.

Specific Phobias

Some of our OCD patients describe their disorder as a phobia rather than as OCD. Several years ago, we received a phone call from a prospective patient asking whether we treated phobias about walking through doorways or down sidewalks. When we asked a few more questions, it became apparent that the person calling was compelled to touch doors or drawers before she opened or closed them, to touch objects a certain number of times and in a certain way before she picked them up, and to engage in specific movements when she walked outside, sometimes reversing these movements several times. We spent a goodly amount of time on the phone with the caller, explaining that she really didn't have a phobia but, rather, was suffering from OCD.

The difference is that, instead of engaging in rituals, people with phobias practice avoidance. More than 12 percent of Americans experience at least one phobia in their lifetime—and it would not be surprising to find that those people who have OCD also have a specific phobia. Phobias are so common partly because people can be afraid of just about anything—bees, bugs, snakes, blood, needles, water, heights, dogs, cats, elevators, flying. You name it! For convenience, phobias can be grouped into categories: animal-related (including insects), environmental (e.g., storms, water, heights), blood-injury-injection-related, situational (e.g., tunnels, bridges, flying, driving, enclosed spaces), and other (e.g., choking, vomiting).

No one is sure what causes a phobia. Some phobias, such as fear of the dark, are common in childhood; as we get older, we grow out of them. And some individuals *can* blame their parents for their phobias. Researchers believe that phobias can be learned, so if a family member is afraid of heights, it's possible that her child will observe and learn that same fear. Genetics, brain chemicals, and trauma can contribute to phobia development, too.

Symptoms of a phobia include the following:

- An irrational fear of some situation, object, or organism
- An immediate, intense anxiety when you encounter that situation
- A strong desire to avoid the object of your fear, and a tendency to go to great lengths to avoid it in your daily life
- Understanding, in many instances, that your fear is irrational
- Feeling anxiety just thinking about encountering the object of your fear

You may not need treatment for your phobia; if it doesn't interfere with your life, it technically is not a disorder. However, if your phobia grows to the point where it interferes with your relationships or work or other areas of your life that are meaningful to you, then you might need to get help.

As with other anxiety disorders, cognitive behavior therapy is what is recommended for the treatment of phobias. In many cases, the behavioral part of CBT is highly effective and has a long history of being used to treat phobias. With behavior therapy, you would learn to tolerate staying in proximity to what it is you fear until your anxiety subsides. And then you would do this all over again until, with enough repetitions, you were no longer afraid of the object or situation. Many clinicians also include the cognitive component of CBT, which helps to challenge the fear-related thoughts that contribute to your phobia. In most cases, medications are not helpful when treating a specific phobia.

Post-Traumatic Stress Disorder

Post-traumatic stress disorder (PTSD) is triggered by a traumatic event—one that happened to you or that you witnessed happening to someone else. Most people associate PTSD with soldiers returning from war, but in our clinic we see it in survivors of sexual abuse, car accidents, natural disasters, and a number of other situations as well. (A slightly different diagnosis, acute stress disorder, may be given to individuals in the immediate aftermath of a trauma.) PTSD symptoms usually start appearing within three months of the event, but in some instances they can be dormant for years before arising for the first time.

PTSD is unique among the anxiety disorders in that its cause is known: The sufferer has invariably experienced, witnessed, or confronted a traumatic event that involved actual or threatened death or injury, or a threat to the safety of oneself or others. The symptoms associated with this disorder fall into three major categories:

- Persistent *reexperiencing* of the traumatic event as indicated by recurrent, intrusive recollections of the event (e.g., images, thoughts); recurrent upsetting dreams; acting or feeling as if the event were recurring (e.g., flashbacks, a sense of reliving the experience, illusions, or even hallucinations); distress over internal or external cues that resemble some aspect of the trauma; and physical reactions or symptoms in response to some aspect of the trauma.

- Persistent *avoidance* of any aspect of the trauma and *numbing of responses* as indicated by several of the following: efforts to avoid thoughts, feelings, or conversations associated with the event; avoidance of activities, places, or people that arouse these recollections; inability to remember an important aspect of the trauma; diminished interest in or participation in significant activities; feelings of detachment or estrangement from others; restricted breadth of emotional responses; and a sense of a foreshortened future (e.g., does not expect to have a career, marriage, etc.).

- Persistent symptoms of *increased arousal* as indicated by at least two of the following: difficulty falling or staying asleep, irritability or anger outbursts, difficulty concentrating, always feeling as if on alert, and startling unusually easily.

With PTSD, some terrible, legitimately tragic situation has occurred. As you may recall, some of the fears that fuel OCD involve this kind of catastrophic thought. Imagine being involved in a car accident that resulted in someone's death. The trauma from that would be understandable. But for a person vulnerable to OCD, this kind of trauma might also set off fears about driving itself, such as concern over possibly running over someone. The rituals would then involve checking whether this was indeed the case. This is an example of how PTSD and OCD can coexist.

PTSD can worsen over time; the disturbing episodes may occur more frequently or last longer, or they may become more upsetting. For PTSD, cognitive behavior therapy is the treatment of choice, sometimes combined with medication. At least one study, however, has found that in cases of serious depression accompanying PTSD, the response to behavioral therapy for OCD was diminished.

Spectrum Disorders

Long after you finish reading this book, researchers still will be debating about which illnesses should be called "obsessive-compulsive spectrum disorders."

Some would include every disorder with repetitive symptoms, from autism to compulsive gambling. Others would add impulse control disorders, such as pyromania or compulsive shopping. The Canadian Medical Association took a stab at defining spectrum disorders: "These disorders and OCD are said to overlap in terms of phenomenologic features, clinical course and treatment response; may share a common pathophysiologic basis and genetic predisposition; and often occur comorbidly."

The debate over what is considered obsessive-compulsive (OC) spectrum is over what is omitted from the above definition—the function of obsessions and compulsions. As we noted previously, in OCD obsessions cause anxiety and compulsions serve to neutralize that anxiety. From the perspective of learning theory, compulsions are considered negative reinforcements because OCD sufferers interpret the function of their compulsion (the reduction of anxiety) as something that is useful to them, which then increases the likelihood that they will continue to use their rituals to manage their anxiety. Unfortunately, the relief gained by ritualizing is short-lived and only further disrupts the OCD sufferer's life. With many of what are broadly termed OC spectrum disorders, the so-called compulsive behaviors do not provide negative reinforcement. Instead, they provide positive reinforcement. For example, winning is a positive reinforcement for gambling. And even if the compulsive gambler isn't winning, there is always the possibility that the next toss of dice or hand of poker will bring home a jackpot. Likewise, individuals who are compulsive shoppers find pleasure in buying things. The positive outcome of their "compulsive" behavior increases the likelihood that the behaviors will continue. Thus, in OCD, compulsions are negative reinforcers, whereas in some of the spectrum conditions, compulsions are positive reinforcers.

In actuality, many of these so-called compulsive behaviors are not compulsive at all. The term "impulse control disorder" more accurately describes conditions such as compulsive gambling, shopping, stealing, sex, and drug addictions, although the latter two groups fall into different diagnostic categories entirely. People with impulse control disorders are drawn to harmful activity; people with OCD will do almost anything to avoid it.

For the purpose of demystifying OCD, we will include only those disorders that fit most closely with our definition.

Body Dysmorphic Disorder

People who have body dysmorphic disorder (BDD) are convinced that some aspect of their appearance is unattractive, disfigured, or grotesque. It might be a real flaw that they're focusing on, but their concern about it is distorted and excessive, to the point of an obsession. They may not be able to control their own negative thoughts about their looks, even when friends and family reassure them that they look just fine.

BDD sufferers are preoccupied with their perceived flaw and often undergo cosmetic surgery to correct it. However, because they have

BDD, they don't believe the surgeries were successful (even if they were) and they remain unhappy. They may also move on to a new "flaw," aggravating the BDD even further.

According to one estimate, one in fifty people are affected by BDD. Many are perfectionists in their teens and 20s, focusing largely on their faces. About 30 percent of those diagnosed with BDD also have OCD, and 60 percent also have major depression.

Patients with BDD often develop checking rituals, repeatedly checking themselves in the mirror (or, on the flip side, avoiding mirrors altogether) to reassure themselves that they don't look bad. Excessive grooming is common, and they usually spend at least one hour every day thinking about or being preoccupied with their "defect."

In our clinic, we've seen that patients with BDD sometimes withdraw from their social lives because they're afraid that people will notice their defect. Their relationships become difficult and they tend to perform badly at school and work because their obsessions about their looks interfere with their normal thinking and activities.

Not surprisingly, people with BDD are at high risk for depression and suicide; as many as 29 percent of them have tried to end their lives. The disorder affects men and women in equal numbers, but with a couple differences: Men are more likely to resort to substance abuse and remain single, whereas women more often have comorbid panic disorder.

The best treatment for BDD is exposure and response prevention (ERP), along with cognitive therapy—a combination recently found to be more effective than medications. If you've been diagnosed with BDD, your treatment is likely to center around ERP with an emphasis on tolerating uncomfortable situations and their associated feelings and thoughts—a process known as "exposure," which you'll learn more about in the next chapter. You'll also learn in therapy about relaxing and managing your anxiety.

Trichotillomania (Hair-Pulling Disorder)

Our hair adorns us. It frames our faces, accents our eyes, and enhances our identities. So when someone is compelled to pull out her eyebrow hairs by the roots, or create bald patches on her scalp from pulling out hair, it's hard to understand why she doesn't just stop.

Trich is classified as an impulse control disorder—in other words, a disorder in which you can't resist doing something that is harmful to you or to another person. Hair-pulling episodes can be triggered by a bad mood, loneliness, fatigue, or anxiety as well as for reasons that the sufferer can't articulate. For some, it is a simple urge to pull gray hairs or hairs of a certain shape or coarseness. Still others do it for positive reinforcement—the simple act of pulling hair feels good to them—or for negative reinforcement—to distract themselves from boredom or anxiety. Most know they're doing it and are ashamed. Others don't even realize that they are pulling until they see a pile of hairs on the floor. And some sufferers will pull hair from less obvious places like their arms or legs, underarms, or genital area.

Trich does present complications beyond appearance. In some cases, the hair won't grow back because the follicles have been damaged. In other cases, patients have suffered intestinal obstructions because they swallow the hairs and a hairball becomes lodged in their stomach or intestines.

The most accepted approach to treating trich is a behavioral treatment known as *habit reversal*, which is sometimes combined with relaxation, awareness training, and ERP.

Skin-Picking

Patients with trich aren't the only ones who try to hide evidence of their compulsive behaviors. Skin-pickers, too, often camouflage evidence of their compulsions with makeup, Band-Aids, or a scarf. Some individuals with BDD skin-pick in an attempt to correct some defect related to their skin. At times, they will stand in front of the mirror for hours, trying to "even out" their complexions by picking or squeezing just one more blemish or trying to create a smooth, even surface—which ultimately doesn't work because of the damage that's resulting from the picking. Some patients pick their skin mindlessly, purely as a habit, while for others the picking is deliberate. And, like trich, skin-picking seems to have a soothing effect. The damage, scarring, can be permanent.

The treatment approach, as with trich, is habit reversal.

Tourette's Syndrome

A disorder that begins in childhood, Tourette's is marked by motor and vocal tics, and occasionally with swearing outbursts. The tics can come and go as the child grows into adulthood, sometimes escalating in periods of stress. Head-banging, eye-poking, and lip-biting are other occasional symptoms.

The tics associated with Tourette's are under partial voluntary control. What this means is that someone suffering from Tourette's may be able to resist engaging in the tic—at least for a brief period. However, this ability to resist is not without a cost. The tics resume with an explosive outburst. In addition, as with OCD sufferers, people with Tourette's will recognize a premonitory urge; they will know that there is an impending tic, much like people with OCD will know that an obsession triggers an urge to ritualize. Tourette's can be contrasted with the stereotyped movements of other disorders that typically have an earlier age of onset; are more symmetrical, rhythmical, and bilateral; and primarily involve the extremities (e.g., flapping the hands).

In treating Tourette's, the aim is to relieve any discomfort that might be caused by the tics, but not to eliminate the tics themselves. Certain medications can help to suppress the tics. CBT is helpful if OCD is present with the Tourette's. Habit reversal has also been found helpful in treating the disorder.

Hoarding

We've talked about hoarders—individuals who collect mountains of old and new clutter that eventually fills every room of the house. To a hoarder, nothing gets "wasted," and if the hoarder happens to need an item in the future, it will be on hand—providing it can be found amid the disorganization.

The clutter becomes an obsession and a compulsion. Hoarders will recognize themselves in this list of symptoms:

- Inability to get rid of anything
- Constantly acquiring more items that they don't need
- Keeping bags or boxes of old bills, magazines, junk mail, and newspapers
- Saving used food containers
- Cluttered rooms
- An impairment in social, occupational, and financial functioning
- Serious procrastination problem
- Inability to make decisions
- Inability to organize possessions in any room
- Becoming more attached to clutter than to people
- Refusing to allow others to handle the clutter

Hoarding transcends age, gender, and level of affluence, although it does seem to affect older adults with greater frequency. It leads to social isolation, though the converse also can be true: Some people resort to hoarding as a remedy for loneliness, interacting with salespeople either in person or online in their quest for acquiring more "stuff." Many hoarders are perfectionists and may worry for hours about what to do with each small item.

Hoarding isn't a problem that can be left alone. Most hoarding hides a host of unsanitary conditions and health risks, such as rodents, insects, and waste (e.g., human and/or pet excrement, decaying food). The piles can become a fire hazard, not to mention a source of embarrassment.

Currently, some very experienced clinical scientists are involved in research on hoarding. So far, what we know is that the methods for treating OCD can be adapted to some of the issues that are unique to hoarders. This is clearly an area to which you will have to "stay tuned" in order to be informed about how the cognitive-behavioral treatments are developing.

After a thorough evaluation and diagnosis, your therapist may want to start you on a program of cognitive-behavior therapy, so that you can examine your compulsion to hoard and learn some organizational and decision-making skills. Such skills are a major focus in the treatment of hoarding.

KENNY'S HOARDING STORY

By the time he finished high school, Kenny's reputation as the neighborhood "computer dude" was solid. It was a way to distinguish himself from his buddies, which hadn't always been easy. Kenny wasn't a particularly assertive guy; he hadn't tried out for any sports teams and wasn't even a great student.

But he understood computers. And he collected them. He hated to see a broken or outdated computer being thrown away; in his mind, there was no such thing as an obsolete PC. So when friends or his parents' employers invested in new equipment, he rescued the abandoned hardware and gave it new life. Kenny gathered up printers, laptops, PCs, modems, even old copiers, and somehow made them useful again.

At first, he gave the renovated hardware to fellow students who couldn't afford new computers. Then he began selling them, creating a substantial income to pay for college. However, the computers kept coming. "Every day I'd get a few more," he says. "On some days, I'd get a lot more, and I started stacking them in every room." Kenny became a hoarder. His parents, who also lived in the house, were squeezed out of their own living space. Kenny convinced them that he could catch up with the backlog, so they accommodated him, even to the point of losing their bedroom. In the spring of Kenny's junior year in college, his parents moved to a tent in the backyard. Kenny rigged up space heaters and kept a clear path to the inside toilet, and assured them that he would clean out the house before the weather turned cold.

The family lived in Ohio, so camping in the backyard was not an option for the winter. As October approached, then the end of October, Kenny's parents knew their son's hoarding was out of control and they had to do something—or freeze to death that winter.

Kenny's parents had accommodated his hoarding to the extreme, and Kenny wasn't able to recognize the severity of his disorder. Fortunately, one of their neighbors was a city housing inspector, and upon seeing the family's plight he knew just what to do.

The inspector called the Municipal Housing Court and explained the situation to the judge. The judge had had other hoarding cases come before him, so he knew about the problem and the need for a good diagnosis. He fast-tracked the case and, within a week, despite the anxiety it caused Kenny but with his grudgingly given agreement, the home was cleared of all but a few computers, the parents were sleeping in their own bedroom, and Kenny was meeting with a clinician and learning for the first time about the disorder that had compelled him to collect hundreds of pieces of computer equipment.

What It All Means to You

Scanning the lists of symptoms for each comorbid condition and spectrum disorder, you probably will gain an appreciation for the difficulty involved in diagnosing the various disorders whose symptoms so closely resemble each other. What's more, you can see how these secondary illnesses, some of which are quite powerful, can wreak havoc on a treatment plan and stand in the way of recovery from OCD.

It may also be a little scary if, as you've been reading, you realize you probably have more than one of these conditions. Your reaction is not uncommon. What we honestly tell our patients is that often there are common threads among the different disorders; in other words, the underlying beliefs that are fueling these conditions frequently overlap. For example, someone with OCD may engage in checking in order to ensure he has done something perfectly, may have social anxiety disorder because he is fearful and embarrassed that his inability to do things perfectly will be noticed by others, and may be depressed by his failure to achieve perfection. So while technically he may qualify for several diagnoses, a knowledgeable clinician can help him tease out what these common threads are—and his underlying theme of perfectionism will become a focus for treatment.

Further, you've most likely noted that CBT is the treatment of choice for all of the comorbid and spectrum conditions we've described. Rest assured that the basic principles you learn in dealing with any one of the problems you may be experiencing can easily be adapted to address the specifics of the other conditions.

If you have OCD, you must carefully assess the symptoms of *all* of your possible disorders. A mental health professional can be instrumental by providing you with a comprehensive diagnostic evaluation as well as by helping you understand the implications of that evaluation and what treatment is available. There is no doubt that overlooking a comorbid condition can hinder treatment.

You've also seen that some conditions referred to as "obsessive-compulsive spectrum" disorders really aren't OCD-related at all; they are impulse control problems or entirely separate conditions that some people regard as "spectrum." Yet, they can coexist with OCD and must be treated if you want your OCD symptoms to stop.

Now that you've been given all the background on OCD, you're ready to read the next two chapters, which will show you how clinicians actually treat the disorder: with cognitive behavior therapy, including exposure and response prevention, and sometimes with medication as well. This is where the ride gets bumpy—but also where your triumph over OCD really begins.

Frequently Asked Questions

Q: I have OCD, and I worry a lot—usually when I can't finish my rituals. How many disorders can one person have?
A: It's true that a person can have more than one disorder. Generalized anxiety disorder is characterized by excessive worry and many people with OCD can also suffer from GAD. However, if your rituals are interrupted and you are worrying about what might happen as a result of not completing them, this is most likely OCD, not GAD. On the other hand, OCD may have gotten its start as worry. Like obsessions, worry is an intrusive thought. However, in GAD, worry is pervasive—it's not about just one thing—and there are no rituals. Given the overwhelming nature of obsessions, they can easily mask

the presence of GAD and it may not be until your OCD symptoms are under better control that your GAD will become more apparent. So, it's entirely possible that you have both OCD and GAD.

Q: *Why are some disorders called "spectrum" and others aren't?*
A: The term "spectrum" refers to disorders that are not OCD but appear to be related to OCD. For example, hoarding and trichotillomania are both considered to be spectrum conditions. There are compulsive behaviors involved, and people diagnosed with these conditions describe urges that are similar to the urge to ritualize. There is currently a debate over what is (or isn't) a spectrum condition. We have included in our discussion only those conditions that, like OCD, involve repetitive behaviors that are negative reinforcers. What differentiates the other spectrum conditions from OCD is that the compulsive behaviors are positively reinforcing—it feels good when a compulsive gambler keeps gambling because winning is so positively reinforcing. A more neurobiologically oriented clinician would say that the same areas of the brain may be involved in OCD and obsessive-compulsive spectrum conditions.

Q: *What about kleptomania and pyromania—Are they OC spectrum disorders?*
A: No, kleptomania (compulsive stealing) and pyromania (repeated setting of fires) are not, by our definition, in the obsessive-compulsive spectrum. Even though anxiety builds in the person before these acts are committed, and the person experiences pleasure or relief afterward, if the tension and relief are restricted to stealing or fire-setting the disorders would be diagnosed as kleptomania and pyromania only, not as OCD-related conditions. The American Psychiatric Association classifies these conditions in the *DSM-IV* as impulse control disorders, not as anxiety disorders. This gets a little confusing since trichotillomania also falls into the same *DSM-IV* category.

Q: *How can depression affect OCD treatment?*
A: Depression robs people of their motivation and enjoyment in pursuing interests. It can be paralyzing, and a person with depression

might not be able to complete his ERP successfully—an obstacle you will learn more about in the treatment chapters to follow. Treating the OCD patient's depression is imperative; most clinicians want to treat the depression as soon as possible so the patient can make progress in his OCD treatment.

Q: *A friend was recently diagnosed with body dysmorphic disorder. Is this a "fad diagnosis," considering that most women hate their bodies?*
A: *Body dysmorphic disorder* is more serious than just a focus on weight or wrinkles. Patients with BDD are excessively preoccupied with a minor (or even imaginary) flaw, and the obsession causes great anxiety. BDD sufferers constantly check their appearance in mirrors and ask others for reassurance that they look all right, and many get repeated surgeries because they're not happy with the outcome. Treatment might involve such exercises as removing all mirrors from the home and leaving the house without wearing makeup; it may also include medication.

SIX

The Good News About Treatment: What Works Best

OBSESSIONS AND COMPULSIONS emerge as symptoms in multiple illnesses, as you read in the previous chapter. Yet, even though they're defined by a host of different symptoms, they all can be treated with the same general approach: cognitive behavior therapy. CBT is sometimes augmented by prescription medications, which are discussed in detail in Chapter 8.

Changing Your Behavior

CBT is a form of treatment that attempts to change undesirable thoughts and the resulting behaviors and emotions. The cognitive component of the therapy works on people's beliefs and ways of thinking, helping them to dramatically reduce their fears and anxieties. The behavioral component addresses their actions. The basic idea behind CBT is to teach people with OCD how to better understand and manage their obsessional beliefs and related anxieties so they no longer need to engage in compulsive behaviors, or rituals.

If you have OCD, your therapy will involve a specialized form of CBT called *exposure and response prevention*, or ERP. (Some people prefer to call it "exposure and ritual prevention.") ERP typically emphasizes the *behavioral* part of treatment, as opposed to focusing exclusively on the patient's *thoughts*. Using *exposure and response prevention,* you are *exposed* to whatever causes your anxiety (e.g., something that you believe is contaminated) and then *prevent* yourself from using your rituals (e.g., washing) to manage the anxiety. Ultimately, by "facing your demons" you learn that your fears are unfounded. In recent years, ERP has been expanded to more fully incorporate the cognitive component of therapy—the component that will help you to better understand and alter the beliefs that fuel your fears. Indeed, this new knowledge will enable you to carry on with your life, to confront anxiety-creating situations whenever they occur, and to use adaptive means, rather than rituals, to cope with your fears.

Sounds simple, doesn't it? If only it were. This chapter includes the stories of several OCD patients who underwent ERP and succeeded—but as you will see, their treatment involved a great deal of work, and the exposures were frightening, at least initially.

Exposure and Response Prevention, the Cornerstone of OCD Treatment

Much of the work involved in OCD treatment involves ERP. The notion that confronting the source of your fear enables you to live with it originated in the late 1960s and was affirmed by additional research in later years. Exposure in OCD treatment takes two primary forms:

- *"In vivo exposure"* involves actually doing what you fear. As you will read below in our descriptions of actual treatment procedures, we generally begin a patient's ERP program with activities that produce lesser amounts of anxiety and work our way up to situations that he or she fears most. For example, we might initially ask a hoarder to discard the contents of one drawer (as opposed to an entire house) or a person with harming obsessions to hold a nail clipper (as opposed to a chef's knife).

- *"Imaginal exposure"* (also sometimes called "imagined exposure") is utilized when *in vivo* exposure isn't possible. Or, it can be used as a way to prepare individuals for *in vivo* exposure. As an example, recall Jonathan's story in Chapter 4. Jonathan's therapist couldn't realistically ask him to harm his family, which was his greatest fear. Instead, Jonathan and his therapist developed a script wherein he described in elaborate detail all the horrific things he imagined he might do to his family. The script also included what Jonathan thought the consequences for his harming behaviors would be. For homework, Jonathan reviewed the script—a process that, understandably, made him very anxious. He did not allow himself to avoid handling knives, for example. In fact, he would walk around with a paring knife or a pointed pair of scissors in his pocket. The more times he reviewed the script and didn't ritualize or avoid, the less anxious he became when actually handling sharp objects. Jonathan became more and more convinced that despite the extremely distressing nature of his intrusive thoughts, he could choose not to act on those thoughts; in short, he realized that his thoughts were very different from actions. And, even more important, he learned that he could tolerate the anxiety without having to resort to rituals.

ANNE COULTER'S ERP TREATMENT

She doesn't want to sound overly dramatic, but Anne says she honestly credits ERP with giving her back her life. Medication relieved her depression and took some of the edge off her anxiety, but the CBT showed her how to manage the OCD and, she says, "put me back in control. ERP is what led to real and lasting relief from the symptoms that made me feel miserable and exhausted every day."

Now she says that undergoing ERP was one of the most rewarding experiences of her life, but also one of the most difficult. It required her to face the very things that she feared the most—the unrelenting thoughts that kept racing through her mind and caused so much doubt. "Then, when you're filled with that consuming anxiety," she says, "you aren't allowed to perform the rituals you've been using to try to alleviate it. ERP really challenges you to focus on getting better."

But it works, and in Anne's case it worked relatively quickly.

Anne's treatment involved an intensive course of CBT, which meant working with a therapist five days a week for several hours each day. She took a medical leave of absence from her job so she could devote all of her energy to her treatment program. Some of her therapy took place in her therapist's office, but most sessions happened at her home, since that's where she had struggled with her numerous checking obsessions.

The treatment started with the therapist asking Anne to list a "hierarchy" of situations ranging from those that caused her only mild anxiety to those that created the most dread and held the greatest power over her. One of the most challenging of these exposure exercises involved her gas stove.

"At first, I had to turn on a burner so I could see the flame, turn it off with my eyes closed, and then leave the kitchen without checking to make sure the burner was off," she says. "My therapist had me sit in the living room while my anxiety level spiked and then came down." Working together they repeated the exposure again and again. Each time she repeated the exposure, her anxiety level decreased a little more until it felt fine to leave the kitchen without checking.

Later she performed the same exposure with all four burners— turning them all on, turning them all off without checking, and then leaving the room. Her anxiety level was higher than with only one burner, but it decreased as she repeated the exposure over the next hour, just as it had before. Then she "graduated" to turning on all four burners, turning them off, and leaving the house to walk around the block without checking. Again, her anxiety was intense at first, but it diminished each time she repeated the exposure until eventually it didn't bother her at all.

Anne recalls another difficult exercise involving her alarm clock; at various times in the past, she had spent hours checking it before going to sleep at night in order to be absolutely certain that the alarm was set. With this symptom, there was no way to work up to the exposure gradually. However, she did come up with a strategy: She set the alarm, then covered the clock with a tissue so she wasn't able to see the settings. For the first few evenings, she gave in to her urges and checked the clock several times to make sure she had set the alarm. But soon she was able to resist the compulsion and could fall asleep without checking the alarm at all.

One of her hardest homework assignments involved writing letters, cards, or e-mail messages to people and deliberately misspelling or omitting words. Her exposure list had included reading and rereading handwritten notes dozens of times to be sure she hadn't made any mistakes; with this exercise, however, people she knew would see the errors. The e-mail aspect of the assignment was especially difficult since her software highlighted the misspelled words; she felt as though the mistakes were staring back at her. "It was excruciating at first," she says, but like the other exercises, she got to the point where she also could complete this one without checking.

On the days when her therapist left the house after a home visit, she reminded Anne that they had agreed to a "complete and total ban on checking." The following day, Anne had to report how well she had kept to their agreement. For the first two weeks she almost always had to confess to slipups. But by the end of three weeks, even though she still felt anxiety in some situations, she could report that she'd lived up to the checking ban.

"ERP gave me the tools I need to manage my OCD for the rest of my life," she says, "or at least until there's a cure. My OCD has never disappeared entirely, but now I usually think of it as an aggravation rather than a disability."

The distress that ERP causes is necessary and even deliberate. OCD sufferers need to experience the anxiety, rather than ritualizing or avoiding it, in order to discover that they can manage it. Their fear stems from irrational thoughts about a situation. For instance, Jonathan's harming obsessions were triggered by his driving past a funeral home or watching a violent movie. But, as you will read in Jonathan's continuing story, ERP taught him that such beliefs made no sense—that there was no connection whatsoever between driving past a funeral home and stabbing his wife or child.

The exposure component of his ERP program actually brought Jonathan to the point where he could change his thought patterns— and this, of course, was the cognitive part of the therapy. Jonathan learned to evaluate, interpret, and respond to a particular situation— driving past a funeral home—in a more positive way. In his case, this meant being able to simply drive on the same street as the funeral home and continue on his way, as a healthy person would do.

Initially, Jonathan's way of looking at funeral homes was *distorted*. What the cognitive component of the therapy gave him was the benefit of *cognitive restructuring*—a way of seeing his distorted thoughts for what they were, challenging them, and replacing them with healthier, more accurate thoughts, attitudes, and beliefs—evoked, in this case, by Jonathan's ERP assignments. The exposures truly did work in tandem with the cognitive component of the treatment. With his newly developed perspective, Jonathan could no longer "logically" connect driving past a funeral home with harming his family. His therapy taught him to manage his anxiety in that situation, allowing him to function well enough to understand, on the spot, that such thoughts made no sense.

CBT works for all types of OCD symptoms. If your symptoms have you checking constantly, for instance, it's likely that you carry a distorted sense of responsibility about something terrible happening to your home or family. Many patients obsess that if they are careless enough to leave the stove on, the house will burn down because of their negligence, or that if they merely leave on a light, an electrical fire could be sparked and it would be their fault. This distorted sense of self-blame or responsibility, along with the inclination to attribute excessive importance to a particular thought, might even arise when the OCD patient says something negative about a loved one (e.g., "If I call off work saying my wife has the flu, she could get pneumonia and it would be my fault"). In short, ERP coupled with cognitive therapy gives you an opportunity to test out whether what you fear actually occurs.

It's important to keep in mind that everyone has intrusive thoughts. We all occasionally think things that we shouldn't. All of us have checked to make sure we have our keys as we walked out of the house, or wondered whether we left the coffeemaker on. By contrast, people with OCD misinterpret ordinary situations and fear that those situations will put them or their loved ones in danger. In their minds, for example, messy shirts in a drawer could invite chaos of all sorts. Straightening them to perfection puts control back in their hands: It means everything will be all right. But the ritual of straightening and aligning things brings only momentary certainty and control into their life; when the OCD sufferer sees a crooked picture frame or a rug that's out of place, the perfection-distortion takes hold again and the rituals reoccur.

With ERP, however, you will no longer need that certainty to get through the day; you'll have learned that it isn't possible to exert control over most things in your life. You might still feel a bit of anxiety when you notice a crooked picture on the wall, but you can simply straighten it—or not—and move on without getting involved in lengthy rituals. When treatment is successful, you no longer need the reassurance that rituals falsely promise.

JONATHAN'S ERP TREATMENT

Jonathan's story is a perfect example of a case where *in vivo* exposure alone does not fully work for an OCD patient. You'll remember that Jonathan obsessed about harming his family, even his little girl— terrible thoughts that finally led him to seek help for his disorder.

His ERP assignments: "I had to write a lengthy movie script about stabbing people I loved," he remembers. "It was so painful because it had to be as gory and graphic as possible. I had to describe how I would take a knife and slaughter my family, chop my kid to pieces, splash blood all over the place. I had to describe what the walls and floors covered in blood looked like, what the sounds and smells were. It was awful. At first, I couldn't stand having those thoughts about my family. I was terrified to pick up a knife or a pair of scissors."

But Jonathan recorded his script and listened to it, over and over, and became accustomed to the violent images. "You start thinking about it from a little more distance, like an objective third person. The more I listened, the less afraid I was of those thoughts because I knew they weren't real," he says. His therapist coached him to listen to his tape (an imaginal exposure) and then to put a sharp knife in his pocket and walk around the house knowing he had a knife with him (an *in vivo* exposure). Jonathan was able to connect his gradually lessening level of fear with the knowledge that just because a knife was handy, he wasn't going to use it to harm anyone. It wasn't in his nature to be a cold-blooded killer. Instead, he was a caring husband and father with an overly developed sense of responsibility.

Some aspects of his obsessions he did deal with directly, such as his avoidance of sharp objects (as described above) and his fear of funeral homes. In the past, he took long detours to avoid driving past a funeral home or cemetery, whereas once he began ERP, he not only drove past funeral homes, but if a funeral was under way he parked his car and went in to look at the deceased person. "I attended I don't know how many funerals of complete strangers," he says. "I walked right up to the casket and looked at them. If family members were nearby, I offered my condolences and then left."

Jonathan was able to complete his treatment without any medication. Looking back, he thinks some meds would have eased his anxiety a bit. Today, Jonathan accepts frequent speaking engagements—as, in his words, "an important part of my ongoing recovery." He gives talks to mental health organizations about his OCD experiences, and he usually points out that combining ERP and medication therapy is the answer for many patients.

Jonathan tells audiences he knows what each person is thinking: "No one behaves as badly as me." You're in an emotional cocoon, he says—but when he finally joined a support group, it was a revelation.

"I thought, my God, there's someone else who can't go to a funeral!" No matter how drastic your symptoms might be, he adds, nothing you're doing or thinking is unique to you.

His best advice: Get out of the house and get into a support group, because it can be your lifeline. "Understand that you may never be totally cured of this illness, and that new obsessions can develop. But with education, treatment, and support groups, you can learn how to manage them."

Your ERP assignments might include not only exposing yourself to the situations you fear—the "E" in ERP—but actually staying in that situation for as long as it takes for the intensity of your fear to decrease by at least half. That process is called *habituation*, and it involves becoming accustomed to the anxiety associated with an activity or situation by remaining in it until you experience a marked decrease in your anxiety level.

For example, children who are afraid of the water can be taught gradually to first put their feet in the water, then to enjoy wading, and then to walk in deeper water, until finally they are able to totally immerse themselves without panicking. They are habituating, or becoming comfortable in that situation.

Healthy people habituate all the time, in all sorts of situations. Consider what happens, for example, when cookies are in the oven. When you first walk into the kitchen, you can smell the cookies baking. But if you stay in the kitchen, the smell seems to disappear unless you leave and come back in. Your nervous system would become overloaded if it had to keep sending you messages about the smell of cookies. Instead, it turns down the stimulus, since it is nonessential. So how does this relate to anxiety-producing situations? Almost everyone is a bit nervous when they have to speak in front of a group. Even people who do a great deal of public speaking will describe feeling anxious as they begin a presentation. After a minute or two, however, their heart stops racing, their palms stop sweating, and they become more relaxed. They understand that the discomfort is temporary and nothing to be fearful of. We all know people who once were afraid of flying in planes but, in circumstances that called for them to fly often, weren't so frightened anymore. By changing their behavior and flying in spite of their fears, they were able to change their thoughts and feelings about flying as well.

The better able we are to remain in or habituate to situations that make us fearful, the less afraid we are. The same principle applies when people are in treatment for phobias and other anxiety disorders as well as when they are getting ERP treatment for OCD. Habituation is a key factor in exposure-based treatment.

Another key ingredient in ERP is the "P"—the prevention of rituals. Studies have shown that when people with OCD continue to practice even a few rituals, they really haven't stopped believing that the situation is dangerous and, thus, are not likely to manage their anxieties well. The best outcomes happen when patients understand this at the outset; so, in our clinic we always make sure our patients understand our expectations—and that we understand theirs as well.

For some people, it's also important that the therapist be willing to *model*, or perform, the exposure. Those who have a harming obsession like Jonathan's and whose ERP includes watching violent movies or walking through a cemetery might find it beneficial to have a therapist who modeled their assignment. Likewise, for some patients, it's very helpful if their therapist accompanies them on an exposure. Therapist-directed exposures allow the clinician to instruct and observe, or in some cases to model, what it is the patient should be doing. Or, if the patient's ERP has stalled, having his therapist along on an exposure exercise may allow the two of them to problem-solve where the difficulty lies.

As important as it is that the therapist be willing to reinforce your recovery by performing exposures alongside you, it's even more important that you are willing to do the exposures on your own. We should point out that the research literature supports the use of both therapist-and self-directed exposures. The value of one versus the other depends on the severity of the OCD, the types of obsessions, whether overvalued ideation is present, and, perhaps most important, whether you have access to someone trained to provide ERP in your community. If a therapist isn't accessible, your only resource may be to do self-directed exposures. But if you do have a therapist, it is critical that he or she disengages from directing ERP and encourages you to do more and more on your own. In short, whether it's a matter of modeling or therapist-directed exposure, you need to begin doing the hard work of ERP on your own. There's no better way for you to bolster your confidence and confront your fears.

Sarah's ERP Treatment

Sarah's contamination fears, you'll recall, were triggered by a dead mouse in her apartment. Her ERP plan would have to include some of the dirtiest exercises possible.

Although she lives in Chicago, Sarah found help at the Eastern Pennsylvania Psychiatric Institute in Philadelphia. She lived at the hospital during her three weeks of treatment because she wasn't able to care for herself. Her treatment began with images of germs crawling all over her, as therapists cautioned her not to wash her hands. She had yet to do any actual exercises, but already, she said, "I felt contaminated."

On the second day, Sarah and her therapist went to a public bathroom and sat on the floor—an extremely difficult move for her. Her psychologist laid his palm on the floor and asked her to do the same thing. After a few minutes, she said, "It didn't feel so horrible. There's something reassuring about having the therapist there with you. It makes you feel safer." She wanted to wash her hands, but instead, the doctor touched his arms and face with his dirty hands and asked her to do the same thing. Then she was told to touch his face: "It was even more ghastly," she said, "because then I was contaminating him, too." Yet as she kept her hands on his face and her own, she was already beginning to realize that her actions may have felt gross but were not dangerous.

The following day, they returned to the same bathroom and she was told to touch the toilet seat, then to touch her therapist's shirt and face, and, eventually, to touch both of their mouths with her dirty hands. "Then I had to lick my lips so I would feel I had ingested the contamination," she says. That day, she had to eat lunch and dinner in the hospital cafeteria without washing her hands after the ERP session, and she was instructed to choose food that had to be picked up with her dirty hands. After that day, she wasn't allowed to wash at all except for a five-minute shower at the end of each week.

"At home, that shower would have taken me at least an hour," she says. "Nobody came to tell me my time was up, or drag me out of the shower, but I really wanted to get better."

On weekends, Sarah visited her sister in Washington, D.C. During her first visit, her sister gave her a gift that still touches her today: She rolled a cough drop all over Sarah's slept-on sheets, then popped the cough drop into her mouth. "That was like a miracle," Sarah said.

In later sessions, Sarah was escorted through some city neighborhoods and instructed to give money to street people and shake their hands. On one excursion she was taken to an adult video store. She would use public restrooms, then have to eat an apple or other food without washing her hands. "I felt I had no control over anything," she says. Once she was told to touch a dead pigeon; another time it was dog excrement. Then her worst fear materialized: During one of their sessions on a bathroom floor, her therapist pulled a dead mouse out of his pocket.

"I nearly jumped twenty feet," she says, but then they sat for hours, stroking the dead rodent. The next day, she surprised her therapist by pulling a dead mouse out of her own pocket. She knew she was ready to go home.

Today, Sarah reports few obsessions or compulsions. "They take up maybe thirty seconds on some days, and some days there are none," she says. She has incorporated exposure into her life and still doesn't wash her hands before handling food. "That's my way of saying 'Screw you, OCD—I'll take my chances'."

Whatever the exposure exercise, many of our clients find it helpful to monitor their response prevention—in other words, to track and write about their success in avoiding rituals. You might find, as many have, that monitoring in itself can help you resist them; indeed, each act of monitoring is a reminder that rituals are negative. And each time you resist the urge to respond to your fear with compulsive behavior, you are a little closer to recovery.

Frequently Asked Questions

Q: Do CBT and ERP really work?
A: First, remember that ERP is a form of CBT. Without a doubt, ERP is the most effective way to defeat OCD. Overall, studies find a 50 to 80 percent reduction in OCD symptoms after twelve to twenty sessions of ERP. Emphasizing the cognitive component of therapy alone to treat OCD is a newer innovation; while it has been successful, it doesn't have the same established track record as ERP. However, most therapists who use ERP may be indirectly incorporating elements of cognitive therapy in any case, since exposures help to challenge the beliefs that form the core of OCD.

Q: If my OCD is treated successfully, it will never return—correct?
A: Unfortunately, there's no permanent cure for OCD—but you should leave therapy equipped with enough information and strategies to keep yourself from ritualizing again. Many patients schedule follow-up appointments once or twice a year, just to reinforce their successful recovery. Others will seek out support groups in their community as a means of maintaining their treatment gains. If you have been living with OCD for some time, it's like a comfortable pair of old shoes. There may be a gaping hole in the sole, but when your feet hurt you really want to be wearing those shoes, despite the fact that they aren't really functional. If you have largely recovered from your OCD and you go through a very stressful time, your inclination may be to use a ritual to help you overcome the stress and anxiety. While you shouldn't be hypervigilant about rituals cropping up, you need to be attentive to the potential for falling back into old, dysfunctional, OCD-related patterns.

Q: I saw a psychiatrist for my phobias—which involved fear of driving over bridges and of riding in elevators—and the treatment sounded a lot like my friend's ERP assignments for her OCD. Please explain.
A: Phobias often are treated behaviorally—treatment focuses on exposure to the fear-causing phenomenon. However, rather than ritualizing,

people with phobias avoid the situations they fear. In your case, we're guessing you were told to drive over progressively higher bridges and to take repeated elevator rides. So yes, ERP for OCD is similar to exposure treatment for phobias—just without the ritual prevention component.

Q: My compulsions keep me safe, so why would I go through ERP and give them up?

A: Your compulsions do not keep you safe. You have obsessions about terrible things happening to you or your family—a horrible disease, your house burning down, a car accident—and your compulsions are an attempt to ease the anxiety caused by those obsessions, but they do not keep you safe. Checking the stove and window locks *once* could help keep your house from burning down or being burglarized, but checking them for hours doesn't accomplish anything useful. In fact, you are paying an extremely high price for this maladaptive OCD belief.

Q: Would ERP work with other impulse control disorders, such as compulsive gambling or sexual addiction?

A: Each disorder is different. For some disorders in the obsessive-compulsive spectrum, such as hoarding, ERP may be a beneficial treatment. For others, such as compulsive gambling or sex addiction, exposure and response prevention isn't the treatment of choice. If you think you have an anxiety disorder or a disabling condition of any kind, it's best to talk to a clinician to see which treatment approach would be best for you.

Q: Is it absolutely necessary to see a professional in order to treat my OCD?

A: It's not always critical to see a clinician; it is possible to design your own plan of ERP and treat yourself. However, only a professional can firmly diagnose that your condition is, in fact, OCD. Also, you may need medication to help with other conditions that arise during your treatment, such as depression or overwhelming anxiety. A treatment plan, drawn up by a professional in collaboration with you, will give you the quickest and most effective route to recovery. And it is crucial that you see a professional if you are experiencing thoughts of suicide or if you are abusing alcohol or drugs or if your OCD is putting you or your family at risk.

Q: In what other ways might my recovery be facilitated by clinician-guided therapy?

A: One additional benefit of clinician-guided therapy is the clinician's experience in treating OCD and his or her ability to customize your ERP program so that you realize maximum success in the early stages. A trained professional can select exposure items that would be lower on the hierarchy as your starting point, so that you could build on the confidence of early successes. And, your clinician would know how to assess your progress along the way and make adjustments accordingly. Another advantage of working with a clinician is that he or she will know how to help you if you get stuck. Sometimes, our patients don't realize that they are distracting from an exposure while doing the assignment; as a result, it's hard to move up the exposure hierarchy since items lower on the list really haven't been mastered. But a clinician can spot that distracting behavior and bring it to the patient's attention. A clinician also may be better able to work with a family member or friend who is willing to be your OCD coach. This is especially the case if family members have been involved in facilitating your ritualizing or are frustrated with your OCD behaviors.

SEVEN

What to Expect from Treatment, Step by Step

IF YOU CAME TO OUR CLINIC for help with your OCD symptoms, you would talk to a clinician who would first evaluate your disorder and its effects on your life. In collaboration with your therapist, you would put together a treatment plan. Your ultimate goal would be to get to the point where you didn't need to perform rituals.

You learned in the previous chapter about the cognitive component of cognitive behavior therapy (CBT) and how important exposure and response prevention (ERP) is to the process of getting well. You also read several accounts of OCD patients who used ERP to conquer their rituals, so you know that the route to recovery can be difficult and frightening—but you saw that for those patients, the outcome, a return to normal lives and relationships, was worth every bit of effort. We hope that the information we have provided and the experiences of these veterans of the treatment process are helping to demystify both OCD and the process of recovery.

We thought it would be worthwhile, now, to walk you through a generic course of OCD treatment as it would unfold in our clinic. As you read along, imagine yourself as the patient. Apply the various steps to your own symptoms. By the time you complete this sample "treatment plan," you will have a good idea of what might be involved in the treatment of your disorder. If you are working on your own, you will have the tools to help yourself deal with your OCD; if you are working with a therapist, these steps will be a helpful adjunct to your treatment.

ERP: What to Expect

Step 1: Setting Goals and Objectives

In your first actual treatment meeting, once a clinician has completed your evaluation, you and your therapist would start getting to know each other. This process involves setting goals and objectives for your treatment. To do that, you can simply ask yourself: What do I want to accomplish? If I woke up tomorrow and everything was better, what would that mean? What would be different? By determining a clear set of goals and objectives, you will have a road map to help you gauge your progress.

Most of our patients identify a broad goal for treatment. An example might be, "I will get my OCD under control," or, "I will get back to the way I was before OCD was running my life." Your treatment plan may include just one goal or it can include more than one. It is likely that at least one of your goals will focus on your OCD. If you are also experiencing depression, alleviating that might constitute a second goal for treatment. If you have multiple goals, you will need to prioritize them. Trying to address all of your goals at the same time would be overwhelming.

We then would ask you to help us better understand your goals. Indeed, we work with all of our patients to develop objectives. Objectives are realistic and measurable ways for both the clinician and patient to assess progress toward achieving a goal. For some patients, an objective might be to ride the subway to work and not have to scrub themselves after they get there, or to flush a toilet using their bare hand rather than holding a paper towel or using their foot to turn the handle. For others, an objective might be to check the locks and doors only once before they leave the house—and then get in the car and drive away.

In your own case, of course, the objectives would fit your OCD symptoms. You can add or refine objectives as you go along, and you should have more than one objective for each goal. However, you do not have to specify each and every objective; just provide a reasonable number of examples so that you can characterize what you would like to accomplish.

The goals set by our patients don't always involve just behavioral rituals. They may instead have a goal that focuses on their obsessions or on mental rituals. In this case, the goal might be, "I will be less bothered by my intrusive thoughts." And an objective that relates to a goal of this type might be, "I will spend less than ten minutes a day obsessing," or, "I will reduce my belief in my obsession to less than 10 percent."

On the following page is a Goals and Objectives Worksheet for you to complete. If you are working with a therapist, it might be helpful to bring this with you to your first appointment—or at least to have given some serious thought to your goals and objectives. If you are working on your own, this is an essential first step.

Step 2: Managing Physical Symptoms of Anxiety

Before progressing any further, we would like to teach you how to manage your physical symptoms of anxiety. Like setting goals and objectives, learning how to manage anxiety symptoms is an important step in helping you to prepare for undertaking ERP.

The situations that trigger your OCD symptoms usually bring on severe anxiety; if you're going to manage your symptoms and eliminate your rituals, you must first get your anxiety level down to where you can function in those situations *without* resorting to rituals. Thus, in our clinic we would teach you diaphragmatic breathing, or some other relaxation technique—something that is easy to perform, that you can learn quickly. We would be giving you a tool, enabling you to reduce your anxiety so you can start your treatment. Not all therapists teach these techniques. But we find them useful because many

GOALS AND OBJECTIVES WORKSHEET

Instructions: List your goals and objectives. Remember that a goal is a general statement of what you want to accomplish. (If you were to wake up tomorrow and your OCD was gone, what would be different?) Objectives are specific, realistic, and measurable ways that you can assess your progress toward your goals.

Example:

Goal #1:   I will be less preoccupied with my contamination fears.

Objectives: 1a. I will be able to sit on the ground outside and not shower afterward.

1b. I will be able to use my household cleaning products, like window cleaner, and not use rubber gloves.

1c. I will not wash and disinfect any items that I buy and bring into the house.

1d. I will spend less than fifteen minutes per day obsessing about germs.

My Goals and Objectives:

Goal #1:

_____

Objectives:

1a. _____

1b. _____

1c. _____

1d. _____

Goal #2:

_____

Objectives:

2a. _____

2b. _____

2c. _____

2d. _____

Goal #3:

_____

Objectives:

3a. _____

3b. _____

3c. _____

3d. _____

of our patients want to have a tool they can quickly master as a first step in treatment. The use of anxiety management skills has a secondary purpose as well: It will help you to become proficient at rating your anxiety levels. This process plays an important role in ERP.

Diaphragmatic breathing, at least in principle, is easy to master. There are two key elements: (1) gradually slowing your breathing rate down to a point where you are comfortable and (2) breathing through your nose. Some of our patients will report that they already know how to do this, so we ask them to demonstrate. More often than not, they take a very deep breath in and then exhale it forcefully through their mouth. This method isn't paced breathing. In fact, it's a terrific way to hyperventilate! We don't want you to do that. Instead, try to avoid forcing air in or out. Diaphragmatic breathing should be relaxing. As a test, place one hand on your belly, just above your belt, and the other hand below your collarbone. If you are doing the breathing correctly, the hand on your belly will be moving the most. We don't, however, encourage you to get all caught up in whether you are doing this "right." Just know that if you slow your breathing rate down, you will begin to automatically use your diaphragm to breathe. It's what you do when you fall asleep, so it's a skill you already have. Once you think you have the basics mastered, try to practice this skill for ten to fifteen minutes twice each day. When you first sit down to practice, rate your level of anxiety on a 0-to-10 scale. A 10 is the most anxious you have ever been; a 0 means you are so relaxed you are almost asleep. After you have completed your breathing exercise, rate your level again. In the beginning, you may find that your anxiety level drops only a little. As you get better at this skill, you should be able to lower your anxiety level more efficiently.

A few words of caution regarding any relaxation exercise are worth noting. Many of our patients are used to feeling anxious. Thus, when they try to relax, their body reacts in an unexpected way. Instead of becoming calmer, they find that they become more anxious. In fact, there is a term for this: "relaxation-induced anxiety." If you find that after a few minutes you're feeling more anxious rather than less so, stop practicing. Instead of forcing yourself to practice for fifteen minutes, use a shorter session—for example, three minutes—as your practice time.

(Decide on how long your practice should be based upon when you start to feel anxious.) Increase the number of daily, three-minute practice sessions until you're getting a total of twenty to thirty minutes of practice. You want to be sure that you have as few interruptions as possible when you practice. So, you may want to turn off the phone and make sure that someone is watching the kids or that they're asleep, and also that there are no pets nearby who want to unexpectedly jump into your lap. Practicing with music on is fine; just be attentive to the type of music you plan to listen to. We have had to convince some patients that heavy-metal music doesn't really facilitate relaxing!

We have included a Relaxation Log to help you keep track of your practice sessions and how well you are mastering this technique.

FORM 7.2

RELAXATION LOG

Date / time of day	Beginning level of tension	Ending level of tension (0–10)	Where practice took place	Comments or problems
0 = no tension/anxiety, almost asleep 10 = the most anxious you have ever been				

Physical Wellness and OCD

Clients often ask us whether exercise or a new diet plan is compatible with OCD treatment. Our response is an enthusiastic "Yes," but with a caveat.

Getting physically healthier will boost your positive feelings about yourself and should help you to succeed with ERP. However, it's important that you share your planned wellness program with your clinician because some elements of it may affect your medication or other aspects of your current treatment. Here are some pointers to keep in mind:

- Too much caffeine can disturb your sleep and affect your energy level, so you may wish to decrease your intake. But be sure to do so slowly. Stopping all caffeine abruptly will cause you to have headaches.
- Tell your clinician not only about your diet plan but also about any supplements you're taking and any exercise you're doing so he or she can be sure you won't be working against your own good efforts.
- Don't allow your wellness plan to become another ritual, or to distract you from the more difficult parts of your exposure hierarchy.
- Embarking on a fitness program is always a good idea, but be realistic about how many things in your life you can change at once.

ERP is hard work; so is taking on a diet and exercise regimen or some other self-improvement goal. Make sure you have carefully considered whether you have the energy to tackle all of these changes simultaneously, or if you'd have a better chance to succeed going at it more gradually.

Once you have outlined your goals and objectives and begun practicing diaphragmatic breathing, you are ready to begin the hard work of ERP. Recall the basics of exposure and response prevention from our earlier discussion: You put yourself in the anxiety-causing situation and, as always, you feel anxious. But instead of leaving the situation or ritualizing, you stay in that situation until the anxiety level is reduced by at least half. (Most patients report that they get pretty good at gauging their anxiety in this way; it quickly becomes easier for them to measure when they've cut their fear in half.) The idea is to stay there long enough to see for yourself that nothing catastrophic happens in that situation and that your anxiety level does, in fact, come down.

If you have OCD with contamination symptoms, touching the floor and then rubbing your hands across your body feels like a dangerous thing to do. For most people, it might be distasteful or gross, but they wouldn't see it as dangerous. If you perform that action as part of your ERP, you, too, would discover that nothing bad happens when you touch your face with dirty hands. In short, ERP builds a case against ritualizing by showing you that what you fear the most will not happen.

This is not to say that your anxiety necessarily disappears altogether. But it will diminish as *you learn to tolerate it*. It takes practice; if you get to the point, for instance, where you can touch your face, mouth, and eyes with dirty hands without washing, or can hold a public bathroom doorknob until your anxiety is cut in half without taking a shower until the next day, you will have accomplished a great deal. And as your exposure time builds, you'll come to know: "If I do this enough times, I'll know I'm not going to die from it."

You can expect homework assignments to be a major component of your ERP program. If you are working with a therapist as part of an intensive treatment program, you will probably spend at least one hour performing ERP exercises during each session. Similarly, if you are working with a therapist in a traditional outpatient setting, it is likely that a portion of the session will initially be devoted to therapist-directed ERP. But in either case you should plan to allow an additional hour each day for homework.

The amount of time you spend engaging in ERP is vital to your recovery, so it's not in your best interests to skip days or take shortcuts. In the case of ERP, more is definitely better!

Step 3: Developing Your Exposure Hierarchy

We understand that overcoming OCD involves considerable fortitude and a great deal of courage. But it's important to underscore that we don't ask our patients to tackle the things they fear the most at first. We work systematically by asking our patients to develop an "exposure hierarchy"—a rank-ordered list of their feared situations. You, too, should be able to build a hierarchy of your triggers—those thoughts and situations that cause you to ritualize. You may already have a sense of what your rituals are, but it's important to fine-tune this information so you can design a plan for stopping them. In this section, we will help you to develop and refine your personal hierarchy.

The therapists at our clinic often ask patients to begin keeping a list of everything that causes even the slightest twinge of anxiety, all the way up to the biggest symptom-causing events. If your obsessions are about contamination, for instance, can you drop a pencil on the floor and simply pick it up without feeling any anxiety? How much anxiety would there be if you dropped a pencil outside on the sidewalk? What would happen if you dropped your house keys into the toilet bowl? Would you feel a slight pang of anxiety in these situations, or would your anxiety reach the level of a full-blown panic attack? How about if a neighbor were to ask you to wipe her baby's nose or change a diaper? It's essential that we know what triggers your OCD, so we would try to help you work up a list that covers as many situations and differing levels of anxiety as possible.

We've found that some patients cannot provide all the information we need at this stage. There are several reasons why this might happen:

- The patients may have lived with their symptoms for so long or have such limited insight that they cannot see that their behaviors are rituals. Alternatively, they may discount their rituals as being situation specific. Some obsessions, especially those that trigger lesser amounts of anxiety, may no longer even seem to be obsessions; likewise, the associated rituals are discounted.

- The patients may have become so adept at avoidance that they are unaware of things they are no longer doing. For example, if a clinician asks someone with contamination fears whether she can use a public restroom, she may say "Yes." But if the clinician does not ask her whether she can touch the faucets or the door handle without using a paper towel to protect her hands, items that belong on the hierarchy may be missed.

- The patients may be embarrassed by their obsessions and their rituals. This is easy to understand; they recognize that taking hours to leave the house because they're straightening or scrubbing isn't normal behavior. They may minimize the impact that OCD has on their life.

- Sometimes, obsessions or rituals are so distressing to patients that they have difficulty even discussing them. When this happens, we try discussing less serious fears. For instance, we might make an agreement with the patients that, once they've made progress on certain less-anxiety-producing exposures, we will begin to add the bigger items to the list.

It's important that you be brutally honest with yourself and provide your therapist with as much information as possible. With this info, we will be able to help design a list of situations that is relevant to the specifics of your OCD. This list will form your exposure hierarchy, and your success at completing the progressively more difficult exposures will mark your improvement.

Your exposure hierarchy will basically consist of a rank order of triggers and rituals ranging from 0 to 100. Bear in mind that the ranking is not rigid; it can be adjusted at any time throughout your therapy. In our clinic, we address items in increments of 5. So, as we list your items, we'll need to know, for instance, What would have a score of 100? What makes you the most anxious—using a public toilet without washing your hands? Touching a dead bird? Or, as with Sarah, touching a dead mouse?

Then we move down to 50: What makes you just half as anxious as that worst-case situation? Hugging a person who is HIV-positive, perhaps, or eating grapes without washing them? What behaviors would give you a ranking of 25—handling magazines in a doctor's office waiting room? Then we might jump up to 75—sitting on the floor in a bus or train station?

Then we refine the list even further. Touching a light switch might be a slight (or major) anxiety trigger for you, but not all light switches are the same. Does it feel the same to flick a light switch in a hotel room as it does in a neighbor's house? How about one in your own home, after one of your kids touched it, or an outdoor porch light versus an indoor switch?

Tracking your anxiety or rituals in this way is a rigorous task, but it's important to be as specific as possible. We don't want items on your hierarchy that are too broad because then we won't know what may be triggering your anxiety. If driving gives you OCD-related anxiety, you need to specify whether you become anxious at all and/or at the same level on a freeway, on bridges, at a crosswalk, in a major city, on streets that are bumpy, and on roads in the countryside. For example, if you don't feel compelled to retrace your route to make sure you didn't run someone over when driving down a particular country road, it doesn't make sense to have this as a hierarchy item. By the same token, simply including "driving" on your list isn't specific enough because it may be far more difficult for you to be driving in a school zone when children are standing at the crosswalk than to be driving on a freeway.

Some hierarchy items need to be broken down a little differently. These may involve duration, for instance. Going back to our example of dropping a pencil on the floor, would your anxiety level vary depending on how long you held the pencil after picking it up? Likewise, would it be harder if you couldn't wash your hands (or the pencil) for fifteen minutes, thirty minutes, an hour, a day, or not at all? Obviously, our preference is that you not ritualize at all after an exposure—but for some people, gradually expanding the amount of time to reach this goal is their best chance at success.

Also, on those occasions when you can't quite decide whether a situation is, for example, a 60 or a 70 on your hierarchy, err on the side of making it more difficult. Doing so will decrease the probability that you have misgauged the difficulty.

Once you have accumulated a list of the triggers and rituals that will form your hierarchy, you need to consolidate the information all in one place. We have included an Exposure Hierarchy Worksheet on which you can organize your hierarchy items.

The "nuance" of these broader situations is what will make ERP work for you, and it's different for everybody. Once we have your hierarchy set, we can begin to design ERP to combat the triggers and rituals that are specific to you. In most cases, we would start by addressing items with rankings of 20 or 30 and lower. If you are working on your own, you should likewise begin with the easier items on your hierarchy.

OCD often takes more than one form. Some patients might have checking and washing symptoms; others might have washing and harming symptoms. For those individuals, we can take one of several approaches; we can work on *all* of their checking obsessions and compulsions first, then move on and address all of their washing symptoms.

Or, we can devise a plan that cuts across the *types* of symptoms and works on all of them by *level*—that is, we could first treat all of their symptoms with rankings of 20 and below, then all of their symptoms ranked at 25, then all symptoms ranked at 30, and so on. From this perspective, too, every patient is unique; we would work together to create the best treatment plan for each particular lifestyle, including yours.

First, before addressing your thoughts, we would work on at least a few of your lower-level symptoms using ERP, eliminating your need to do rituals in those lower-anxiety situations. This would help build your confidence and start getting you accustomed to dealing with your OCD in a more adaptive way.

One word of caution is in order here. Many of our patients extend their perfectionism to completing their hierarchy; they get caught up in trying to decide what the right number for an item is.

EXPOSURE HIERARCHY WORKSHEET

Your exposure hierarchy should include triggers that generate varying amounts of anxiety and cause you to engage in rituals. You can include items at the same degree of difficulty, but it's helpful if the overall list covers the broadest range possible on your hierarchy. If you are trying to decide on just where to put an item on the list, err on the side of making it more difficult. Hierarchy items should also be specific. Refer to "Step 3: Developing Your Exposure Hierarchy" in Chapter 7 if you need more information about how to build your hierarchy.

Difficulty Level	Hierarchy item description
100	
95	
90	
85	
80	
75	
70	
65	
60	
55	
50	
45	
40	
35	
30	
25	
20	
15	
10	
5	

If this is happening to you, try a different strategy. Instead of rank-ordering your items, group them into categories: "easy," "moderately difficult," and "hard." Likewise, it's important to avoid getting caught up in how many items should be on your hierarchy. You need to have enough breadth across anxiety-producing situations that you can select easy exposures and then move on to items that are more challenging but not overwhelming.

Step 4: Beginning ERP—Let Your Hierarchy Be Your Guide

Once you have completed your hierarchy, the next step is to use it! Making progress up your hierarchy is what your treatment goals are all about. You need to remember that the point of ERP is not to avoid or eliminate the anxiety and the intrusive thoughts but, rather, to learn how to *tolerate* them without ritualizing.

Exposure, ideally, would be planned. In our clinic, the therapists might accompany you on an exposure in session, and they would always give you a homework exercise. For instance, when at home, you would deliberately drop a pencil on the floor, then pick it up and hold it until your anxiety diminished by half, and then go back to what you were doing—or even better, you would repeat the exposure. You might also use the diaphragmatic breathing you have been practicing to bring your anxiety level down even further than the halfway point.

The exposure process itself is straightforward. Begin by picking an item from your hierarchy that you want to try. This first item should be one that will generate only a little anxiety so you will have the opportunity to learn how to master the skills needed to do ERP and build your confidence. You don't want to select an exposure that will cause you to panic! Next, decide on where you will do the exposure and then follow through. For example, if you have contamination fears, a relatively easy exposure might be to grasp the bathroom doorknob at home. Once you've selected this as your assignment, decide when you will actually do the exposure. You may opt to do the exercise as soon as you get home from work. Implement your plan and, while doing so, note what your anxiety level is. Let's assume your anxiety level increases to 20 on a scale of 0 to 100 when doing the exposure. You will need to continue to hold on to the door handle until your anxiety drops to at least a 10. Also be aware of how long it takes for your anxiety level to drop. Once your anxiety is lowered by half, you can use your breathing skills (or the cognitive coping strategy that we discuss later in this chapter) to further lower your anxiety.

Completing your exposure exercises could take just a few seconds, or considerably longer. But no matter how long it takes, your anxiety will eventually lessen—it's not possible to stay anxious forever. Obviously, once you complete the exposure, you should not ritualize. In the current example, this would mean that you do not wash your hands after holding the doorknob. Instead, you just go about your usual routine. You might even want to repeat this exposure a little while later.

There are a few "rules" that will help you get the most out of an exposure.

- Though you may be tempted, don't focus on being able to ritualize at some later time. Some of our patients will breeze through an exposure because they remind themselves that no matter how anxiety provoking it is, in a little while they can wash, check, and so on.

- Likewise, be careful not to allow reassurance seeking to sneak in as a way to alleviate your anxiety after an exposure. In our example, if after a while you asked a friend, "You can't get AIDS from grabbing a doorknob, can you?" this seemingly innocuous question could defeat the purpose of the exercise. And remember that searching the Internet for answers to these sorts of questions is also a form of reassurance seeking!

- Some people find very subtle ways to distract from their exposures. One of our patients became very talkative while doing hers. In fact, her progress on her hierarchy was very impressive. But when we asked that she not talk during her

exposures, she found the tasks to be much more challenging—
her talking was a way of distracting herself from fully experiencing the anxiety associated with the exposures. Talking is
just one form of distraction. Be attentive to any sort of behavior that you find yourself doing routinely in these sorts of situations and then refrain from that behavior. If you find that
it's harder to do the exposure, you may have been distracting.

- Remember that exposures need to be repeated. Successfully
  completing an exposure once doesn't necessarily mean that
  you've conquered the obsessions and compulsions associated
  with that item. Indeed, it's always a good idea to go back and
  repeat the "easier" items on your hierarchy; doing so allows
  you to cement your success and your skills.

Earlier, we alluded to the need for you to plan your exposures.
The planning aspect of selecting exposures is important because, for
instance, if you were to accidentally drop a pencil at work, you might
sit there full of anxiety, unable to pick it up despite having succeeded
at the same planned exposure at home. Planning exposures and having a detailed hierarchy help to prevent you from thinking that you
are not making progress or feeling defeated, especially if you are confronted with a situation that is more anxiety provoking than what
you have been practicing. In our clinic, we would ask you to set aside
the time to work on specific exposures and to be thoughtful—to
fully engage in the exercise. Then, if you drop a pencil at work, you
would be equipped to say to yourself, "I've been really good at mastering this at home. Maybe the current situation is unexpected—
maybe I can handle it here, too. If I can't, then I'll know where it
belongs on my hierarchy." That said, sometimes the best-laid plans go
awry. You may have honestly believed that there would be no difference between dropping a pencil at home and dropping one at work.
Instead, you find that the work situation is unexpectedly more difficult. This sort of thing happens. It's hard to anticipate all of the in-
tricacies of every situation. Understand that you did your best, rerate
the difficulty level, and move on.

We noted that, ideally, you do not ritualize after having completed an exposure. But if you do "slip" and ritualize, be honest and tell your therapist during your next appointment. That way, the therapist will know that you need an effective strategy for preventing rituals and can work with you on creating that plan. Likewise, if you are working on your own and notice that rituals are creeping back in, don't ignore, avoid, or dismiss it. Do something proactive. Rituals are often an easy trap to fall back into, so if you catch yourself in a ritual, be attentive to the need to initiate response prevention.

In helping you to plan and perform these exercises, we would learn more about your anxiety and rituals. For instance, continuing the above example, we might ascertain that workplace anxiety is an entirely separate category, or that retrieving the pencil is more difficult in some situations than in others. Perhaps it's easier to pick up the pencil on a carpeted floor than after it has rolled under your desk and is sitting among the dust bunnies. We would refine your hierarchy so that workplace-related items were better integrated into it—at a higher level, if necessary. That's why we always tell patients that the hierarchy is flexible—we expect to learn more about everyone's anxiety and rituals along the way.

We should note here that some clinicians might require patients to completely abstain from a ritual for a specified period of time. One example of this approach is a "no wash" protocol that we have used; it entails asking patients to go without washing altogether, even if they are going to prepare food for other people. (Recall Sarah's "no wash" experience with ERP, which we described in the previous chapter.) This approach takes the pressure off with regard to how much of a normal, daily activity is permissible for someone who can't separate an acceptable level of the activity from a ritual.

So that you can have a clear sense of your progress, we've included an Exposure Log for you to complete. Having you keep track of your exposures, along with your beginning and ending levels of anxiety and the amount of time you spend with each exposure, is a good way of remaining aware of your progress (and of knowing whether and when you're getting stuck). It also keeps you honest about just how much you are practicing.

EXPOSURE LOG

Exposure item and level	Practice day and number	Anxiety level at start of ERP	Number of minutes to decrease anxiety by half	Ending level of anxiety
Driving around the block early in the morning - 25	Friday: 1 2 3 4 5 Saturday: 1 2 3 4 5	30 30 30 25 25 30 25 20 20 15	10 12 8 8 8 10 10 10 8 8	15 15 15 10 10 15 15 10 10 8

Exposure item and level	Practice day and number	Anxiety level at start of ERP	Number of minutes to decrease anxiety by half	Ending level of anxiety

Step 5: Normalizing Behaviors

While completely abstaining from a ritual for a period of time is a highly effective strategy, it can also be misused. We talked to one woman with contamination triggers who never washes her hands now after she uses the toilet. We don't think that's a productive outcome—instead, it is a form of avoidance. Guiding that patient to a normal hand-washing routine after she has completed several days of contamination without washing would be a better outcome.

Part of setting goals and objectives and eliminating rituals is deciding what constitutes "normal" responses and behaviors in anxiety-triggering situations. Some patients become so caught up in their OCD that they lose sight of what the "normal" level of an activity is. It's not unlike dieting: If you are accustomed to overeating, you may not know what an average-sized portion of food is. With food, of course, it's easy to figure out—there are labels on most products that give you calorie counts or a means of assessing how much is too much. Making this determination is harder when it comes to OCD.

One way to figure out what this "average" amount of a behavior might be is to ask or to observe. With respect to some rituals, such as washing your hands after using the bathroom, you may be able to observe people in a public restroom. In other instances, you may need to survey people you trust, or who understand about your OCD, regarding the amount of time they spend washing their hands after using the bathroom, how long they shower, how often they check to see if they have locked the doors, or how frequently they wash their bath towels after they have been used. Don't ask just one person; ask several. Once you have the answers to your survey, calculate the "average" and use it as your guideline.

Step 6: Paying Attention to Your Thoughts

ERP has been the mainstay of OCD treatment for years. Recently, however, researchers interested in treatment have also been giving some attention to the role of thoughts, especially OCD-related beliefs, in treatment. Examining your thoughts—the cognitive component of therapy—is much easier once you have some perspective based on having reduced your ritualizing. At that point, as you continue your ERP, you can begin the process of separating facts of a situation from your unrealistic fears.

Some people with contamination obsessions, for example, believe that they will come to harm or that they may cause harm to others as a result of their becoming contaminated and passing that contamination on to someone else. What, we would ask, do you know for sure? On any given day, how many people in this world come into contact with floor germs? The answer, we would assume, is millions. And we would then ask, "Have you seen anything on the news indicating that people died or became horribly ill because they touched the floor or ate a cracker that fell on the floor? Is there an epidemic going on that most of the world's population is unaware of?" The answer, of course, is no—so our next question would be, "What do you make of that information?" You would have to conclude that touching the floor isn't likely to be harmful. And you would know—at least at those times when you are not overwhelmed with anxiety—that this is true.

What this set of questions illustrates is that when you are caught up in your obsessions, you may have not correctly assessed the probability that you could become sick from touching the floor or eating something that dropped. Rather, your OCD causes you to believe that it is highly likely that you would get sick. One way of testing this out is to create an experiment. This is exactly what I did in working with one of my patients who sincerely believed that, if she touched the floor in a public restroom and then touched someone she knew, that person might become horribly ill. She touched the bathroom floor and then shook my hand. I then licked my hand. I promised that I would get word to her if I became so ill that I couldn't make her next appointment. Needless to say, I was in perfect health for her appointment a few days later.

You can accurately predict that some situations will happen. Floors will be dirty, kids will have runny noses and bring home germs, and, once in a while, you will leave a window unlocked. It happens to everyone. What people with OCD misgauge and misinterpret is the *probability* that a catastrophic outcome will occur and/or the *severity* of the outcome. These are two kinds of cognitive errors. The probability is high that touching the floor won't kill you, that wiping a child's runny nose won't give you a life-threatening disease, and that a little rain on the windowsill won't bring disaster on your family.

What about severity assessments? How bad would it really be if you weren't perfect? If you left the house wearing two different-colored socks, would people really think there was something wrong with you? If you didn't read and reread the same paragraph until it was just right in your mind so that you could get a perfect score on a test, would it really matter if your grade was lower than an A+? The task here involves how you are going to reconcile your beliefs with the outcome of an experiment—or an exposure. Can you tolerate the consequence of being less than perfect? How bad would it really be? On the other hand, if you believe that if you didn't check the burners on the stove and it would be your fault if the house burned down, that would be a severe consequence. However, there is an interaction between probability and severity that is being overlooked. The probability that not checking the burner would result in a fire is infinitely small. Is it worth spending hours of checking to prevent something that is so unlikely to occur? In this case, probability outweighs severity.

One of our patients, Elena, was a new mother. Prior to her pregnancy, she had no problems with anxiety or OCD. However, shortly after her child was born, she began to have intrusive thoughts about whether something terrible would happen to her child as a result of her not being a good mother. She baby-proofed everything it was possible to baby-proof and walked through the house innumerable times checking to make sure everything was safeguarded. She lay awake most of the night so she could check on her newborn every few minutes. She asked herself, "What if I missed an electrical outlet? The baby might stick her finger in there and be electrocuted." She similarly obsessed over, "What if the baby stops breathing in the middle of the night? If I don't check on her, it would be my fault if something terrible happened."

Elena began her treatment in our clinic by practicing ERP exercises from her hierarchy; then we began to work on challenging these thoughts. We first looked at the reality. One of the first steps was helping Elena to realize that she was a new parent and that many, if not most, parents experience fears about this huge change in their lives. So while her concerns were normal, she was preoccupied with them excessively and they were interfering with her ability to enjoy being a new mother. Elena's child wasn't even crawling yet, so the probability that she would poke her finger into an outlet was very small. And as we noted above, Elena had gone through the house (and had her husband and mother do likewise) to make sure that everything necessary had been done to ensure that it was baby-proofed. After examining what she had done and what childcare experts recommended, Elena concluded that she had done as much as any diligent, good parent could do to make sure her child was safe.

Regarding the issue of feeling responsible for making sure that her child continued to breathe while asleep, we had Elena do a different sort of homework. (Remember from Chapter 4 that *inflated responsibility* is one of the six core beliefs affecting OCD sufferers.) Specifically, we asked her to do some research on sudden infant death syndrome (SIDS). What she found out was that it doesn't occur all that frequently, that having the baby sleep on her back was one means of prevention that she had already accounted for, and that occurrence of SIDS is not the fault of a parent. Further, when Elena weighed whether she would be able to best care for her baby if she had more sleep versus waking up every half-hour, she realized that not sleeping was not in the best interests of her child. She had to stop checking both on her baby-proofing and on whether the baby was still breathing (these two issues were the major focus of her ERP) as well as change her beliefs about what being a responsible parent meant.

During the course of her ERP, Elena wrote down what her thoughts were. By examining her thoughts in each of her exposure situations, she was able to see that being completely responsible at all times was not achievable. She was able to put into perspective that as a parent, she was going to make mistakes and she could not protect her child from every bump or bruise. In fact, sometimes falling down wasn't so bad. Her job was to be the best parent she could be, and to avoid being overly protective. As a result of changing her beliefs about what it meant to be a responsible parent, she was able to stop ritualizing. As you can see from the Changing My Thoughts and Beliefs Worksheet she filled out, we were able to identify how Elena's beliefs about responsibility were helping to fuel her OCD.

Elena ultimately completed a number of worksheets in response to the items on her hierarchy that caused her to obsess and/or ritualize. These reflected other belief domains in addition to variations on the theme of responsibility. In the beginning, Elena truly believed that if she did not perform her rituals, something bad would happen and that this would be proof of her being a bad mother. But when she began to examine and dispute her thoughts, she found that she also believed she had done her best and that her rituals were not really alleviating her fears. Indeed, examining her thoughts and beliefs helped her put her fears in perspective. Her belief in the evidence outweighed her obsessional fears.

Treating OCD with Medication

Not everyone being treated for OCD needs a prescription medication as part of the treatment. But OCD is a disorder that can create overwhelming anxiety and distress—and these symptoms can be forceful enough to prevent patients from successfully managing their ERP assignments. In those instances, psychiatrists often will prescribe a class of antidepressants called serotonin reuptake inhibitors (SRIs), which, as we discussed in Chapter 3, are effective in normalizing the serotonin function in the brain. SRIs have the capacity to tame OCD symptoms so that patients can carry on with their recovery program.

Summing It All Up

One way to better understand the ERP-related process of disputing obsessional beliefs is to think of it in terms of climbing a steep hill. As you walk toward that hill, you are getting prepared for the climb (setting goals and objectives, developing your hierarchy, practicing paced breathing). Then you start the hard work of climbing up (selecting, planning, and undertaking the actual exposure). Eventually

CHANGING MY THOUGHTS AND BELIEFS WORKSHEET

Ritual	Anxiety-producing thoughts/ obsessions	Beliefs[1]—and rationale for the beliefs	Evidence to dispute[2] how likely this is to happen	Evidence to dispute[2] how bad it would be if it did happen
Checking to make sure the house is baby-proofed	I have to check all of the outlets or else something bad might happen to the baby. If something bad happens, it would be my fault. I'm a terrible mother.	Inflated responsibility—It will be my fault for not having checked thoroughly enough if the baby gets hurt or is electrocuted.	I've gone through the house twice myself and my husband and mother have checked all of the outlets, too. I read the book my doctor recommended about how to baby-proof everything and followed the directions. Given how much I've done, it's really unlikely that anything bad will happen.	It would be horrible if something happened to the baby. However, I have done the best job any parent could do to protect my child. As much as I would like to, I can't protect the people I love from everything bad that could possibly happen.

[1]**Beliefs:** overestimating the importance of the thought, ability to control thoughts, inflated responsibility, inability to tolerate uncertainty, overestimating the threat, perfectionism

[2]**Disputes:** What do I know? What evidence is there that is counter to what I'm saying to myself? What are the facts? Is what I'm expecting achievable, reasonable, or even desirable?

Ritual	Anxiety-producing thoughts/ obsessions	Beliefs[1]—and rationale for the beliefs	Evidence to dispute[2] how likely this is to happen	Evidence to dispute[2] how bad it would be if it did happen

[1]**Beliefs:** overestimating the importance of the thought, ability to control thoughts, inflated responsibility, inability to tolerate uncertainty, overestimating the threat, perfectionism

[2]**Disputes:** What do I know? What evidence is there that is counter to what I'm saying to myself? What are the facts? Is what I'm expecting achievable, reasonable, or even desirable?

you reach the top, where you become more objectively aware of how hard the climb was, at which point you can begin the gradual descent back down the other side (waiting for your anxiety level to begin to decline). Once you've caught your breath and your energy starts to return, you can reflect on the experience (using paced breathing and cognitive restructuring to further lower your anxiety and dispute your obsessional beliefs).

The next chapter explains the various medications used in treating OCD, their strengths and side effects, and how they work alongside an ERP program.

Frequently Asked Questions

Q: Sometimes I get thoughts that I don't want, but I'm not tempted to act on them or perform any ritual. Are they part of my OCD or separate from it?
A: Everyone has intrusive thoughts. It's normal. Whether they are OCD-related may depend on whether you give them a great deal of credibility as opposed to shrugging them off and going about your day. Alternatively, are these unpleasant thoughts connected to a real-life situation? For example, if you've recently had some unusual expenses or were told that there are going to be layoffs at your job, do you have a fleeting thought about being evicted or having your car repossessed? Such thoughts, however unwanted, are normal reactions to being low on cash, and you needn't change your ERP program because of them.

Q: I live in a tiny farm town in Wyoming. The nearest city is about ninety minutes away, and I have no idea if any psychiatrist there is experienced in treating OCD. Where can I find help?
A: You don't need a psychiatrist to be treated for OCD. Many psychologists and other healthcare professionals—social workers and counselors—treat OCD. If you live in an isolated area, your best bet is to contact the Obsessive-Compulsive Foundation (OCF) at 617-973-5801 or www.ocfoundation.org. OCF's website will point you toward an OCD specialist near your town. Also, take a look at Chap-

ter 12, the resources chapter of this book. You'll find a lengthy list of places where you can find help.

Q: If I contact someone for OCD treatment, will I have to be admitted to a hospital?
A: Thanks to the development of CBT and ERP, as well as SRI medications to help OCD patients, relatively few people with OCD need hospitalization. However, for those whose symptoms are so severe that they cannot function at home or in society, a hospital stay is an option until their symptoms become manageable. The best way to determine whether your symptoms are so severe as to warrant hospitalization is to be evaluated by a professional.

Q: My therapist suggested that I attend support groups for my OCD. How would they help me?
A: Your therapist's suggestion was a good one: Support groups can be immensely helpful for people with OCD. Their benefits include the following: (1) Because OCD symptoms can isolate a person from family and friends, support groups help patients feel less alone. (2) Many OCD symptoms are embarrassing; support groups help to cut through whatever shame the patient may be feeling. (3) Supporting others in your group will take your focus off yourself and your anxiety, and help you realize the contribution you can make to other people's lives. (4) You will meet other OCD patients who have made great progress in their recoveries, and hearing about their experiences can motivate and inspire you.

EIGHT

The Role of Medication in Recovery

MEDICATION IS ONE ASPECT of conquering OCD symptoms that may not be necessary for all OCD patients, but for many it is essential. By the same token, there are some OCD sufferers who take medication only and do not include ERP as part of their treatment. Like many clinicians, we encourage our patients to consider all available forms of treatment that have research to support their use.

Recall the biology lesson in Chapter 3, where we discussed neurotransmitters (especially serotonin) and the role they play in OCD. Now that we know about behavioral therapy, and how successfully OCD symptoms can be tamed using ERP, it's easy to forget that one theory of OCD implicates lopsided chemicals in the brain. From this perspective, a real, physiological imbalance is behind the obsessions and compulsions associated with the disorder. And, just as medicine can sometimes help you stop coughing or make your headache go away, medication can sometimes help stop the obsessions and compulsions of OCD.

So, your next question may well be, If medication can remedy my OCD symptoms, why bother working so hard at ERP? Why not just pop a pill and be done with it?

The fact is, many kinds of medications do relieve anxiety, and that's how they generally are used in treating OCD. It's an important role because OCD is an anxiety disorder and if you can feel less anxious, you'll be better able to perform your ERP and manage your treatment and recovery. Antidepressants are the most commonly prescribed type of drug in this country, according to a 2007 study by the Centers for Disease Control. In addition, there is accumulating evidence that while medication and ERP work differently, they both influence areas in the brain where OCD-related neurotransmitters are found. Medication and ERP work differently but can work effectively in concert.

One of the key differences between medication and ERP is what happens once treatment stops. The treatment outcome literature informs us that, in many cases, once medication is discontinued, OCD symptoms return even among those people who responded very well to pharmacotherapy. Moreover, although the research subjects who were treated with ERP do at least as well as the people receiving medication, once formal treatment stops, only the ERP group continues to improve. With ERP, you learn skills you can continue to employ. If you are like many OCD patients, medication alone isn't enough to eliminate symptoms; it plays a supportive role, enabling you to make the best use of ERP to manage your symptoms, especially once you have completed treatment. Other patients' OCD is so severe that they need medication in order to get their anxiety under sufficient control to start ERP. Still others may find that medication alone will provide considerable relief from their OCD symptoms and choose to not pursue a course of ERP. We encourage you to consider all of these options.

Keep in mind that these are *prescription* medications we're discussing. That means only a physician can prescribe these drugs. If you have been treating your own OCD symptoms successfully, then you won't need to add medication to your regimen. But if you are seeing a professional, or considering treatment with a therapist, then the topic of medication is likely to come up at some point. This chapter will enable you to be an informed consumer about the medications used in treating OCD.

This next section won't be quite as technical as Chapter 3—but there's a lot of science here. If you want to get a deep understanding of OCD meds today, you might want to skim that third chapter again before you continue, so as to refresh your memory on neurotransmitters, synapses, and such.

How Medications
Are Used in Treating OCD

Behavior therapy for OCD was first used in the 1960s. Back then, no medications were known to be particularly helpful in treating OCD. Only in recent years, as we've learned more about anxiety and its relationship to chemical imbalances in the brain, have medications been recognized as reliable OCD treatments.

As we have noted, the most commonly prescribed drugs for OCD patients are serotonin reuptake inhibitors (SRIs), because they help to regulate serotonin and "inhibit" its premature reuptake. In the 1990s, SRIs were widely used for treating depression. Scientists soon discovered their effectiveness in treating anxiety disorders, and today they are prescribed not only for OCD, but for panic disorder, social anxiety disorder, and PTSD as well as other anxiety disorders and depression.

Prescribing the correct medication for any individual, however, is tricky. Obviously, any physician can prescribe a psychotropic medication, even if that doctor isn't a psychiatrist. But we strongly encourage our patients to seek medication treatment from a psychiatrist—preferably one with experience and expertise in treating anxiety disorders and/or OCD. Half a dozen different drugs are used in treating OCD today; and technically, all are antidepressants. When a patient is being evaluated for treatment, the physician must consider whether an unrelated condition, such as epilepsy or brain injury, could be causing OCD-like symptoms.

If a patient has a comorbid diagnosis, such as Tourette's syndrome, obsessive-compulsive spectrum disorders, or trichotillomania, an SRI might not be the first choice for medication management. For most

OCD patients, however, the doctor will go right to an SRI. There are several of these available for OCD treatment; based on your individual medical and medication histories, a psychiatrist will be able to carefully assess which one is best suited to you.

Dosage, cost, and side effects will also be factored into the decision because, among the drugs used in treating OCD, none stands out as the "best" or "most effective" for all patients. So, the answer depends partly on your particular symptoms. For instance, if you're so fatigued that you can't get through the day, you may need a different drug than would be appropriate if you were suffering from insomnia. Sometimes the best approach is trial and error. It's a time-consuming strategy, but it might be the only way to determine which drug will have the strongest impact on your symptoms and ensure that you experience the fewest side effects.

Like many drugs, the antidepressants used in treating OCD take some time to become effective. You can't take one of these medications tonight and watch your OCD symptoms disappear by the weekend—although on rare occasions, some effects are noticeable within a few days. In most instances, these drugs must accumulate in your system for at least three weeks, and sometimes as long as three months, before your doctor can determine whether they are effective.

Like the process of selecting a medication, the medication trial process can be somewhat complicated. This is one of the main reasons we encourage you to see a psychiatrist. Determining whether you have had adequate time to experience the benefit from an SRI or other drug used to treat OCD is very different from being prescribed a two-week course of antibiotics. If the first medication doesn't help your OCD, the doctor probably will want to wait a week or two before starting another, to avoid any possible interactions. Alternatively, with some medications, your physician may be able to "cross-taper"—that is, reduce the dose of the first medication while starting and/or increasing the dose of the new medication. Don't let these "false starts" or second tries discourage you; they're very common. In fact, about one-third of patients receiving medications for anxiety disorders find themselves taking at least two prescription drugs, often at the same time. This is especially true of patients who are both anxious and depressed. Some doctors prefer to "kick-start" drug therapy for the first few weeks by prescribing both a faster-acting benzodiazepine (which is an antianxiety medication) and a slower-acting SRI. Then, as the SRI builds in your system, the doctor will very gradually taper your dose of the benzodiazepine.

You can see, then, how much patience you will need in order to find the right drug—one that matches your body and brain chemistry. If you have an allergic reaction to the medicine, or an unpleasant side effect, you'll want to ask your doctor about trying a new prescription, adding even more time to the process. If you don't notice any unpleasant reaction to the drug but also see no improvement in your symptoms, the doctor may want to increase your dose in order to determine whether that new dosage brings about any positive change over the next few weeks, before switching to a new medication.

In some cases, psychiatrists augment the SRI with a second medication to maximize results. This process works to enhance the effect of the SRI. In other cases, a second medication is added to better address specific OCD symptoms that the SRI may not be optimally resolving. As we noted, for some individuals an SRI may be augmented with another antianxiety drug such as a benzodiazepine. For other patients, the augmenting drug could be what's known as an "atypical antipsychotic"—a fairly new drug usually used in treating schizophrenia and other psychotic illnesses. These drugs tend to be effective for those groups of OCD patients whose physicians believe it is not just the serotonin neurotransmitter system that is involved but the dopamine system as well. Likewise, sometimes a mood stabilizer may be added.

Augmentation can be effective in the following common situations:

- When the patient has a coexisting depression or other condition
- When the patient has Tourette's or a tic disorder
- When the patient shows persistent anxiety

In any event—whether you see progress or not, or have any side effects or not—it's a good idea to keep careful notes about your medication experience, including dosages and how you were affected. Likewise, if in the past you were prescribed medication for OCD or any other mental health problem, you should let your psychiatrist know what medication was prescribed, how long you took it, whether it worked (or not), and whether you had any side effects. This information can help a new physician select the best medication regimen for you as well as allow your doctor to educate you as to whether you had an adequate trial of a previous drug. In addition, if you need to find a new doctor in the future, or you decide to seek a second opinion on any aspect of your treatment, your notes and records will hold valuable clues as to your future treatment.

ANNE COULTER'S MEDICATION STORY

You probably remember Anne from earlier chapters—one of the "lucky few," she says, who was diagnosed with OCD the first time she visited a psychiatrist even though it was the late 1980s and OCD wasn't widely recognized then.

This is not to say that Anne's recovery came easily, however. "Needing to take pills made it seem as if there was something 'wrong' with me," she explains, "and I fought the idea at first. I kept thinking I should be able to stop the thoughts and rituals on my own, without drugs." But that approach had been unsuccessful for years.

The possibility of getting relief is what finally changed her mind. "OCD and the depression that accompanied it were crushing me, and making me feel more and more isolated. If medication could reduce the anxiety and lift the black cloud over my head, I decided it would be worth it," she says.

She began by taking Prozac (fluoxetine), one of the few effective drugs prescribed for OCD at that time. Her therapist cautioned her that she wouldn't notice any results for a few weeks, but Anne stuck with the treatment plan and gradually started feeling the difference.

She desperately hoped that the Prozac would ease her anxiety— and it did, somewhat. "But its greatest gift," she says, "was cutting through the depression." As the weeks progressed, Anne felt more energy and more optimism. That outcome, she says, was what empowered her to take on the tough work of ERP for dealing with her OCD.

"Before taking medication, I couldn't imagine how I would be able to face my obsessions in such a rigorous way," she recalls. "But when I felt less depressed, I was able to find the motivation and courage to commit to the entire treatment process."

Ultimately, Anne says, medication made ERP possible for her, "and ERP gave me back my life." She stayed on medication through her intensive course of treatment and for several years afterward, switching to Luvox (fluvoxamine) when it came on the market. This drug, she believes, was much more effective than Prozac in relieving her anxiety: "Luvox helped me hold onto the huge gains that ERP had enabled me to make as I learned to manage my OCD."

Anne has been off of medication for well over a decade now, but she understands that someday OCD could intrude into her life once more. "If that happens, I know that a prescription from my psychiatrist can help get me back on track," she says, "and that's very comforting."

The OCD Medications

Six of the seven drugs listed below help to alleviate OCD symptoms by regulating serotonin in the brain. We've presented them here in some detail so that if your doctor wants to prescribe one or more of these drugs, you can turn to this section and refresh your memory about each one of them specifically.

The drugs are listed by their generic names, followed by their brand names in parentheses. If you have been reading about these medications and how some of them are used to treat depression, a word of caution is worth noting. The doses of these drugs for treating depression are usually at the lower end of the range. When these medications are used to treat OCD, higher doses of these drugs are typical. This is another reason why we encourage you to see a psychiatrist for your treatment, since a specialist will be more experienced in prescribing these drugs in their effective dose range. In addition, you cannot directly compare the dose of one drug to that of another since they may be calibrated differently. For instance, a starting dose of one medication may be 50 milligrams (mg) and it may be increased up to 300 mg daily, compared with a drug that is started at 20 mg and increased to 80 mg per day.

Clomipramine (Anafranil)

Used overseas in treating anxiety for more than thirty-five years, in 1989 clomipramine became the first drug approved by the Food and Drug Administration (FDA) for OCD treatment in the United States. It still is considered the first-line OCD medication by many clinicians. You might hear it referred to as a "tricyclic" antidepressant, similar to Tofranil (imipramine), because of its three-ringed chemical structure. Clomipramine still is arguably the most effective drug in controlling OCD symptoms, but it also produces a number of unpleasant side effects, including constipation, low blood pressure, fatigue, dry mouth, weight gain, dizziness, and decreased libido. We've heard patients at our clinic comparing it to an antihistamine because it makes them extremely drowsy, but this side effect can be minimized if the drug is taken at bedtime.

Clomipramine is one of the slower-acting OCD medications, rarely producing an improvement in symptoms before four weeks of treatment and often taking three times as long.

Fluvoxamine (Luvox)

Another long-established OCD medication, the SRI fluvoxamine, started undergoing OCD testing in the late 1980s. Its initial effects often can be seen in less than six weeks, and they continue to build over the following months. Patients report a number of side effects, but they are milder than those felt by patients taking clomipramine. These side effects include nausea, drowsiness, headache, insomnia, and dry mouth.

Fluoxetine (Prozac)

Widely known for treating depression, fluoxetine has been prescribed in the United States since 1987. In fact, it was the first of the SRIs to be prescribed in this country. When given in fairly low starting doses of 20 mg/day, its side effects are mild; they include restlessness, fatigue, nausea, respiratory discomfort, headache, and dry mouth. Even among patients who are not depressed, fluoxetine has been proven effective in combating OCD symptoms. Prozac takes a considerable period of time to reach an effective level in your blood. A similarly long period is required for the drug to wash out of your system if you need to be switched to another medication.

Paroxetine (Paxil)

The side effects from taking paroxetine are somewhat different from those caused by the other SRIs approved for OCD treatment. Constipation and dizziness are the most common of these, but nausea, sexual dysfunction, and weight gain may also be experienced. If you have a bowel or blood disorder, your doctor is likely to prescribe an SRI other than paroxetine first.

Sertraline (Zoloft)

Sertraline's side-effect profile is also slightly different from that of the other SRIs listed here. Nausea, diarrhea, sexual dysfunction, and both sleepiness and insomnia can be expected, whereas nervousness is usually not a problem. Another dichotomy in sertraline's side effects: weight loss and loss of appetite.

Citalopram (Celexa)

A relative newcomer to the SRI field, citalopram is approved for treating depression but has also shown effectiveness in treating OCD symptoms, in children as well as adults. Its side effects include nausea, sleepiness, and dry mouth.

Escitalopram (Lexapro)

Approved by the FDA in 2002 for treating anxiety disorders, escitalopram is associated with side effects similar to those of the other SRIs discussed here. This drug is a close relative to citalopram, as its generic name suggests. Because the two drugs are so chemically similar, they should not be taken together. We elaborate on drug combinations later in this chapter, in the section on side effects.

JILLIAN'S OCD MEDICATION EXPERIENCE

At 36, Jillian was on track with most of her life goals. A registered nurse, she was earning a good salary in a profession that helped other people, owned her own home, and, while she didn't have a husband or boyfriend, was living a full life. She could honestly say she was a happy person—until her OCD symptoms began.

The event that triggered Jillian's symptoms didn't even involve her directly. One of her colleagues administered the wrong dosage of a blood pressure medication to a patient, and the patient nearly died. All of the nurses vowed to double-check instructions before they gave meds in the future.

But Jillian went beyond double-checking dosages. She started checking patients' blood pressure at least twice, reading their entire charts several times, and changing bandages that were still clean. Finding a "good vein" to start an IV took long minutes. Her checking began to intrude on her personal life; she took her own temperature every evening, checked her breasts for lumps every morning when she showered, and continually checked her skin for suspicious moles.

Jillian's checking rituals probably were noticed earlier than would be the case with other OCD sufferers, simply because she works in a healthcare setting. Her colleagues easily persuaded her to get help, and her doctor started her on a program of ERP and, to ease her anxiety, a prescription for clomipramine (Anafranil).

After only a month of treatment, Jillian had cut her checking rituals substantially—but she had gained ten pounds. The following month she gained five more, and another six in the fourth month.

She knew it was the medication that was causing her sudden weight gain, and told her psychiatrist that she needed to complete her treatment without the medication. "The extra pounds are making me even more anxious!" she said to the doctor. "I need a new plan."

Jillian and her doctor discussed whether she should be switched to a different medication, start behavioral treatment, or do both. Together they decided she could handle her ERP as they were tapering her off of the Anafranil. They revised her treatment to include a weight-loss plan and a reasonable program of exercise. She walked and did a little strength training.

Her new weight was stubborn; after six months on the new plan, she had lost only half of the pounds previously gained—but she was determined to succeed. Over the next season she kept to the same amount of exercise but stepped up the intensity, and cut about 150 calories from her daily diet. Three months later, all of her new weight was gone and her OCD symptoms were under control. At times she was tempted to check her weight several times a day, especially when she felt bloated, but she resisted even that form of checking and resolved to weigh herself just once every two weeks.

Side Effects of OCD Drugs

As you've read, all the medications used to treat OCD carry at least mild side effects. Some of those uncomfortable feelings dissipate quickly, but others continue for as long as you take the medicine.

WEIGHT GAIN, BIGGER APPETITE WITH OCD MEDS

Is there any side effect more infuriating than packing on the pounds? Like some OCD patients taking SRIs, you may notice frequent cravings for carbohydrates and sweets. Until your body adjusts to the new medication, stock up on low-calorie snacks to feed your cravings. Like many side effects of medications, food cravings and weight gain are often temporary—and by watching your calories and boosting your exercise, you can help ensure that the aftereffects are temporary as well. If the weight gain is a cause for concern, as in Jillian's case above, discuss it with your doctor.

Side effects seem to follow patterns, with SRIs causing fewer problematic side effects than tricyclics such as Anafranil. Whatever discomfort you're experiencing because of your medication, don't hesitate to talk with your doctor about this issue and what alternatives are best for you. All OCD drugs are prescribed in different doses; perhaps your clinician started you at a dose that was too strong for your system. Regardless of the reason for the side effects you are experiencing, it is important that you talk to the physician who is prescribing the drug; don't simply stop taking the medication unless your doctor instructs you to do so.

Three additional words of caution. First, if you are experiencing side effects, do not reach for an over-the-counter medication without first speaking to your physician or, at the very least, the pharmacist who has a record of all of the medications you are taking. Not all medications can safely be taken together. They can interact. As you know, some household cleaners can be harmful in combination; for example, the fumes from mixing bleach and ammonia can make you very sick. The same can be true of medications. **You must let all of your doctors know which medications you are taking, including vitamins and herbal supplements. Do not take even a cold medication without first speaking to a physician!**

Second, even if you've stopped ritualizing, **you must never stop taking a prescription drug unless your doctor has given you a discontinuation plan**, which will taper you off gradually. Abruptly stopping a medication on your own can have disastrous consequences. If you think you're ready to stop taking your SRI, talk to your doctor about discontinuing it. Generally, it's helpful for your therapist and your prescribing physician to work together to develop a taper plan so that all of the coping strategies you need will be firmly in place.

Last, **do not share your medications, especially with your child**. If, for example, you think your child may have OCD, do not share your SRI (or any medication, for that matter) with him. A few years ago, the Surgeon General issued a warning against the use of antidepressants in treating children and adolescents—especially children who are depressed. This warning was warranted by research indicating that use of antidepressants by children is associated with an increased risk for suicidal thinking and behavior. It is critically important to have a psychiatrist closely monitor anyone in this age group who is being prescribed an antidepressant.

Below is some essential information about the possible side effects of OCD drugs. Remember: Since everyone's body reacts differently, your experience with medication side effects may be different from that of a friend or family member who is taking the same prescription.

- *Fatigue.* Serotonin helps to regulate our "inner clock," which tells us when to sleep and when to be alert. It's no surprise, then, that drowsiness and general fatigue are common side effects of drugs that affect our serotonin levels. It's for this reason that many doctors suggest taking an SRI before bedtime. If you find that you're waking up in the morning still feeling tired, ask your doctor if you can take your pill earlier in the evening. This may help to offset the period when you'd otherwise be most affected by fatigue since you'll be asleep for the greater portion of that time.

- *Insomnia.* Paradoxically, given that we just mentioned fatigue as a common side effect, some people feel more keyed up and have trouble sleeping as a result of taking an SRI. If this has been your experience, ask your doctor if you can take the medication earlier in the day rather than during the evening. Most of the SRIs are meant to be taken once per day, so the time you take the medication may be less important than your taking it close to the same hour each day. In addition, you may want to monitor your sleep for a week or two; if it doesn't improve, discuss other possible solutions with your doctor.

- *Dry mouth.* Tricyclics are famous for producing dry mouth! Although this side effect is not immediately harmful, dry mouth can eventually cause cavities as a result of insufficient saliva to rinse the mouth. We recommend a little extra dental hygiene, such as additional mouthwash rinses and dental checkups. In addition, sugarless gum and sugar-free hard candy can help to stimulate saliva production.

- *Constipation.* The remedy for constipation caused by OCD meds is the same as for constipation brought about by other causes: more water and fiber, which you'll find in whole-grain breads and veggies with "roughage," such as cabbage and broccoli. Prune juice is another popular antidote. If that doesn't help, ask your doctor whether you should use an over-the-counter stool softener or fiber supplement.

- *Diarrhea.* Mom said to eat apples or drink apple juice, and she was right; they're often helpful in treating diarrhea. Also stay away from anything that might stimulate your GI track, such as caffeine, for a few days.

- *Low blood pressure.* Especially among OCD patients taking tricyclics, low blood pressure is a frequent side effect. If you're feeling dizzy after starting one of these meds, especially when you stand up or turn over too quickly, you may have had a blood pressure drop. Slow down—don't take a chance on falling—and ask your physician if the side effect will go away or, alternatively, whether another medication would be better for you.

- *Urinary retention.* The inability to urinate not only is uncomfortable; it also can lead to bladder problems, including urinary infections. Make sure that you call your doctor if you are having this problem.

- *Headaches.* If you have a history of headaches due to stress, you might want to ask your doctor if the medication you use for your headaches is compatible with what he or she is prescribing. If you do not have such a history and suspect that the OCD medication is causing your headaches, check with your doctor since headaches can result from a blood pressure problem or other medical issues.

- *Decreased libido.* A common complaint about SRIs is decreased interest in sex and problems with sexual performance. In both men and women, SRIs can cause a diminished sex drive. In addition, women may experience an inability to have an orgasm while men might experience an inability to have an erection. Several SRIs, such as Celexa, are less likely to cause such problems. And the addition of another medication can be used to treat the sexual dysfunction directly. Talk to your doctor; this problem is frustrating but treatable.

- *Tremors.* Antidepressants used to treat OCD sometimes cause hand tremors. Your doctor may want to prescribe another medication.

- *Nervousness.* If you're already being treated for an anxiety disorder, you may find it difficult to recognize added nervousness caused by your medication. If you do sense a new, slightly agitated quality in yourself, try to stay away from coffee and colas or any food or beverage that has caffeine. And relax—as this is one side effect that usually disappears a few weeks after it begins.

CAN BRAIN SURGERY OR STIMULATION HELP OCD?

For a tiny subgroup of OCD patients, several high-risk treatments are available—but only as a last resort. These include neurosurgery, deep brain stimulation (DBS), and repetitive transcranial magnetic stimulation (rTMS).

- *Neurosurgery.* In severe cases of OCD in which multiple attempts at appropriately administered behavioral and medication treatments have failed, clinicians might suggest neurosurgery. The operation can take one of two forms: cingulotomy or capsulotomy. These procedures, which target parts of the brain known to be dysfunctional when OCD is present, involve severing some of the fibers in the brain in order to disrupt the OCD "circuit." However, you should be aware that a surgical approach does not guarantee a cure for OCD. Studies have shown that nearly half of OCD patients who underwent these surgeries still had diminished OCD symptoms up to ten years following the procedures. In addition, a small proportion of them experienced seizures (5 percent) or infection (1 percent) after the surgeries.

- *Deep brain stimulation (DBS).* Deep brain stimulation involves implanting electrodes in certain sites of the brain, with the goal of stimulating surrounding tissue. In previous years, DBS was used primarily for treating Parkinson's disease and a few other neurological conditions. But in February 2009 the FDA granted Metronic, a manufacturer of DBS equipment, a "humanitarian device exemption" that will allow the limited use of DBS for the treatment of intractable OCD in fewer than 4,000 patients. Research on this procedure indicates a 40 percent reduction in symptoms after one year of DBS use by the twenty-six patients studied. One advantage of deep brain stimulation over surgical intervention is that it is reversible and adjustable. The electrodes can be completely removed if the stimulation does not work. Experts warn, however, that deep brain stimulation involves brain surgery, carries potentially severe complications, and should be performed only at centers with proven expertise.

- *Repetitive transcranial magnetic stimulation (rTMS).* This treatment, which alters brain activity using a magnetic field, has been effective in treating depression and schizophrenia. Unlike surgery or DBS, however, rTMS is completely noninvasive. Only three studies of this approach to OCD treatment have been performed; a major review of these studies found that there is presently a lack of evidence supporting the effectiveness of rTMS for OCD.

What to Expect from OCD Medications

It makes sense that, because OCD is a chronic disorder, the medications used to treat it must be taken for the long term. This doesn't necessarily mean forever, but most researchers agree that unless the drugs are taken for a year or two after the symptoms are controlled, the risk of relapse is high. That risk is greatly diminished, however, if the patient has also undergone cognitive behavior therapy (CBT).

Stopping a medication abruptly can bring on withdrawal symptoms or a surge of anxiety or depression. The rule of thumb practiced in our clinic is "Start low and go slow." Medications are started at a low dose and gradually increased to their clinically effective range. OCD patients on medication should plan to take their prescription for at least a year, then be weaned off of it gradually. (There are exceptions, of course: Some people will need to be treated for a longer period, whereas others will need to discontinue their prescription after a brief time.) If OCD symptoms return, the same medication is likely to be prescribed again. Alternatively, if symptoms worsen while the doctor is tapering down a patient's dose, the tapering may be stopped to see if the symptoms stabilize and then the discontinuation process may be started again.

We wish we could tell you that all people taking medications for OCD will be able to stop their medication and be OCD free. While this can happen, it's also possible that you may need to continue taking a reduced dose of your medication for the rest of your life. (A small proportion of OCD sufferers have to stay on their maximum therapeutic dose for life.) In addition, there may be times that you will have to stop taking your medication. For example, if you are considering becoming pregnant or are in need of surgery, you should make sure to discuss your medication with your physician since under these circumstances the OCD medication may have to be temporarily discontinued to protect a fetus or avoid interaction with other drugs you will need.

In rare instances, a person's OCD meds will stop working. (In the case of some spectrum disorders, particularly Tourette's syndrome and trichotillomania, an antidepressant can appear to work well for weeks, even months, then suddenly lose its effectiveness. As silly as it sounds, this loss of effectiveness is called "serotonin poop-out.") When this occurs, we encourage our patients to discuss the problem with their prescribing physician, who will typically evaluate their medical history and consider changing the dosage, changing them to a new drug, or designing an augmentation plan.

Frequently Asked Questions

Q: *What's the limbic system, and what does it have to do with treating OCD?*
A: The limbic system is part of the "midbrain," which is a primary center for memory as well as for emotions, including anxiety. Since anxiety is a major component of OCD, medications used to treat OCD will affect this part of the brain.

Q: *My psychiatrist wants to prescribe an anxiety medication for my OCD treatment, but I hate taking drugs. Will I become addicted if I take this medication?*
A: Although it is possible to become addicted to prescription medications, most drugs prescribed for OCD patients are antidepressants that will help them control their anxiety so they can successfully complete their CBT—and these SRIs and tricyclic antidepressants are not considered to be addictive. In many cases, the antidepressants are a temporary measure—but they also can be a lifelong commitment. You should share your concerns with your doctor and learn about all of your medication's side effects, so that you can make an informed decision about taking the drug. If you are prescribed an antianxiety medication, such as benzodiazepine, you can become physically dependent on the drug. However, this is very different from being "addicted." It's more like having a cast on a broken leg—it's something that is necessary for the healing process. If you are struggling with anxiety during exposures, being on a scheduled dose of this kind of medication may help you to effectively engage in treatment.

Q: I keep hearing about a drug's "half-life." What is that?
A: Half-life refers to the amount of time it takes to eliminate 50 percent of a medication from your body. It's an important factor for your clinician to consider when choosing which medication to prescribe for you, at what dosage, and for how long.

Q: How will my doctor know which drug to prescribe for my OCD?
A: The medications most often prescribed for OCD patients are serotonin reuptake inhibitors, which, though classified as antidepressants, are widely used to treat anxiety disorders including OCD. Each of the six most commonly prescribed SRIs (or seven, if you include the tricyclic antidepressant Anafranil) is effective in treating some patients. Unfortunately, however, there is no way to predict which of those medications will be best for any one person. Together, you and your doctor should consider each drug's side effects, your medical history, the cost of the medication, and other relevant factors and decide which may be the right medication for you. It's possible that you'll try more than one medication before you find one that works best for you.

Q: What if the drug prescribed for me is working but I can't tolerate the side effects?
A: If the side effects of your medication are uncomfortable, discuss this with your doctor. He or she may recommend that you lower the dosage or switch to another medication. Sometimes, side effects from SRIs are temporary—but if they're serious, you shouldn't try to endure them or stop the medication on your own unless your doctor advises you to do so.

Q: My treatment combines CBT and medications, and I'm making good progress—but this whole effort is wearing me out. I can barely stay awake during the day. Is it because of the drugs I'm taking?
A: Some of the medications used in treating OCD can cause fatigue. And in some people, the same medications can cause insomnia, which has the same effect of leaving them feeling tired all the time because

they're not getting enough sleep. You need to be alert during the day, so discuss your concern about fatigue or sleep with your doctor. It's possible that a small adjustment, such as taking your meds at a different time of day, will have a considerable effect on resolving the problem. Alternatively, your psychiatrist may suggest adding a medication that can help combat your insomnia or discuss nonpharmacologic strategies to help improve your sleep.

Q: Are there any new and exciting OCD treatments on the horizon?
A: We've already discussed two new treatments—DBS (which, as noted, was recently approved on a limited basis by the FDA) and rTMS. A third one is also showing promise: Researchers, notably those at Massachusetts General Hospital in Boston, have used a drug called d-cycloserine to augment exposures in OCD treatment. This medication seems to consolidate memory; those taking it report a significant improvement in the effect of ERP.

NINE

Children and OCD

REGARDLESS OF YOUR AGE or life stage when you realized you had OCD, it's important to understand how OCD works in children. You may discover that your symptoms were trying to emerge years earlier than you realized Or, more important, you may recognize OCD in some child or teenager you know.

It seems like a cruel trick nature plays on children, that a disorder capable of robbing their ability to live normally—studying, building friendships, pursuing sports or artistic dreams—would hit so many of them, so hard. About 1 in every 200 children is likely to have OCD. Many are unaware that they're living with the disorder since, in some of the forms it takes, children ritualize only in select settings and at certain times of the day. But legions of others suffer teasing and bullying from schoolmates because of their undiagnosed "strange" behaviors and are met with constant annoyance or even hostility from their parents and siblings because their actions disrupt family life.

By now you know that, in adult-OCD cases, there are circumstances when it might be acceptable to self-treat instead of getting professional help—specifically, at those times when the disorder is causing little disruption in your life. With children, however, it's essential to get a diagnosis and have a clinician guide the treatment, even when the OCD is on the mild side. There are two reasons why we emphasize the need for a careful diagnosis. First, children's physiology is different from that of an adult. It is important to make sure that the behaviors you're observing are, in fact, OCD rather than behaviors associated with some other condition that requires medical treatment—or normal behaviors that, with maturity, will disappear. Second, children are rarely capable of fighting off OCD's symptoms (which some pediatric therapists refer to as "brain hiccups") on their own. Even with the help of a supportive family, there will be times when efforts to treat OCD will contribute to power struggles and bad feelings among family members. Thus, in most cases, we suggest consulting with a professional who can provide objectivity and plan strategies to help you work with your child in overcoming OCD.

Another reason why professional involvement is so important with children is that parents and siblings are naturally tempted to accommodate a child's symptoms and participate in the rituals. They simply want to help the child get past the discomfort. In fact, they may help the child to avoid or prevent "trigger" situations, not realizing that they're only feeding the OCD. When parents, other family members, even teachers reassure or accommodate rituals, it shows the youngster that rituals are an acceptable way of dealing with obsessions—the complete opposite of the message you want to send!

Like adult OCD patients, children undergoing ERP treatment learn to avoid becoming overwhelmed by their obsessions and to stop ritualizing in response so that they can stop being distracted by their symptoms and ultimately get better. This is the most effective path that parents of children with OCD can take. In the overwhelming majority of cases, more than 80 percent, they are able to reach that goal. If you have a child who exhibits OCD symptoms, it's important for you to remember that OCD really is like a hiccup in the brain—it is *not* part of your child's true personality and, with the right treatment, it can be eliminated.

You also should keep in mind that neither you nor your child caused the OCD. It is an illness, and it's nobody's "fault." You read about the causes of OCD in Chapter 3. Fighting at home, pressure to excel in school, financial troubles—situations related to problems such as these may trigger OCD's episodes, but they do not cause this disorder.

Several years ago, researchers at the National Institute of Health, led by Dr. Susan Swedo, came across an unexpected circumstance regarding childhood-onset OCD: They found that some infections, most notably group A–hemolytic streptococcus (GABHS) infection—strep throat or scarlet fever—might trigger a sudden case of OCD in children who were genetically at risk for the disorder. If you suspect your child has OCD, the following symptoms could be painfully familiar: In addition to the GABHS infection, these include sudden changes such as separation anxiety, irritability, and abrupt mood shifts, along with motor and vocal tics, and obsessions and compulsions. This special variety of OCD is known as pediatric autoimmune neuropsychiatric disorders associated with streptococcus, or PANDAS.

PANDAS is believed to be caused by strep-related antibodies that attack an enzyme in the basal ganglia (especially the caudate nucleus) and other parts of the brain associated with OCD symptoms. As we noted in Chapter 3, communications between neurons suddenly become dysfunctional. Other normal childhood phenomena, such as nightmares, also show up as symptoms and, in some cases, math and handwriting skills become impaired. The variety and acuity of symptoms can make pediatric OCD, and especially PANDAS, difficult to recognize. You should also be aware that few investigators have been able to identify streptococcal virulence factors or genetic markers for PANDAS. As a result, the concept of PANDAS is subject to considerable controversy.

This isn't the first time doctors have noticed PANDAS, though. During the seventeenth century, a British physician named Thomas Sydenham noticed that some children with strep infections developed a tic condition that eventually was named Sydenham's chorea. When modern researchers noticed the connection between tics and OCD, they started looking for previous strep infections in those children, and found them.

We have since learned that PANDAS presents suddenly, always after a GABHS infection, and always in preadolescents. (The average age of a patient with PANDAS onset is 7 years.) For parents of children

with either a GABHS infection or OCD, however, it's important to remember that most strep infections do *not* trigger OCD, and most children with OCD have not experienced a GABHS infection. In fact, only
as few as 10 percent of the cases of childhood onset OCD are thought
to be explained by post-streptococcal infections.

Pediatric OCD Looks a Lot Like Adult OCD

Even if their OCD was identified or diagnosed years into their adult
lives, about half of adult sufferers say that their symptoms began while
they were children. Interestingly, young boys with OCD outnumber
girls with the disorder, but by the time they reach their teen years,
those gender distinctions disappear.

In terms of the behaviors involved, adult and pediatric OCD are
remarkably similar. Children are plagued by intrusive, unwanted obsessions and they try to alleviate their distress by acting on compulsions—
either physical acts, such as checking or hand-washing, or repetitive
mental exercises, such as counting or silently reciting a poem over
and over.

Also, as with adult OCD, such intrusive thoughts interfere with
the child's "work." OCD can make it difficult for the child to concentrate in school, study for exams, interact normally with friends, or
complete assignments. This can be particularly challenging for teachers. On the one hand, the perfectionistic OCD student hands in
beautiful assignments and in many cases is the "perfect" student—
she gets good grades and is a delight to have in class. On the other
hand, if the assignment is to be completed in class, the teacher may
observe her inability to hand in a paper unless everything is checked
and rechecked, or appears "just right." Such students might stay awake
far into the night, copying their schoolwork dozens of times until it
"feels" right to them or reading and rereading paragraphs—all of
which makes assignments a nightmare. Sometimes group projects become problematic because the child with OCD wants everyone else's
work to be perfect as well, thereby disrupting peer relationships.

These behaviors can progress to the extreme, until eventually the student cannot attend school at all.

Following are the most common forms of pediatric OCD.

Contamination Issues

Washing/cleansing and contamination are among the most prevalent concerns among children and teens with OCD. Sometimes their obsession is an overall fear of germs, compelling them to wash their hands dozens of times during the day. This form alone would cause them to miss class time and avoid interacting freely with desks, books, materials, and other students. Playing with toys used by others is out of the question among these children. If their OCD remains untreated, they probably won't be able to participate in sports, drama, or other extracurricular activities when they get to high school. Jostling up against fellow students in a crowded hallway or using a school bathroom could cause major distress for these youngsters.

Harming Obsessions

As with Jonathan, whose stories appear in several chapters of this book, some children with OCD harbor intrusive fears that they may hurt a parent, sibling, or friend or that if they don't do something to keep the people they care about safe, it will be their fault if harm befalls them. These children might also assume disproportionate responsibility for harmful events, such as a burglary or fire or natural disaster that had nothing to do with them. In addition, they worry about allowing a harmful image or thought into their minds, such as strangling a classmate or punching a younger sibling, because having those thoughts is just as bad as harming the person—a process known as "thought-action fusion."

Sexual Obsessions

Just as adults with OCD might experience intrusive thoughts about sexual matters, children also have such thoughts; but the difference is that it can be much more difficult for children or teens to talk about their obsessions, even to a clinician. Children and teens are apt to practice avoidance regarding their sexual obsessions. If the intrusive thoughts are about sex with some "forbidden" person, such as a priest, teacher, or older relative, then the child might avoid that person in order to avoid the unpleasant images. He also might devise lengthy mental reassurance rituals, constantly telling himself that he isn't a bad person and doesn't really want the sexual contacts he has imagined, or engaging in distractions such as reciting the alphabet or repeating a nonsense phrase.

Hoarding

It may be difficult to envision young children as hoarders, but they do exist. Their hoarding just happens on a smaller scale: They may save old scribbles or candy wrappers, filling a box under their bed or their school desk with the trash. In many cases, the hoarding "kicks in" when they leave their parents' home and can totally control their own "stuff," often because they think they might need it at a later time.

Superstitions/Magical Obsessions

Superstitions are among the most common symptoms in pediatric OCD. A child might truly be afraid to step on a crack in the sidewalk, or believe that if a traffic light changes before she counts to ten, for instance, or if a certain boy turns back to look at her before he crosses the street, then some positive or negative outcome will occur.

Somatic Obsessions

Some young OCD sufferers are viewed by their families as hypochondriacs because of their imagined or feared illnesses. The same concerns may sometimes be mistaken for or actually be body dysmorphic disorder (BDD), which, as we have noted, manifests as an obsession about a physical flaw that doesn't exist. Many children with somatic obsessions are reassurance-seekers, continually asking parents, doctors, and nurses for reassurance that they are healthy.

Scrupulosity

Religious obsessions involve guilt and fear of being judged by God as a bad or immoral person, whereas religious compulsions can take almost any form ranging from pious or charitable acts to scrubbing away the perceived immorality. Children with religious obsessions also might ask for repeated reassurance—in this case, wanting to be told that their sins are forgiven, that they are not doomed to hell, and that God loves them.

Perfectionism

As the label implies, children with perfectionist obsessions want everything done perfectly, whether it's their schoolwork or household chores, even the combing of their hair. They are also afraid to disappoint their teachers and parents. During the time that perfectionist children are in treatment for their OCD, it can be helpful to inject small doses of reality into conversations with them, such as by asking, "And what would be so terrible about having one sock lower than the other? What would be the consequences of having a wrinkle in the corner of your paper?" They can be taught that excellence and perfection are two different things and that no one is perfect.

RICK'S CONTAMINATION SYMPTOMS AND TREATMENT

When Rick was very young, he and his parents seemed to be a storybook-perfect family—spending weekend mornings at the park, walking the family dog, attending church together every Sunday. They were easygoing and comfortable with one another, at least until Rick's OCD symptoms appeared. When OCD joined the family, Rick's parents behaved as many do—with the kind of anger and disdain that only isolates the OCD sufferer and feeds the disorder.

Rick's contamination fears entered their family life gradually. As the obsessions and compulsions grew, his relationship with his parents deteriorated. If you asked him today, Rick wouldn't be able to tell you when his symptoms first began. He remembers, as a little boy, hating "sticky fingers" after he ate a cinnamon bun or fried chicken or potato chips, and he avoided those foods most of his life.

Along the way, almost everything came to feel "dirty" to him, especially if it had been handled by other people. He insisted that everything in the house be spotless and sanitized and, at the same time, his parents became progressively more resentful of his strict requirements about cleanliness. If something was spilled on the kitchen counter or if Rick spotted dust on the staircase, he criticized his parents for being slobs. Their lives together became one long argument—contamination seemed to be Rick's single focus while his parents were more concerned about his poor grades and, in their view, dysfunctional social life.

The anxiety created by touching doorknobs and sitting in chairs used by others was a constant in Rick's life. Naturally, it interfered with his concentration, causing his grades to suffer. None of his teachers knew that he was actually a really bright guy. Even Rick didn't recognize his own talents. His parents, not knowing how to support a son who was a "bundle of nerves" in their eyes and apparently couldn't succeed at anything, weren't able to hide their disappointment. As Rick's OCD grew over the years, they continually criticized and belittled him, sometimes resorting to calling him "lazy" or "a loser" or a "neat freak" when they felt especially frustrated. He began to sink into depression.

Rick wouldn't allow friends to come to his house—he didn't want them contaminating his things. He stopped doing sleepovers at friends' houses because he was forced to eat with their silverware, use their bathrooms, and sleep in their beds. In middle school, he carried his own school supplies, including brushes and paints for art classes. By the time he reached his senior year, Rick had never played in a team sport and had no friends; his classmates had long ago labeled him weird.

Rick's first turning point arrived in the form of a school counselor—or, as he refers to her today, his "angel," Mrs. Mendez, whose brother had been diagnosed with OCD and had undergone ERP. His symptoms were mostly checking, but she learned a great deal about OCD during her brother's treatment and suspected that Rick's problems were due to OCD during their first meeting.

Mrs. Mendez then met with Rick's parents, who were relieved that their son's problem might be treatable, and she referred the family to a nearby mental health clinic for assessment. Rick's OCD symptoms, along with his anxiety and emerging depression, were easy to diagnose. The doctor prescribed Celexa (citalopram), an antidepressant that had proven effective in combating pediatric OCD. In addition, Rick was able to start ERP and to make progress within weeks.

After just three months of treatment, Rick no longer showed outward signs of anxiety or depression and was able to behave normally in public buildings, including his germ-filled school. He still washed his hands several times during the day and carried a hand sanitizer in his pocket, but his rituals no longer interfered with schoolwork and his grades were beginning to improve. His parents attended support groups to learn the best techniques for helping him recover—and, much to everyone's delight, by telling people about his OCD, Rick was making great strides toward no longer being the object of ridicule from his classmates or his siblings.

How Pediatric OCD Is Different

In the process of reading earlier chapters, you may already have recognized differences between adult OCD and the circumstances surrounding your child or teenager's disorder. Some experts believe that children who exhibit certain temperaments may be more likely to have OCD—one way of explaining, according to these scientists, why some children exposed to more challenging family environments or other stressors might develop OCD symptoms while others do not. Children whose reactions to situations are more emotional and negative, they say, might show the connection between OCD and temperament most strongly. However, other personality traits, such as shyness, sociability, and activity level, appear to have no influence on whether OCD symptoms developed.

Research has also found that the thoughts, or cognitions, of children with OCD are quite different from those considered typical among adults. All children have routines and small, personalized rituals. The mere fact that a child insists (often loudly!) that certain procedures be followed at bedtime doesn't mean the child should be diagnosed with OCD. Indeed, one study found that two-thirds of preschool-aged children express concern over routines and symmetry. Such order-related thoughts are viewed by experts as positive and necessary to the child's development of a sense of control and self-confidence later in life.

However, such normal and positive thoughts and rituals differ from OCD-related obsessions and compulsions—not in their nature but, rather, in frequency, intensity, and the level of distress they cause. Obsessions, remember, are *unwanted* thoughts that intrude and create distress and the need to neutralize them with rituals. The same rituals—straightening a sock, erasing a messy-looking word on a school paper—could be considered ordinary, even positive, behaviors among children who do not have OCD.

For an OCD sufferer, the compulsion to perform such actions—and to repeat them many times over—is impossible to resist. If a person without OCD were to see a crease in the corner of a paper, she would probably shrug it off, if it even registered in her mind at all. But for children with OCD who need things to be perfect, that little crease presents a challenge from which they cannot turn away.

The family environment, too, plays a bigger role in pediatric OCD than in adult OCD. One study found that OCD symptoms are more likely to emerge, or to linger more stubbornly, in families where parents fail to show support and confidence in children's ability to complete challenging tasks successfully than in families where parents show more support. The same is true in families where parents don't reward their children's risk-taking or independent behavior. Note, however, that this particular study might have been limited by the fact that it was conducted entirely with children who already had been diagnosed with OCD.

Other studies appear to affirm the old saying "Like father/mother, like son/daughter." In cases of perfectionism, at least, having perfectionist parents seems to contribute to the likelihood that children will develop OCD symptoms. Apparently, the children mimic the parents' behaviors and standards; and if they can't "measure up" to those standards, anxiety appears, followed by compulsions to ease the unpleasant, anxious feelings. Indeed, as yet another study has shown, perfectionism and precision are the traits mentioned most often by teenagers with OCD when asked to describe their family members.

Before Treatment, Talking to Your Child About OCD

If you are becoming increasingly convinced that your child has OCD, it's important to begin talking to your son or daughter about getting well. Your child needs to decide to get well and to do the work necessary to be healthy again. It's not enough to recognize OCD as a problem, or to realize that its intrusive thoughts and compulsions are symptoms. Even though your child didn't choose to have OCD, he or she must make the choice to stand up to the symptoms and be well again—and you both should understand that while recovery won't come easily, it will be worth the effort.

Having read the first part of this chapter, you know that accommodating rituals only perpetuates them. Indeed, if you have been accommodating your child's rituals, now is the time to talk about stopping. Once you have enlisted the help of a therapist, ERP will help you and your child deal with unwanted obsessions without bringing back the rituals that have dominated your lives. It's a good idea at this point to talk about that good outcome and to prepare to step back into a supporting role. Your child will be the one to perform the ERP, at his own pace, and the clinician will show you how best to take on the job of ERP coach.

One of the most productive ways you can prepare for your child's OCD treatment is to do an informal inventory of his symptoms even before you sit down with a professional. Keep in mind that *only a* mental health professional, preferably someone with expertise in treating pediatric patients, can properly diagnose a child or adolescent and decide the best course of treatment. The parental assessment you will undergo initially is intended only to help you understand the depth of your child's disorder, so that you can better communicate with the clinician and gauge your child's progress through the prescribed treatment plan.

One tool used by many clinicians during the course of treatment is the "fear thermometer," an easy-to-understand version of the adult exposure hierarchy developed by John S. March, M.D., who is an expert in the area of pediatric OCD. (Recall our discussion of the exposure hierarchy in Chapter 7, under **"Step 3: Developing Your Exposure Hierarchy."**) Kids can readily picture this thermometer: At the bottom with a score of "1" are those symptoms that will be easiest to tolerate; and as the "heat" builds up to the "10" position, the symptoms become progressively more difficult and fear-generating and, thus, are tackled during the latter stages of treatment. (*Note:* We've sometimes found in our clinic that older teens prefer measuring their progress with the adult hierarchy rather than with the fear thermometer used by younger children.)

Some therapists ask patients to begin their ERP with just one example of the obsession and to follow that example up the thermometer. For instance, number "1" for a child with perfectionist fears might be to slouch in his chair while at school until the first break (e.g., recess or lunch). A more difficult task, one rated "4," could be to forget to bring an assignment to class. And "10," the most anxiety-inducing task, might be to turn in the first draft of his homework, even though it's messy with words crossed out, wrinkled edges, and eraser smudges.

In all probability, your child's clinician will want to do the first interview and assessment with you present for all or part of the session. (*Note:* Older teenagers may want to be treated more like adults and to have their privacy respected. So, don't feel left out if the therapist asks to meet with your teenager without you in the room.) These early meetings provide us with an opportunity to collect the wealth of information we will need to devise the best treatment plan possible for your child. They also allow us to establish the roles you and your child will play during his treatment. Of course, if the child is embarrassed or afraid to talk about his symptoms, which often happens in cases of sexual or religious obsessions, then we will honor the child's feelings and schedule some interview time with him alone.

Treating Pediatric OCD: What to Expect

As you and your child embark on the road to recovery, perhaps your most important task will be to clear the air. Forget about the disruptions to almost every aspect of your family life that were caused by the OCD; forget about the hostilities and fighting, too. Those days are behind you. It's important now to be positive and to look forward to your child's return to health—and a normal life for the entire family.

If the clinic treating your child's disorder is current on OCD research and treatment options, ERP will be the intervention method used by the clinicians there. Depending on your child's symptoms, it's possible that medication may also have a role in his treatment. According to a number of authoritative resources, including the *Surgeon General's Report on Mental Health* and pediatric pharmacology textbooks, research has shown that combining medication with cognitive therapy (which, just as with adults, involves changing unhealthy thought patterns) and exposure and response prevention (which entails exposure to the problem, without indulging in a ritual response) in treating children often is more effective than using either CBT or ERP alone.

The side effects of medications that children experience are similar to the ones encountered by adult OCD patients. For instance, weight gain can occur during SRI treatment of teens; indeed, this is an emotionally charged side effect that parents and clinicians will want to keep an eye out for. Other adverse effects, however, carry different implications for children and pre-teens. For example, the side effect of sexual dysfunction may take the form of decreased libido in an adult but manifest as a lack of inhibition in a pre-teen.

For the first several weeks, you and your child will spend most of your time learning about OCD, identifying patterns in your child's obsessions and compulsions, establishing a fear thermometer, and beginning to deal with the lowest-level anxiety and ritual–inducing situations. From the outset, the therapist, and you, will refer to OCD as something outside of your child's true self; you will speak of it in the third person, using the same tone and attitude you would use if you were talking about some very rude, unwelcome person in the room. Speaking of the OCD as an unwanted, unliked third entity helps to reinforce the idea that while OCD is a bad thing, *your child is not bad*. It is the OCD we despise and want to eliminate; the child, who right now happens to be living with this nasty problem, we cherish and support.

Your child will realize that *he*, not you, is responsible for his recovery and needs to take charge of the OCD. As the weeks pass and the treatment evolves, he will gradually see that OCD's reign is coming to an end, as long as he continues to do his therapy homework and does not give in to the urge to ritualize.

As with adult OCD, treatment will center on your child's *response* to the obsessions, rather than on trying to make the obsessions disappear. We know that the obsessions and intrusive thoughts will return from time to time; the goal is to ensure that the individual never responds by ritualizing. As your child becomes more skilled at refusing OCD, the obsessions will diminish in frequency and intensity, and your child's success will build on itself. His confidence will grow, even as he moves up the fear thermometer and takes on more difficult challenges. It will get easier and easier to say no, and to get through the day without interrupting his normal comings and goings to perform rituals.

It's important for parents and young patients to understand, too, that the obsessions diminish as a result of cognitive restructuring but also because the ERP process involves not giving in to the rituals. The obsessions create anxiety and fear because the child imagines some sort of catastrophe arising if the obsessions are not countered by a ritual. Throughout the treatment period, the therapist will gently reintroduce reality, probing again and again as to why one sock lower than the other, a wrinkled paper, or a dirty shirt would bring about a tragedy. (Recall our example above, when we suggested that you ask your child what disasters might happen if his socks were to remain uneven all day.) From these conversations and from directly experiencing the outcome of having uneven socks, turning in a wrinkled paper, or wearing a dirty shirt, your child will develop more rational thoughts and become less frightened by the thoughts and images that once tormented him. This is how ERP in combination with the cognitive component of CBT works; he will see that a wrinkled paper isn't such a big risk after all.

STEFFIE'S SOMATIC OBSESSIONS AND TREATMENT

Only gradually did 12-year-old Steffie's parents notice her fixation on illnesses that didn't exist. They had listened to her complain about stomachaches, a sore arm, and various other afflictions for several years. Her mother lovingly administered whatever over-the-counter medicine was appropriate and didn't pay much attention to Steffie's complaints until a call came from the girl's teacher.

It was the third time in a week that Steffie had asked to see the school nurse, the teacher said. Each visit had been for a different reason—a headache, a stomachache, and something wrong with her ankle. The nurse could see nothing wrong with the girl, and the teacher added, "Steffie had been asking for cough drops, children's aspirin, or just to 'go rest' at least weekly since the school year began."

Fortunately, Steffie's symptoms had not taken over her life—her schoolwork wasn't suffering, and she was able to sing in the school choir and play on the girls' soccer team. Steffie's teacher had read about children who try to get attention with physical symptoms and suggested that Steffie's parents take their daughter for an evaluation by a professional trained in pediatric psychology or psychiatry.

Her parents were embarrassed when the teacher called; they'd been slightly disturbed by her complaints but had wanted to give Steffie the benefit of the doubt, and they thought—or, perhaps, hoped—that she would "grow out of it." Were they neglectful parents, they asked the teacher? Should they have been the first to suspect their daughter had a potentially serious problem or was a budding hypochondriac? They were reassured, both by Steffie's teacher and later by her therapist, that OCD's symptoms often sneak up on people. And sometimes the methods that kids use to seek attention from parents and teachers, even those that build very gradually, can be seen as clues to an underlying disorder.

Steffie was diagnosed with OCD. The clinician conducting the evaluation spent a great deal of time asking Steffie about her various symptoms. She wanted to be sure what the problem really was, since children sometimes complain of physical symptoms in response to conflictual situations. (In particular, her intention was to rule out circumstances like arguments at home between Steffie's parents or between Steffie and her siblings, or bullying situations at school.) But Steffie herself was concerned that even the normal "growing pains" that kids experience or the nervous feeling she had when her teacher called on her in class were signs of some terrible illness that needed to be treated. She was also preoccupied with the possibility of getting sick all the time. If she saw an advertisement on TV for a cold medicine or heard a news broadcast about someone contracting meningitis at a school all the way across the country, Steffie would think, "What if that happens to me? I could get sick and make everyone in my family sick."

Steffie and her therapist embarked on a program of ERP. Steffie no longer had access to cold medicines or other remedies, and she wasn't permitted to visit the school nurse regardless of how she felt. When her ERP was completed three months later, she not only had lost the urge to ritualize by behaving like a physically sick person but was able to hear stories about someone who became sick without running to her mom to explain how sick she felt. Steffie now understood that feeling anxious didn't mean she was ill. Likewise, she had become comfortable with the idea that if she or a family member got sick, it didn't mean that something catastrophic would happen: She'd gotten the flu (and measles and mumps and even knew a classmate who had his appendix removed) and recovered. In short, she knew that OCD was like a monster under the bed—if you keep thinking there's a monster there and never look, the monster gets bigger and scarier. But if you do look under the bed, you find out there's really not a monster there. Steffie could stare her OCD monster in the face and laugh!

Fine-Tuning Treatment

We should note, too, that several alternative forms of CBT have been found effective in treating OCD symptoms, including group treatment. As recently as 2004, Dr. Paula Barrett's research showed that 88 percent of children who underwent individual CBT treatment were symptom-free when the treatment was completed, but also that 76 percent of those treated in a group setting had conquered their OCD. Moreover, those success rates held firm eighteen months later.

One marked similarity between treating adults and children with OCD is noncompliance. ERP does not always progress smoothly. Children sometimes lapse into ritualizing for reasons that seem understandable but still need to be addressed:

- They lapse into ritualizing out of habit and forget to do the appropriate response prevention.

- They are moving up the fear thermometer but find the new exercise more frightening than they had anticipated, and they don't complete it or they become discouraged and don't want to continue to do exposures.

- Their treatment has eased their symptoms to the point where they've lost their motivation to continue; the current level of anxiety created by their obsessions feels manageable.

- They lapse into feeling that their anxiety won't diminish unless they perform the ritual.

In most instances, if the child truly was ready to perform the next exercise, additional coaching and prompts by the therapist, and later by parents, may be all that's needed to get the ERP back on track. If the child is too overcome by fear, then perhaps that task should be moved higher up the fear thermometer and a simpler exposure assigned in its place. Or, the exposure may need a slight alteration. For example, instead of asking the child to wear the sweat-stained shirt for a week, ask him to wear it for one day; instead of refraining from any copying of schoolwork once it's completed, allow it to be copied just once. Sometimes success means just taking smaller steps. These kinds of adjustments to a hierarchy are not easy to anticipate and should be viewed as "fine tuning" rather than as failures.

Clinicians and parents will work closely together on this aspect of the treatment process.

A Success Checklist— for Parents and Other Caregivers

As your child learns what it takes to succeed, parents also can monitor their own "success checklist" of behaviors to ensure their child's recovery from OCD:

- *Keep kindness at the top of your list.* If OCD makes you miserable, imagine what it's doing to your child. Treat your child as if his illness were the flu or measles. Give kind support at every opportunity—but stop short of accommodating rituals. We can't emphasize this last point enough. Parents often tell us that it breaks their heart to have to set this limit, because it is so upsetting for their child. But it's essential to keep some perspective; after all, if your child had diabetes, no matter how much he pleaded you would not allow him to have a meal of ice cream, cake, and candy. You would tell him that you understand he's feeling deprived and that this is a lousy way to feel, but the price for eating sweets is just too high. The price for giving in to rituals is also too high.

- *Remember, you're not in charge of this.* Avoid giving advice to your child; even gentle prodding could push him back into ritualizing. Support your child's choices regarding OCD and leave the advising to the clinician.

- *Cheer him on at every opportunity.* "That was awesome! You're much stronger than the OCD! Gimme five!" Even when an exposure is too difficult or scary for him to complete, remind him of his achievements thus far and assure him that you know he's going to win.

- *Always refer to OCD in the third person.* Some therapists even ask the child to give OCD a nickname—"Almost Gone OCD" or "Creepy OCD"—some name that reflects its total lack of value.

- *Be lavish with praise, but don't make it sound as if you're "grading" the child.* Saying "It must make you feel so good to climb another degree on the fear thermometer" is better than saying "You're handling this like a pro." The latter statement could create even more anxiety for your child, because it introduces pressure to please you. If you're having trouble coming up with compliments that don't put pressure on your child, ask the therapist to help you create a few. You'll soon catch on.

- *Notice your child's accomplishments in other areas and praise those as well.* Much of your child's life has nothing to do with OCD. If all you are doing is praising progress related to overcoming the OCD, it overemphasizes the OCD to the exclusion of everything else. Look at all of the areas in your child's life for positive behaviors and good outcomes, and applaud them.

- *Don't try to step up the pace.* Your child will decide, with the clinician's help, how slowly or quickly you should stop accommodating his rituals. Keep to that schedule, even if you think your child is capable of progressing more quickly. Don't hesitate to ask your child's therapist for guidance on how to best take on the role of coach.

- *Create rewards for milestones achieved.* The rewards don't have to be elaborate—a movie or zoo outing, special flip-flops, a new book bag, or choosing the movie for the family to watch. Ask your child what he would like as a reasonable reward. (Sometimes, the parents' idea of a reward is different from their child's.) The idea is to celebrate yet another step toward conquering OCD fears.

- *Remember that your child isn't a miniature adult with OCD.* Regardless of how mature he seems as he grasps the implications of his disorder and performs his exposures, bear in mind that he's still a kid. His emotional maturity will guide him; in this one instance, your expectations don't count.

- *Make sure that other family members and teachers are aware of ERP and its role in your child's recovery.* Your child's siblings should be involved in his treatment plan, especially if they've participated in his rituals in the past. Likewise, his teachers should know that he is undergoing treatment for an illness and, if possible, adjust his workload during his weeks of treatment. (Teachers may also have become unwitting partners in his rituals.) Everyone who deals with the child should be primed to point out that "It's the OCD that's talking" if your child is asking for reassurance or asking others to do the rituals for him.

- *Remind your child, if necessary, that this is* not *a never-ending project.* Although your child is in charge of his treatment and setting his own pace, it may benefit him to realize that this difficulty won't last forever—and, more specifically, that his formal exposure homework will end in a few months.

Keeping Up the Good Work

Getting rid of OCD's rituals will be cause for celebration—but it is important for all involved, especially your child, to keep their antennae sharp for signs of OCD's return. In fact, you probably should expect minor setbacks; as we mentioned earlier, for some people the obsessions never disappear entirely, but your child can choose not to respond to his with rituals.

You and your child will be given maintenance strategies. These will probably include periodic exposures that ranked high on the fear thermometer. Help your child anticipate stressful situations that once provoked obsessions and compulsions, and plan on ways in which he can respond. If you acknowledge that there will be occasional lapses and have exposure exercises at your fingertips, it's likely your child can effectively manage his OCD for the rest of his life.

Frequently Asked Questions

Q: Does strep throat actually cause OCD?
A: No. A streptococcal infection can (but doesn't always) trigger OCD in children or teens already at risk. This particular form of OCD is called PANDAS—pediatric autoimmune neuropsychiatric disorders associated with streptococcus—and it is triggered when strep infection–related antibodies attack specific parts of the brain, such as the basal ganglia, that are associated with OCD. It's important to note, however, that most strep infections do not lead to OCD, and that most pediatric cases of OCD have nothing to do with strep infections.

Q: I'm pretty sure my 8-year-old daughter has OCD. Can I design her treatment by myself?
A: While it would be possible for you to design a treatment plan for your daughter, it's most beneficial if you both meet with a professional. Let the clinician know that you are interested in being involved in the treatment and are willing to take on the role of coach. A professional who's experienced in treating pediatric OCD can help your daughter eliminate some symptoms quickly, by feeding her self-confidence and ability to face more serious behaviors; he or she can also help you develop the skills you need to keep the ERP program going at home. In addition, the therapist can provide you with

support in your role of coach and help you to make certain that you don't inadvertently succumb to facilitating your daughter's rituals. Indeed, the therapist will appreciate just how hard it is for a parent to stand on the sidelines and cheer instead of providing reassurance. Also, it's possible that your child would benefit from medication, which must be prescribed by a doctor.

Q: My 12-year-old son's therapist suggested pulling the boy out of gym class temporarily until he can better manage his cleanliness obsessions and compulsions. Is this a good idea?
A: Think back a moment to the fear thermometer. Any child's ERP goals and assignments should begin with those that cause the least anxiety and gradually progress to those that cause more severe distress. If any OCD symptom causes so much anxiety for a child that he cannot move toward recovery, then it might be a good idea to remove the child from the source of his fear, until he is ready to face it. If your son's fears about hygiene are closely associated with gym class, then perhaps a short-term respite from the class would be appropriate. But mastering that class should be one of his ERP goals, and he should work toward being a fully participating class member. Total, long-term avoidance of the class will only make the OCD stronger, whereas taking some smaller steps before tackling this big-ticket item will help build his confidence.

Q: My son's clinician wants us to give his OCD a nickname. What's the purpose of that?
A: Naming your son's OCD will help him to think of the disorder as something separate from himself rather than as a permanent part of himself. It also gives the entire family something to "fight against" instead of fighting with the child who has OCD.

Q: I'd like to see my child speed up her recovery, but her therapist isn't concerned about the slow pace. How quickly should children manage their OCD?
A: Treatment should proceed at whatever pace makes the child most comfortable. As long as she is committed to making her way up the

hierarchy and is reaching her objectives with few relapses, then her recovery is proceeding at an acceptable pace. Keep in mind, too, that the medications used in OCD treatment are very slow-acting and can keep the recovery pace rather slow, whether the patient is a child or an adult.

Q: I think my daughter might lose sight of her ultimate goal in OCD treatment. What's a good way to reinforce it?
A: As with adults, your daughter's therapist will have worked with her to establish her treatment goals and objectives. And however it may have been stated, it's likely that her main goal is to stop ritualizing—to resist OCD's invitation to engage in compulsive behaviors. It might be helpful for your daughter to copy her list of goals and objectives so that she can keep it in her room; or, if she's agreeable, post it in a place where the whole family can see it—such as on the refrigerator. Having a visual reminder of where the therapy started is a great way for everyone to celebrate her progress. A similar strategy can be used with her fear thermometer. If your daughter has a copy of this, she can easily keep track of how far she's moved up on her hierarchy. In addition, if there are activities that your daughter enjoyed but stopped doing because of her OCD, it may be useful to point out how she's now able to engage in those things that OCD deprived her of.

Q: My son comes up with any excuse possible to avoid his ERP homework. This is exhausting me—what can I do to help him?
A: If you're exhausted, just think of how tiring this is for your son! Children's rituals can be deeply ingrained habits—to the point where they actually forget to resist them. They also become fearful that the anxiety won't go away if they don't perform the rituals. If your son is old enough, he may be able to verbalize what is interfering with his ERP homework. One strategy is to suggest to your son that the two of you are a team—and that a team is definitely stronger than the OCD. Try coaching a bit during homework, starting the exposure again, and then reminding your son that nothing terrible will happen if he stands up to the OCD—that doing so will actually weaken the

OCD so it won't cause him so much anxiety in the future. It may be that your son is trying to tackle exposures that are just too hard. If you suspect that this is the case, make sure that his therapist knows he's not doing his ERP homework and that you suspect it's too difficult. The therapist can help to revise the items on the fear thermometer so your son can start building on his successes.

Q: I want to help boost my kid's confidence as he works on recovering, but I know that providing reassurance is a bad thing. What exactly should I say?

A: Reassurance is very different from supporting your child's recovery. Congratulate him whenever he resists the pressure to perform a ritual. Tell him frequently that you love him and believe in him. What you should not say is that ritualizing is "okay, just this once"; nor should you respond to questions that revolve around how well something is done—especially if your child is a perfectionist. OCD is the bad guy now, the enemy that you're fighting together. Your son is the good guy. Rather than asking someone else for reassurance, asking your son what he thinks and then applauding his non-OCD-based reaction will help him to stay on track with his ERP. Keep that distinction in mind and you'll do fine.

Q: I'm a little concerned about maintenance after my daughter's recovery is completed. Are there any tips we can follow?

A: Some professionals recommend a monthly ERP practice session, during which your child would perform an exercise that is very high on her hierarchy. Your therapist can help you come up with the right maintenance exercises. If an event is approaching that once triggered your daughter's OCD, plan for it. Some clinicians recommend extra sleep and a relaxation exercise, even a "booster ERP" exercise, that she can perform when the tension hits.

TEN

How to Help When a Loved One Has OCD

BY NOW YOU PROBABLY FEEL that *you* could write a book on OCD. You've learned about the most up-to-date information on its causes, symptoms, and the latest treatments. But there's one particulår we haven't addressed yet: how to support someone with OCD if you are that person's wife, husband, parent, child, sibling, or friend. We sincerely believe that this chapter, in which we focus on OCD from the perspective of family members and friends, can help to deepen understanding of the disorder and how it affects the people surrounding the OCD sufferer.

Living with a loved one's obsessions and compulsions can strain a relationship to the breaking point. It's impossible to exaggerate the effect that OCD will have on your lives together—or, in many cases, separately—because OCD is a demanding, obnoxious, totally unpleasant disorder. It's critical to remember that the person you care about *has* OCD—it is the person who has the illness. *The illness is not the person.*

This chapter is about those people who give support to someone with OCD. (It's also meant to help OCD sufferers themselves understand the disorder's impact on other people and how to ask them for their help and support.) You will learn about aspects of family life that will shape the treatment outcome and the kinds of steps you can take to help ensure that this outcome is a positive one. You will also learn strategies for moving from a feeling of hopelessness to a much stronger position—that of collaboration and effective management of this problem. We will remind you that, in order to become more empowered, you must take good care of yourself as well as the loved one with OCD, even if this means setting limits that the OCD sufferer may find hard to deal with. Our hope is that, by reading this chapter, you will be able to restore balance in your family life.

Ways of Providing Support to Your Loved One with OCD

Strategy #1: Do Not Do What Comes Naturally

Most of us have had to care for people who are ill. When our "patients" become cranky and make demands, it's only natural that we want to smooth things over, accommodate them, and get past the difficult moment. Strange as it seems, when the person you care about is suffering from OCD, you must resist this impulse.

Watching friends or family members struggle with their rituals is hard. It becomes even harder if they ask you to do their rituals for them. It's not the same thing as bringing a cup of tea to someone who is sick with the flu. If you help with a ritual, those with OCD will expect that the next time they ask, you will help again. And if you don't help, it is likely that tensions will escalate until either the OCD sufferer is overwhelmed with anxiety and is ritualizing furiously or you cave in. And then the cycle repeats.

For instance, if the person with OCD has an "evening up" compulsion, she might ask you to be sure the coffee cups in the dishwasher are aligned perfectly, or that the folders in her briefcase are in the right order, before you both leave for work in the morning. If she is a hoarder, she might expect you to exist in a progressively smaller living space because her accumulated possessions take up entire rooms of the house. Any help with rituals—whether they be cleansing, checking, counting, or some other type of rituals—will only be an obstacle to recovery.

Not all OCD sufferers ask others to engage in rituals for them. Some will instead ask for reassurance. Reassurance-seeking is a form of ritualizing, too, but it plays out differently and, in most cases, a lot more subtly. After all, you're merely answering a question, right?

In fact, you would be doing the wrong thing: Accommodating OCD in any way feeds the illness and makes the OCD more powerful. Following are some of the most common ways that families accommodate OCD in their loved ones:

1. *Reassurance.* Even a small reassurance, such as telling the person, "Yes, I'm certain you turned off the water upstairs," or, "Yes, you washed your hands after you touched the dog," can fuel OCD. Granted, without your reassurance the OCD sufferer will have to check the faucet again or wash his hands again. But with even that small reassurance, you unintentionally became a partner in their obsessions and compulsions. In other words, because you become the "go-to" person who helps to momentarily decrease the OCD sufferer's unpleasant feeling of uncertainty or responsibility, he will keep coming back to you. At first, your reassurance may be sufficient. But, as with all rituals, the initial reassurance loses its potency and the person with OCD keeps coming back, again and again—often with only a few moments between asking, "Are you sure?" As you can imagine (or as you've experienced), it can become infuriating. Yet we recommend, based on our clinical experience, that you tell the person with OCD—calmly and lovingly, but firmly—that you will no longer offer reassurance regarding his rituals because you care about him and want him to get better.

2. *Ignoring the OCD.* It's the classic "elephant in the living room" tendency: When something is happening that makes us uncomfortable, the easiest thing to do is ignore it. When the "uncomfortable" event is OCD behavior, we may stay out of the room while the patient is straightening the fringe on the rug or use the guest bathroom if she is taking her fourth shower of the day—and we just don't bring

it up. When family and friends choose to not say anything or dismiss rituals as just "eccentric" behavior, they are encouraging the patient to ignore the reality of how much negative impact OCD is having on her life and the lives of everyone around her.

3. *Participating.* "Helping" a person with OCD to complete his checking, washing, straightening, or other compulsions is one of the most harmful and enabling choices a loved one can make. It means that the person with OCD does not have to take responsibility for his behavior. It may also affirm to the patient that these behaviors are acceptable and that it's fine to address obsessions by performing OCD-related rituals. Family members who participate in compulsive behaviors often find themselves arriving late to work or social obligations, or missing them altogether because they're at home checking, cleaning, or straightening alongside the person with OCD. What's more, the OCD sufferer may put responsibility for any negative outcome on the person with whom he is sharing a ritual. In essence, it's now your fault if a door is left unlocked and the house is burglarized. In a sense, then, OCD has become the unwanted relative that has permanently moved in and taken over the family. It is a sad, downward spiral, and family members must recognize this and resist the temptation to participate in compulsive behaviors even if they know that doing so will be a cause for conflict. Talk to your friend or family member and let him know that because you care about him, you cannot continue to support his OCD. You can support *him* but not his illness.

4. *Changing your schedule or activities for OCD.* This accommodation is potentially more personally distressing than the others because it means you are relinquishing control of your *own* life to OCD. Many families find themselves giving up small pleasures, such as a weekly bridge game or a patio party with neighbors, because the patient's OCD rituals might still be going on during that time, or might be embarrassing in front of company.

5. *Taking on extra responsibilities.* For example, you might start tending the garden for a friend with OCD who can't handle dirt, fertilizer, and so on. Or, you might do all of your husband's Christmas shopping because he would otherwise insist on "evening up" the amount spent on each niece and nephew and keep shopping until

those amounts were exactly the same. Providing this misguided "help" is similar to engaging in rituals for your loved one in that the intention behind it is simply to make life a bit more bearable for the person with OCD.

6. *Putting up with it all.* As we've noted elsewhere in this book, OCD symptoms can take the form of out-of-the-ordinary behaviors or ordinary behaviors run amok—and it's common for co-workers, friends, and family members to simply dismiss them as quirky. If a supervisor seems overly picky about the tidiness of everyone's desks, or a family has to make a pizza run because the person with OCD is still washing dishes after two hours, who is it harming? The answer, of course, is that it's harming everyone involved. It's disrupting normal work and family decisions and routines. Ignoring the symptoms only allows the OCD to escalate.

Indeed, accommodating OCD actually increases the sufferer's need for more accommodating behaviors on the part of everyone around them. Reassuring a person breeds the need for more reassurance. Ignoring the OCD grows past occasional "smoothing the waters" to become a way of life, and participating in compulsive behavior drags the entire family into the go-nowhere OCD lifestyle.

DEBBIE'S ACCOMMODATING PARENTS

Debbie, a very bright, engaging high school student, was a very high achiever. She had wonderful grades, she was popular, and everyone expected her to be a star. Her parents saw an Ivy League college in her future. During her freshman year of high school, they noticed she often characterized a certain clique of students as "grubby." Debbie described them as coming to school in what looked like unwashed, grimy jeans and sloppy shirts, and as generally looking unkempt. Their appearance was in stark contrast to Debbie's preppy look. Since she was not in class with any of these students and saw them only in passing, her comments about them didn't raise any red flags for her parents until her sophomore year.

It was during that next year that Debbie had two classes with a boy from the "grubby" group—and, as it turned out, he was seated next to her in class. She described the experience of sitting next to him as "making my skin crawl." She was able to deal with this level of contact until one day when she dropped a book and the young man picked it up and returned it to her. Debbie nearly had a panic attack. After class, she raced to her locker and threw the book in and fled to her next class. That evening, her mother walked past Debbie's bedroom and saw her spraying disinfectant on the book and on anything she believed had come in contact with it.

As the semester progressed, so did Debbie's fears and, along with them, her parents' concerns. Just being in proximity of anyone from the "grubby" clique made her feel contaminated. It got to the point where she would come home from school and completely undress in the garage, leave her clothes in a pile on the laundry room floor, and then race to the bathroom to shower. She was completely unable to touch her clothes and asked her mother to wash them.

At first her mother didn't mind being asked to launder Debbie's school clothes (some of which were usually washed after one wearing anyway), but Debbie's demands escalated as her OCD worsened. Debbie's mom soon became perturbed about washing Debbie's clothes on a daily basis, especially skirts and slacks that weren't even dirty. When her mother suggested that Debbie wash her own clothes, a temper tantrum ensued. Then, Debbie began insisting that her mother disinfect all of her books, her backpack, and her shoes and coat. Debbie's mother very grudgingly acquiesced because if Debbie was left to disinfect her belongings, it would take so long that she didn't get her studying done. Anything that had come in either actual or potential contact with things she associated with her school had to be washed or disinfected. As her OCD worsened, even the car had to be disinfected if Debbie's dad or sister picked her up at school. Ultimately, her father became so tired of Debbie's tantrums that he began having the car detailed on a weekly basis.

If the family cat happened to be in the laundry room while Debbie was dropping off her clothes, she would have a meltdown if no one bathed the cat. Not even the cat could ignore how Debbie's OCD was taking over the family!

> What began as disinfecting a book turned into hours of her family's
> time spent accommodating Debbie's OCD. They didn't know how to
> resist her demands. If her mom touched Debbie's clothes, then she
> wasn't allowed to prepare food unless she thoroughly scrubbed her
> hands and arms and wore an apron and kitchen gloves. Of course,
> Debbie would have preferred that her mother showered. At the point
> where Debbie was screaming and crying that her mother would poi-
> son the family if she didn't shower because she'd touched Debbie's
> clothes, her mom called a meeting of the family members and they
> decided it was time to get Debbie some help.

When family members call our clinic asking what they can do, one of our main therapeutic goals is to help them understand that accommodating OCD symptoms will only make the situation worse: Your loved one's need and dependence grow until eventually she is unable to make simple decisions, let alone act as an independent, productive person.

OCD can't help but diminish a family's normal functioning. One study quotes the sister of a 23-year-old woman with the disorder who had "barricaded herself in the living room" because she was afraid the other family members might contaminate her space. She was also afraid to use a toilet because it was dirty, so she filled cans with her urine and solid wastes and stored them in her own bedroom. It was no surprise that the rest of the family felt powerless, confused, and desperate.

Family members who become trapped in an OCD sufferer's demands that they participate in ritualizing are themselves sometimes devastated by the OCD. However, even less dramatic symptoms can destroy a family's normal way of functioning. Time-consuming checking rituals, long hours spent washing one's hands, fear of making decisions—all of these more common symptoms may seem benign when compared to the extreme examples but, nonetheless, can disrupt a family's routines and relationships.

The anecdotal evidence showing such disruption is overwhelming. We can tell you story after story of patients who have come through our clinic; yet, unfortunately, very few scientific studies have examined the effects of OCD on family life. In one of those rare studies, about one-third of family members reported that they responded to OCD symptoms with reassurance three or more times a week, one-third said that they participated in the patient's compulsive behaviors, and one-third reported that they had taken on responsibilities that used to belong to the patient.

Here's the punch line: OCD had taken over the lives of these family members to the extent that 35 percent of them exhibited "moderate" distress levels and another 23 percent were experiencing "severe or extreme" distress.

In another study, 60 percent of relatives (including children, siblings, parents, and spouses) said they observed or participated in their family member's rituals or practiced compulsive avoidance, and 40 percent reported feeling responsible for the person's illness. More than half of them wanted help.

Those statistics might seem startling at first glance, but be encouraged: Based on years of clinical experience we can assure you that, when family members stop their reassurance, avoidance, and other accommodating behaviors, the person with OCD is more successful in treatment.

As you learned in the treatment chapters, exposure and response prevention (ERP) puts the person with OCD in the position of taking risks, setting goals, and beginning to live without compulsive behaviors and unrealistic fears. It is essential, then, that family members understand ERP, too, and support the treatment methods and goals. We will discuss this further—but, for now, keep in mind that we strongly advise you to seek out a professional for consultation if your family member's OCD is making everyone's life a misery. A clinician or support group can provide instruction regarding how best to set limits and follow the patient's ERP plan, so that the entire family can fight the OCD together.

Strategy #2: Watch Your Temper!

To an OCD patient, angry outbursts, put-downs, and blaming are just as harmful as accommodating. OCD is such an exasperating disorder that it poses a big challenge to families to prevent their frustrations from boiling over.

When someone in the family spends hours every day indulging in rituals that keep all of you from experiencing a normal, happy home life, it's only natural that you'll be inclined to scream and get nasty. But you must stop yourself from erupting because your blame or insults will only erode your loved one's confidence, and he may retreat even more deeply into his compulsive behaviors. Remember, the vast majority of people with OCD know that their behaviors are excessive and when they are not overwhelmed with anxiety, they feel terrible about what they are doing to themselves and the people who care about them.

We know it's a tricky balance, keeping your anger in check—but for your own sake as well as that of the OCD sufferer in your family, you have to be very firm in confronting OCD symptoms. Bear in mind, however, that it may be hard for that anxious OCD sufferer to make the subtle distinction between your being overly angry and appropriately firm.

Strategy #3: What to Do If Your Family Member Doesn't Think OCD Is a Problem

With some regularity, we receive calls from family members who want to schedule an appointment for a relative who has OCD. We always ask them to have the person with OCD call us directly. On many occasions, the callers tell us that the person with OCD doesn't really think she has a problem but, rather, it's the family whose lives are disrupted and they can't handle the OCD any more. What this indicates to us is that the OCD sufferer is not ready to start treatment. We tell these understandably concerned and distraught family members that we will consult with them to help increase the treatment-readiness of the relative with OCD. We also encourage family members to abandon what is often their strategy to aggressively persuade, argue, debate, or confront their loved one into starting therapy. Rather, we emphasize that in order for treatment to be successful, the motivation must be the OCD sufferer's own. No matter how much the family wants the person to get better, the family member with OCD must want to get better for her own reasons.

There are a few things that you can do if the person with OCD has not sought out treatment or doesn't think that things are bad enough to get help. First, keep track of what the OCD sufferer is asking of you and what you feel you are sacrificing because of the person's OCD. Don't be emotional about it—just keep an objective record. Set limits. Be clear that you care about your loved one, but that your caring doesn't mean you will become a part of her illness. By no longer participating in her rituals, you are making a clear statement that the responsibility for the OCD rests with the patient, not the family. Indeed, if this new stance of yours increases the anxiety and distress that the sufferer is experiencing, it may serve to make the point that the patient really needs to get help. This kind of discussion cannot occur when you are angry at what OCD is doing to you and others or when the person with OCD is caught up in a whirlwind of obsessions and rituals.

If your loved one has started therapy and gets to a point where you see improvement but OCD is still a problem and the OCD sufferer indicates that she has made "enough" progress and wants to quit therapy, we suggest that you ask to speak with your loved one's therapist. Together the two of you can figure out the best way for you to respond. We encourage family members to continue to stand firm in the face of OCD symptoms and to be direct and straightforward about the negative effect OCD is still having on the family and the extent to which your loved one is still suffering. It is important to be supportive and honest *without* expressing anger, blaming, criticizing, or belittling. Remember that ERP is hard work. Whatever you can do to enhance your loved one's motivation—such as noting how much progress she has made even if she is still struggling with overcoming her rituals or letting her know that you are willing to be a partner in her recovery and not her illness—may help to keep her engaged in treatment.

Harmony in the Household: The Best Prescription for Recovery

We've discussed two extreme kinds of "OCD families":

- Those who accommodate the patient by engaging in reassurance, by ignoring the problem, or by participating in the compulsive behaviors

- Those who dig in their heels and refuse to tolerate the patient's symptoms, criticizing him and, ultimately, contributing to his feeling that he has no control over his life

With either extreme, the OCD symptoms get worse. Home life is even more unstable when family members are split: One person in the household might want to appease the patient, reassure him, and just get past the crisis of the moment, while another might be fed up with his symptoms, resorting to excessive criticism and put-downs, and demanding that the compulsive behavior stop immediately. It's not unusual to see parents being more tolerant and accommodating and siblings becoming angry and critical—especially if the child with OCD is viewed as being treated differently from the other children. Anger in response to this latter situation is easy to understand if the chores assigned to the child with OCD are repeatedly foisted onto a sibling.

OCD isn't so widespread in our society that everyone understands how it plays out. Many people view a patient's inability to control his symptoms as a form of laziness or belligerence. Unless the OCD is treated, the discord only escalates into more hurt feelings and angry outbursts. Alcohol abuse, separation, and divorce are common among OCD families.

There's plenty of shame and guilt to go around: Parents may blame their child's OCD on their own anxiety disorders or on their mishandling of some childhood trauma, while the patient may see his family life crumbling and feel even less confident and in control or blame himself for all of the conflict that is occurring. The home becomes a hostile place where everyone is walking on eggshells and the patient is feeling pressure to "measure up" and stop the family's unhappiness—resulting in a stronger-than-ever need to perform rituals. At least one study found that the severity of a person's OCD was greatly influenced by the attitudes of those around him. So, in a hostile or angry home, the outcome usually is an increase in OCD symptoms. This is especially the case when the person suffering from OCD is trying to keep his symptoms under control and the family has not had the opportunity to learn about OCD—it remains a mystery to everyone.

Fortunately for patients and their families, the converse also is true: Studies indicate that when the patient feels that family members understand what he is struggling with and they are all making an effort to get along and agreeing to be partners in conquering the OCD, symptoms decrease and the patient is able to more easily manage the illness.

MANDY AND KATE: A TALE OF TWO SISTERS

Kate had always found her younger sister, Mandy, to be a little quirky. "She was the one in the family who hated to have sticky fingers," Kate remembers, "so while the rest of us were slurping our ice cream cones, Mandy took hers in a little bowl with a spoon."

Her personal-hygiene focus became a good-natured family joke. She never enjoyed splashing in mud puddles or even swimming in the public pool down the road because she didn't want to get dirty or expose herself to germs. Their parents didn't have to ask Mandy to wash her hands before dinner; she always showed up at the table with clean hands and freshly brushed teeth.

During Mandy's senior year of college, however, their parents were killed in a car accident. Kate already was teaching school and owned her own condo, so they agreed that Mandy would live in the family home as long as she wished.

Over the next two years, when they made a date for dinner together or a night out with friends, Mandy usually was quite late. Kate always excused her; time wasn't that important and, after all, Mandy had just started law school. If she needed an extra hour to study, what difference did it make?

It wasn't until Kate and Mandy were at a restaurant lounge together that Kate noticed Mandy's hands. They were red and raw-looking as if Mandy had been scouring floors for hours. That same evening, Kate saw Mandy in the restroom, scrubbing her hands as if she were trying to remove a stubborn stain. Kate watched her for a minute, then suddenly understood what the late arrivals and lengthy trips to the bathroom signified. Kate couldn't remember where she had heard of OCD but she thought that might be her sister's problem.

Kate confronted Mandy as gently as possible, but she stood firm: "You have to see someone about this," Kate told her. "I'll stay with you in the house for a little while and we'll work on this together."

With very few detours, Mandy's OCD story found a happy ending. Kate did move back into the family home for a few weeks. The day after she found Mandy scrubbing in the public restroom, they went online and learned about some of OCD's symptoms and where in their area they could find help. "She was relieved that I had found her scrubbing and that I understood and didn't chastise or make fun of her," Kate said, "so there wasn't much resistance on her part. We think it might have been triggered by our parents' deaths, though she definitely was harboring her OCD for many years; it just didn't become too serious until that trauma happened."

"When they died," Kate added, "she felt so alone. I don't know if she ever would have taken it upon herself to get help. She really didn't know what was happening, only that she was losing control. When I told her I'd stand beside her and lick this thing, you could almost see her face change. I think we both knew right away that she'd be okay."

Keeping the Family in Context

For many patients, the role of family members in their recovery is key. Just as family members themselves may be asking a loved one to get treatment, quite a few of our patients want their families involved. These patients recognize that one or more of their family members or friends are an incredible source of support.

In cases where family members may be contributing to the maintenance of the patient's OCD, during the course of evaluation or treatment the patient should make note of such occurrences. If the family members are amenable, one of their first steps should be to have their own behavior, and their family life, assessed. You can ask the patient's clinician for such an evaluation, but it's likely that he or she will bring it up without your asking, especially if the patient is a child. Every therapist experienced in treating this disorder now knows that OCD is greatly influenced by what's happening at home and in the patient's various relationships, and the professional will want to consider those factors in designing and implementing a treatment plan. Our clinic would never treat someone for OCD without knowing about her family and how supportive it is—or isn't.

While some families are fed up and at their wits' end over having to deal with a person with OCD and just want the person "fixed," most are happy to be a part of the early stages of evaluation and treatment. Being interviewed by a professional gives them a chance to vent, to explain "their side" of the story, and to get some advice for dealing with the patient. It's quite rare that we see relatives of an OCD sufferer who do not want to express their own frustrations to a professional and ask questions.

Another valuable purpose served by these initial family interviews is that they allow a clinician to expel any stereotypes that might have arisen as well as to provide accurate information, thereby giving the patient's relatives the hope that she *can* get better and that their home life can be normal once again. The more information family members give and receive, the more confident they will feel that they'll one day be able to manage their homes, their schedules, and their relationships again.

At our clinic, family interviews frequently touch on the following questions. You should feel free to take this list with you to your own family interview.

- When did your loved one's OCD symptoms first begin?
- Do you remember what triggered the symptoms the first time you observed them?

- To what extent do you blame yourself for the OCD, or feel responsible for causing it?
- How quickly did the OCD symptoms progress? Did they become more frequent or change along the way?
- In what ways has the OCD disrupted your family life? Would you call it a major burden?
- In what ways (and how often) do you, and other family members, reassure, avoid, or otherwise accommodate the patient's OCD symptoms?
- Do you participate in the patient's OCD rituals?
- Have you taken responsibility for obligations that once belonged to the OCD patient, or have you "assigned" those responsibilities to someone else?
- Has the OCD begun to isolate you or other family members socially?
- Are you ready to commit to supporting the patient's ERP treatment?
- Is there anything about OCD in general, or about your family's situation in particular, that you feel you need more information on?

In short, if your family is being disrupted by OCD and you suspect that this issue hasn't been raised with your loved one's therapist—or if she has yet to see a professional about her OCD—we strongly recommend that your family undergo some type of evaluation or consultation regarding your involvement in her symptoms, the anger level in the house, and the ways in which all the family members are responding to her OCD symptoms.

Family meetings usually are less formal meetings that take place between the clinician and family members with the OCD patient present. We generally don't use any specific forms or questionnaires. Instead, if the purpose of the meeting is primarily informational, once we have our patient's permission to involve the family and what we can discuss, we ask family members about their home life, how it has been disrupted by the OCD, and what their goals are for getting back to a normal lifestyle. On the other hand, if the meeting's purpose is to help the family to stop enabling OCD behaviors, we focus more on problem-solving and working with the patient and the family to develop a mutually agreed-upon plan that circumvents any further disruption to family functioning. Sure, this is very personal information—but sharing it with a professional will help determine all the ways in which you and your family can best support the patient during treatment and increase the chances that the treatment will be a success.

Sign on the Bottom Line: The "OCD Family Contract"

All professionals have their own "style" of doing things, and therapists are no different. We find ourselves using certain exercises because we've seen those approaches work. One exercise that many clinicians favor is the "OCD family contract."

Think of agreements you've signed in the past. The basic elements are

- a statement of the problem or need,
- a statement of the goals and expectations/objectives, and
- a statement of how you will resolve the problem or fulfill the need.

In an OCD family contract, the problem at hand is the need to change *your* behavior—not that of the OCD patient—in a way that will best support your loved one's recovery and stop feeding the OCD. Accordingly, this contract

- examines the situations in which you have been most likely to accommodate the person,
- tracks your accommodating behavior,
- identifies goals and strategies for changes in your behavior, and
- evaluates how effectively these strategies for change worked.

You might find it helpful, before you talk with your loved one's therapist about your home life, to begin your own OCD family contract. We've included a sample below, along with instructions that will get you thinking about the ways in which you might be helping or hindering your loved one's recovery.

Since members of the same family often disagree about the best way to handle OCD symptoms, you might want to make a copy of the three parts of this sample for each family member or friend to fill out. It will be helpful for the therapist to know all the ways in which various people in the patient's life have been accommodating and enabling her. Don't be surprised if you discover you've been accommodating the OCD more than you realized; most families of OCD patients find room for improvement—and new possibilities for helping their loved ones!

Part I of Your OCD Family Contract: When OCD Takes Over

In most cases of OCD, the disorder interferes in ordinary daily routines. Even small decisions or actions that we take for granted can trigger fear and obsessions in OCD patients, causing them to resort to their compulsive behaviors. When this happens, the patient's and family's routines are disrupted, sometimes even destroyed. These ordinary situations include the following:

- Family meal time
- Small gestures of affection or friendship, such as a hug or a handshake
- Shopping decisions and completion of shopping tasks, such as putting away food
- Daily hygiene and grooming
- Housecleaning and other simple chores
- Leaving the house for routine reasons, such as work, school, or social events
- Driving a car, or getting into or out of a car

List daily situations that trigger your loved one's compulsive behavior:

1)

2)

3)

4)

5)

6)

Part II of Your OCD Family Contract: Your Accommodating Behaviors

Now that you've thought about the specific situations in which your loved one exhibits OCD symptoms, describe how you usually respond and how often. For the next week, record below each time you accommodate the OCD, noting the day, time, what the patient was doing, and how you responded. This section will be immensely helpful to you, the family member with OCD, and the therapist in terms of getting a clear idea of how OCD affects your home life, so be sure to record even the smallest, most subtle accommodations on your part. Use extra paper if you need to, or track this information on a daily basis in a small notebook. As the week goes on, feel free to add notes regarding your feelings. Specify whether the OCD and your own behavior makes you feel angry, hopeless, guilty, weary—whatever is happening with you at the time.

	Day	Time	OCD Ritual	Accommodating Behavior
1)				
2)				
3)				
4)				

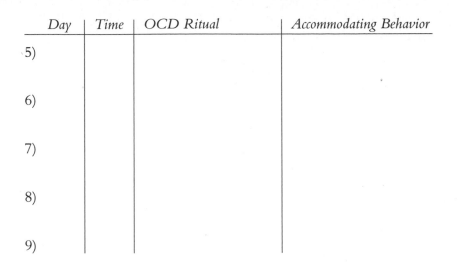

Day	Time	OCD Ritual	Accommodating Behavior
5)			
6)			
7)			
8)			
9)			

Part III of Your OCD Family Contract:
The New Behaviors You've Specified as Goals!

You and your loved one, along with his therapist (if he is in therapy), should review Part II together and talk about the ways in which you have been enabling the OCD. Together, you can determine which of your accommodating behaviors should be eliminated first, based on its frequency and the seriousness of the OCD symptoms to which you are responding. You and he, along with other family members, should be in agreement about your goals as you set them. A guideline to consider is that many therapists who use "behavioral contracting" of this kind prefer to start with very small, easy-to-achieve goals, so that successes can build upon each other and confidence in overcoming what may be overwhelming, disruptive patterns can grow.

As an example, perhaps: You've been reassuring your loved one that he can wash his hands for as long as he likes before dinner. Your accommodating behavior is that you keep the meal warm until he's ready to eat. Or, a more serious accommodation—maybe you've called in sick for him, at those times when his symptoms have prevented him from getting to work on time. Whatever your accommodations, stopping them will be the goals set forth in your contract—one by one, starting with the least severe. The therapist may suggest other goals that involve encouragement and support for the patient. She will make sure that your accommodation goals are in line with the ERP treatment plan.

You can plan your goals for stopping your accommodating behavior in a simple list that itemizes the OCD symptom, how you accommodated it, your new goal behavior, and whether you succeeded. The clinician can decide, with input from you and the patient, how long you should keep logging your new behaviors.

	Date	Time	OCD Symptom	Accommodating Behavior	Goal/New Behavior
1)					
2)					
3)					
4)					
5)					
6)					
7)					
8)					
9)					

MARRIED TO AN OCD SUFFERER: KENDRA, JONATHAN'S WIFE

Remember Jonathan, the man who kept his harming obsessions secret for years, even from his wife? Jonathan's OCD symptoms were always triggered by an approaching family event. When he had obsessions about harming their baby at her first birthday party, he finally knew that he had to tell Kendra about his bizarre disorder. At that point, he hadn't been diagnosed and didn't know he suffered from OCD.

Kendra says today that when Jonathan told her about his harming obsessions, she never saw it coming. "Harming doesn't always have the same outward manifestations as would contamination or checking," she says. "Some of Jonathan's rituals, the cognitive ones, were literally all in his head and hung out there—which made them less obvious to me." And, Kendra adds, their baby had been taking up most of her attention; she simply didn't notice that Jonathan's behaviors had changed.

Once Jonathan revealed that something was wrong, Kendra observed that he was preoccupied with his symptoms—"so much so that he was unable to participate in life." On the one hand, by disclosing his problem to his wife, Jonathan considerably reduced his anxiety about having his intrusive thoughts discovered. However, it was as though his revelation gave him permission to stop doing simple chores like grocery shopping, preparing a snack for the kids, and taking them to school. He made it to work every day, but the effort of appearing normal around outsiders drained him. He was too tired for physical intimacy or family outings. Their relationship became strained and Jonathan's stress level was high. "The changes in him frustrated me," Kendra says. "I questioned whether I could deal with it."

It's difficult, she adds, living with someone who is physically present but mentally absent. His exhaustion eventually caught up with him and he slept so much that he had to cut back his working hours to part-time. The older kids, ages 4 and 6, asked their mother why Dad slept so much. Kendra usually responded by telling the children that Dad wasn't feeling well and changing the subject.

One morning a few weeks after his "confession," Jonathan woke up crying at 1:30 A.M. The couple has a friend in Chicago with OCD and, as Kendra watched her husband cry, she says, "It just clicked. I thought, 'Oh my God, it's OCD.'"

Kendra called their friend, who put them in touch with an OCD specialist. Jonathan was fortunate in that he was able to make an appointment with the clinician the next morning. There was an opening in the clinician's intensive treatment program, which Jonathan then attended every day for the next few weeks. Not only was his wife supportive of his treatment, so was his extended family—his sister from Salt Lake City flew in to help with the kids. Jonathan was receptive to treatment, Kendra says, "but he was convinced he was dying, a new twist to his harming obsession."

She describes those weeks as "depressing. Depression sucks the life out of a person and a family." Jonathan fantasized that he was deathly ill and it got him plenty of attention; people continually asked him how he was feeling and what was wrong. It gave him validation.

One night, Kendra says, "I just freaked out. I yelled, 'Get a grip! Families do not fall apart over leg cramps!' Jonathan was crushed. I'm not sure it was the right thing to do, but it did stop him in his tracks a bit." When Jonathan shared the interaction with his therapist, it became a good exercise in helping him to dispute his health-related obsessions because he was able to work through the thought and conclude that Kendra was right—families don't fall apart over leg cramps.

That was Kendra's only blow-up. "By that time, I had read enough to know that my frustration wouldn't help him recover," she says, "and probably would make things worse. I resolved then to keep my resentment to myself, as much as I could, but also to make sure I didn't start accommodating him. From what I read, I knew he had to bear the full brunt of the effect of his illness or he might lose the motivation to get better." It also helped that Jonathan came back to talk to Kendra about how her perspective on his anxious overreactions could help him to challenge his obsessions. She became a part of his team and a very strict coach!

She continued her tough but supportive stance, telling him more than once that "I can find you a knife or drive you to a meeting—but I'm not going to reassure you, because reassurance will feed the OCD." Once, when he was afraid that his harming obsession would result in his physically harming her, she said, "If you strike me, I will call the police. But I will no longer enable you."

Jonathan's clinician took a firm position with him as well. The two of them closely examined his intrusive thoughts about dying. Jonathan was encouraged to examine the facts. He was learning how to determine whether there was any compelling evidence to support his belief that he was dying versus jumping to a conclusion based on an emotionally fueled obsession. After about two months of treatment, Jonathan finally felt healthier and more optimistic about his future, and he and Kendra were able to begin repairing their relationship.

Kendra now says that if his OCD appears again, she will be prepared. That difficult time taught her to pay attention, she says—"to be connected to what is going on with him." She has a newfound compassion, too, for families of people with mental illness; she had no idea that mental disorders could be so devastating. "I wish our country's health policies were more attentive to this illness," she says. "Medical help for OCD is very expensive and it causes me great sadness to think of the people who can't afford the help they need. I think of the poor children whose parents are crippled with the pain of OCD." Kendra's advice to other spouses of OCD patients: "Be patient with them, but also with yourself. This is not easy work. I would suggest surrounding yourself with loved ones. Reach out for support, maybe a support group, or find an online community for support if there isn't a support group that is located anywhere near your home. Reading about OCD is helpful, too, because knowledge is power and with OCD you tend to feel very powerless when OCD takes over your family."

The Family's Role on the Recovery Team

It's important to understand that you, your loved one with OCD, the therapist, and other family members and friends will be working *together* to help conquer the OCD. The more you agree on your future behaviors, the less you will be enabling the OCD—and the more success you can expect!

As you change your behaviors—no longer criticizing your loved one when OCD symptoms appear, and giving up your reassurances, avoidance, and participation in compulsive behaviors—don't be surprised if you feel some resistance within yourself to this new way of dealing with OCD symptoms. It will be counterintuitive: When someone you love is having a tough day, it's only natural to want to pitch in and make things easier. Or, if the compulsions annoy you, you might be tempted to slip back into your angry mode, accusing the patient of being lazy or selfish, or otherwise criticizing him for indulging in the OCD symptoms.

Don't do it. Adding to your loved one's fears and embarrassment will only make the OCD stronger. Remember that your aim is to conquer the OCD together and that this means being supportive of ERP every day, even if it feels like you are being an ogre. You will not be doing anyone a kindness if you give in to the OCD.

Your behavior toward your loved one will be one of the most powerful factors in his triumph over OCD. Nothing will influence success as much as the support that comes from family and close relationships. Think what it's like to know you have people who love you standing behind you even when times are the toughest. They are your built-in cheering section!

In addition to your personal, daily support of the patient—and your "OCD family contract," if your family and the therapist choose that technique—several adjuncts to treatment can help you support your loved one while maintaining your own healthy stress level. Let's consider each of these in turn.

Support Groups

For patients, support groups can be tremendously important in re-covery. You read in Jonathan's story, in Chapter 6, that he thought it made all the difference for him. But it's also important to know that support groups can be just as valuable to the families and friends of OCD patients! Support groups take several different forms and bring about a number of benefits. If you are interested in learning about such groups for families of OCD patients—and we think all families should consider them—your loved one's therapist can point you in the right direction. A few factors to think over:

- Some support groups are attended by both patients and their families; others are families-only or patient-only. Studies have found that both types are beneficial. Find the kind of group that meets your needs.

- Not all groups are led by a mental health professional. In some cases, the leaders may be people who have overcome OCD; in others, the groups may simply comprise patients and/or families who have come together because of their common experience in dealing with OCD. You need to de-cide what you are looking for in a group and whether the group you've found is right for you. Remember: This is a support group, not a therapy group.

- Although it is very helpful to talk with families sharing the same experience as yours, some groups exist for reasons that go beyond "mutual support." These groups generally educate families about OCD and its effects, as well as about their roles in supporting loved ones with the disorder, with the aim of boosting the families' hope for the future.

- One important benefit of support groups is the sharing of strategies. Families can learn from one another regarding the best ways they've found to support the patient's ERP and strengthening their own non-accommodating behaviors.

- A caveat: If the group is not professionally led or if the members are not screened by a professional, there is no guarantee that everyone in the group will share the commonality of OCD. If there are others in the group whose problems are vastly different and don't fall into the realm of an anxiety disorder (e.g., someone with schizophrenia), the group experience may not be satisfactory. Likewise, if the group has no leader and there is someone present who monopolizes or whose OCD takes the form of repeating rituals—someone who can't be stopped from talking once she starts because if you stop her, she has to start at the beginning again—it may be difficult for others to participate and benefit from the experience.

Family-Assisted Treatment

This term refers to a form of ERP that utilizes the help of family members in a more involved way than simply eliminating their accommodating behaviors. In family-assisted treatment, the clinician gives clear, specific guidelines to a spouse or other adult family member, who then monitors the patient's ERP homework or helps with exposures. In essence, the family member becomes a coach. Studies have shown that when family members are adequately trained by therapists in such matters as communicating support, treatment tends to be especially effective.

Multifamily Group Treatment

Some therapists have begun combining features of family-assisted treatment and family support groups in treating patients who, along with their families, feel particularly isolated. Families collaborate with one another in planning their ERP homework and other aspects of treatment, and suggestions from the entire group are encouraged during their sessions. The success rates are similar to those for patients undergoing individual behavioral therapy, indicating that this approach can be effective for OCD patients and their families in certain circumstances.

We should note here that involving family members in OCD treatment won't work for every patient. In cases where the family environment is extremely hostile, chances are the therapist will hold off on including the patient's family in treatment decisions until his OCD symptoms have diminished somewhat. Bitter or irate family members will need to work with the clinician and the patient in learning to manage their old resentments and frustrations. Likewise, if two family members have OCD, it may be very hard for one of them to be in treatment while the other's OCD goes unchecked. In our clinic, for example, we were treating an adolescent who had perfectionism rituals. His ERP homework was to leave items out on his dresser in an untidy array. Initially, his mother would tidy up while he was at school. After three days of cleaning her son's room, she had an angry outburst about his leaving some of his books and papers sitting out on his desk. His mother was not just accommodating her son's OCD; as we belatedly discovered, she had OCD herself and was resistant to examining how her own behavior was sabotaging her son's progress.

The Ticket to Success: Getting Involved

With the guidance of a good therapist, actively participating in your loved one's treatment should help him recover faster and more effectively than if you had continued accommodating the OCD.

As treatment progresses, keep these pointers in mind:

- If your family member has yet to get a diagnosis, that should be your first step. This may mean seeing a therapist. If your loved one's symptoms are severe, it's unlikely that you will be able to make your way through ERP without a solid treatment plan designed by an experienced clinician. You can't even know for sure whether the problem is OCD or another disorder. In short, your loved one needs a professional diagnosis both to pinpoint the OCD symptoms and to help him and your family decide on how to target them for elimination.

- Support, support, support. Congratulate your loved one every time he completes a difficult ERP homework assignment. Cheering him on will move all of you a little bit closer to recovery.

- Banish reassurances from your loved one's surroundings. Inform his friends, colleagues, other relatives, and possibly even co-workers that such behaviors only strengthen the OCD and work against his recovery.

- Make it clear to your loved one that you understand that he hasn't done anything wrong; explain that you know OCD is a disorder and that it's the OCD that is the source of the problem.

- Once you set boundaries and new rules of the household, stick to them. That includes no longer allowing OCD symptoms to interfere with your daily routines or the routines of anyone else in the household.

- Remind your loved one often that you believe in him, not in the power of the OCD!

Bear in mind that there will be occasions when the patient's resistance overwhelms everyone's effort to steer him toward recovery. In some instances, he may simply refuse to get treatment, or to carry out a treatment plan once he sees how difficult it is to give up his compulsions. This is called "recovery avoidance." In the next chapter we'll discuss why it happens—and, if it's happening to you or someone you care about, how you can put an end to it and get back on the path to recovery.

Frequently Asked Questions

Q: One of my best friends, a sales associate, was just diagnosed with OCD. Does the Americans with Disabilities Act (ADA) require her boss to make any changes at the office to help her recovery?

A: The ADA does not mention OCD specifically, but it does cover mental disabilities. Just how (or if) your friend's company should make any changes depends on many variables specific to her situation. Some companies assist their employees' recovery by granting flex-time, extra leave, or part-time telecommuting. Her best bet is to talk with her boss or someone in the human relations department about her disorder and to specify what she thinks she needs from him or her to aid her recovery. Her therapist also might be able to help her eliminate triggers at work.

Q: I read that OCD is genetic, but my brother is the only one in our family who has it. Why not the rest of us?

A: First, it's very possible that other relatives had OCD but you didn't know it. Or, perhaps several people in your family have the genetic marker for OCD but your brother's was the only one (so far) that was triggered by a traumatic event, by PANDAS if he had a strep infection, or by some other circumstance altogether. Also, it's important to keep in mind that just because a disorder can be inherited, this doesn't mean that everyone in the family will have the gene. A genetic link may increase the probability, but it's not a guarantee.

Q: My wife believes that if she walks a certain number of steps between the bathroom and our bed, nothing will harm us during the night. If she walks the wrong number of steps, she has to start over—sometimes many times. It's a definite mood-killer!

A: It sounds as if your wife has a counting compulsion that interferes with your intimacy. The only way to end that behavior is through ERP; afterward, she will be able to walk to your bed without regard to the number of steps she takes and get into bed after the first walk. The two of you may want to try to implement ERP on your own or talk to a professional about her OCD before her obsession creates compulsive behaviors in other areas of her life. In addition to ERP, you might help your wife to appreciate the obvious. I suspect that you don't count your steps and probably don't walk the same number of steps that your wife does when you travel between the bed and bathroom—and nothing terrible has occurred. What does your wife make of that fact? And what happens when you are on vacation—Is the bathroom the same distance from the bed when you are away from home? What about any other families you know? Does everyone walk that same fixed number of steps between bed and bathroom prior to bedtime? Of course not! When you and your wife are at the breakfast table and she's not confronted with her feared situation, it might be worth discussing this with her. It's likely that she will agree that her ritual doesn't make sense. This is a good first step toward getting her to stop ritualizing.

Q: I hate visiting my mother because of the newspapers, food containers, and other worthless stuff she hoards. It has filled three rooms of her house and now is starting to fill her dining room. I want to empty the house when she's on vacation—Is that a good idea?
A: The problem with your getting rid of her junk is that it could have a seriously negative effect on your relationship with her and wouldn't change her hoarding behavior. In fact, emptying the house could be traumatic for your mother. Chances are that she would just start filling those rooms with trash again. Talk with your mother about hoarding and its consequences (e.g., fire hazards, health risks due to rodents and insect nests) and try to convince her to see a professional who is experienced in treating hoarders.

Q: I know that if I suggest that my mother talk to a therapist, she'll rear up and yell that she's not crazy. How do I bring up her possible OCD without upsetting her?
A: You could try a gentle but direct approach: "I've watched you do some things that seem to take up a huge amount of your time and make you feel miserable. Tell me why . . ." If she seems open to discussing it, give her this book. Do not make any judgments about your mother's behavior; just keep a friendly, objective conversation going,

as if you were talking about headaches or a sprained wrist. Offer to go with her to talk to a professional.

Q: My fiancé is in treatment for OCD. Would it help if I became involved with his therapy?

A: Your fiancé can definitely benefit from your support. Encourage him and applaud his progress at every opportunity. Offer to be with him during his exposure exercises—to observe him, take notes, or even do the homework alongside him (a procedure called "modeling"). You also can watch members of his family and note whenever one of them accommodates his OCD. If it's appropriate, let them know that you're no longer helping your boyfriend with his rituals. If it's difficult for them to resist accommodating him, offer to help them through the rough patch. If you don't feel confident initiating help on your own, offer to go with him to see his therapist so the therapist can train you to help as a coach.

Q: My husband's office is two blocks from mine so we ride downtown together each morning. Lately his rituals take him longer and longer and he's caused me to be late for work several times this month. How should I handle this?

A: First, discuss the issue with him. Be clear that if you don't leave the house by a certain time, you will leave without him—even if that means you are taking the car and he has to make other arrangements. Allowing his OCD to make you late for work is a form of supporting the OCD; it prevents him from suffering the consequences of his behavior. Tell him that you support him and his recovery but not his disorder—and, if he chooses to continue ritualizing instead of leaving for work, that this is not a choice you support.

Q: My therapist wants my husband to accompany me to some of our sessions, but, frankly, I don't want him there. He's been very impatient with me, and even calls me names when my OCD symptoms frustrate him. Do I really need him there?

A: One big question is whether your husband really understands OCD. It sounds as though he is frustrated by the effect OCD has on your life together. It may help if he learns all he can about your OCD—but that doesn't mean he should be a "hostile witness" during your therapy sessions. Tell your therapist about the difficulties in your relationship and find out what strategy may be best, even if it means that she will meet with him alone first (assuming that this is agreeable to you). That way, your husband can talk about the effect your OCD has had on him and, at the same time, the therapist can sort out what he does or doesn't know about OCD. In the meantime, give him this book to read, along with any other resources you think will help him to understand your disorder. But bear in mind that it is ultimately up to you whether and to what extent your husband becomes involved in your treatment.

ELEVEN

What to Do When Someone You Love Isn't Ready to Begin Treatment

FOR MOST PEOPLE, recovering from an illness is a wonderful gift. We're always relieved when our headache fades or our sprained ankle stops hurting. If you've suffered from a serious condition such as heart disease or kidney failure, your gratitude was undoubtedly enormous when your health returned. Newfound wellness can be life-changing. Yet some OCD patients believe they are not ready to begin treatment and thus resist the opportunity to recover from this grueling disorder, even though they know their resistance means that their OCD symptoms will continue!

To clarify: We understand that some individuals exhibit very mild symptoms. They indulge in checking or scrubbing or hoarding behaviors, but not to the extent that their symptoms interfere with their work, friendships, or family life. Their quality of life isn't everything it could be, but they don't feel as if they are suffering. By consulting a few resources (such as this book) and learning about the realities of OCD, they succeed at managing their symptoms without ever talking to a therapist.

Those individuals are different from OCD patients who are not yet ready to initiate treatment or who practice "recovery avoidance." We're referring to people who *need* professional help—who suffer every day, struggling with untreated obsessions and compulsions that make them desperately unhappy. If you are a person with OCD who resists treatment, or if someone in your family is avoiding recovery, then you know that OCD patients themselves aren't the only ones being tormented by this disorder. Their families and friends often feel hopelessness and despair as well. But if that's your situation today, be encouraged: There are solid strategies for persuading OCD patients to take advantage of opportunities to get well.

Why Would Anyone Avoid Recovery?

A number of factors influence an OCD sufferer's readiness to initiate treatment. Treatment readiness—or, perhaps more accurately, treatment unreadiness—is also referred to as treatment resistance, non-compliance, or recovery avoidance, and it wears several different faces:

- *Denial:* The OCD sufferers deny that they have a serious problem: "Maybe I'm a little quirky, but there's really nothing wrong with me."
- *Procrastination:* They acknowledge that they have a problem but say that they're not yet ready to start therapy and will "take care of it later."
- *Minimizing the problem:* They acknowledge the problem but insist that it's "not so bad" and doesn't really affect anyone else.
- *Rigidity:* They can't bear the thought of life without rituals and are not willing to "take the chances" involved in exposure and response prevention. If ERP and recovery mean that these patients must endure big changes, they will choose not to participate.

If you have OCD, you might recognize some of these behaviors—denial, procrastination, minimizing, and rigidity—in yourself. Confronting any big problem head-on is difficult and frightening, but we want to emphasize again that without treatment, you won't get better. For your own sake, and for the sake of your family and friends, it's important to enlist their support and begin your recovery.

How does anyone know that a person with OCD is avoiding recovery? The behaviors are straightforward and easy to spot:

- The person exhibits OCD symptoms but won't talk to a professional about getting treatment.
- The person does talk to a therapist but minimizes the seriousness of the disorder.
- The person provides the clinician with inaccurate or incomplete details about his or her symptoms.
- The person agrees to talk with a therapist or undergo treatment, but then repeatedly misses appointments.
- The person begins a treatment program but fails to complete the homework assignments.

If you live with someone who exhibits these behaviors, you probably are baffled by the noncompliant behavior. After all, you know that he or she wants to get well. The OCD exhausts everyone in the household—Why would anyone resist recovery?

Our patients have described multiple reasons for why they previously were not ready to start treatment or why they avoided recovery. Sometimes, the explanation is surprisingly basic: The person simply cannot imagine a day without obsessions and compulsions. Many patients who have lived with their OCD for years actually cannot remember what it felt like to live without rituals. In fact, their OCD has become such a "normal" part of their life that they no longer recognize it's a problem and don't believe they need treatment.

Following are some other fairly common reasons for recovery avoidance:

- Change is difficult for those stuck in their daily regimen of OCD rituals—so difficult that it's downright scary. They persist in their compulsions because the compulsions *appear* to be a way of coping with their obsessions. The problem, of course, is that the compulsions offer no relief at all; they just keep the person in the grip of OCD.

- Exposure and response prevention, in particular, can be terribly frightening. By its nature, it is about confronting one's worst fears. Some OCD patients honestly believe that they cannot face this form of treatment and, in fact, convince themselves that ERP is for people with milder OCD.

- OCD treatments are not without side effects. Medications used to treat OCD bring a wide array of side effects, and ERP produces anxiety in almost every patient who undergoes it. People who seek help for their OCD usually are informed about these consequences of treatment—or at least *should* be informed. Some, realizing that the path to recovery will carry some sort of discomfort, will choose not to undergo treatment despite the toll that OCD is taking on their lives.

- We see a number of noncompliant patients who have become masterful at manipulating their families into accommodating their symptoms. If they can convince their parents or spouses to manage the household and leave them to their rituals and other compulsions, then they may see no reason to undergo scary ERP treatments or take medications that will produce side effects.

- We've also had patients who stop taking their medications because the prescribed drugs didn't stop their compulsive behavior. These individuals are smart enough to know that the medications often were prescribed to address the *depression* that blocked their ability to complete ERP successfully. But the medications may work slowly and some patients, unfortunately, lose sight of the fact that recovery from OCD can be a lengthy process—especially when the medications involved have been prescribed to ease the way for the ERP program that follows.

- Some OCD sufferers embark on a never-ending search for the "perfect" treatment program. Their anxiety arises as this search becomes a ritual in itself; they refuse to try a new behavior or medication without a guarantee that it will bring them a painless, speedy, stress-free recovery.

- ERP requires a certain amount of time, which in turn takes patients away from their rituals. Thus, in a perverse sense, time itself is a factor in some patients' decision not to get treatment!

- Some OCD patients are without insight into their illness. They place undue value on the role being played by their obsessions and compulsions—after all, it makes perfect sense to be absolutely sure that the burners are turned off so that the house doesn't burn down. These patients may have recognized, at some point in their lives, that thoughts of this sort were anxiety inducing and not the norm—but this is no longer the case. Instead, they now believe that their rituals support such thoughts. This lack of insight is termed "overvalued ideation" and can be a considerable impediment to treatment.

- The path to recovery can be an expensive journey. Even well-insured patients (a shrinking group in today's healthcare climate) are at the mercy of insurance-company restrictions and cost ceilings on mental health care—including therapy, medications, and hospitalization. And then there are the millions of Americans who are underinsured or have no health insurance at all. Therapy and pharmacological treatment can cost a small fortune, especially for a long-term illness such as OCD, and there's no way to determine how many people with OCD symptoms avoid treatment because they simply cannot afford to get the help they need.

Doug didn't think his OCD symptoms—contamination issues—were interfering with his life, at least not in a major way. He owned a small import business and didn't have to deal directly with customers or the items he imported; he had a small staff who took care of those hands-on aspects of the business. Doug spent most of his time in his own office alone, doing paperwork.

In fact, Doug's staff rarely saw him because he thought they were contaminated and wouldn't allow them near his desk. He talked to them only on certain days of the week and refused to handle papers or books once anyone else had touched them. Needless to say, there was a lot of turnover in his little company.

"If people didn't follow all of Doug's rules and restrictions, he wouldn't work with them," reports his girlfriend, Sandy. "He required them to wear plastic gloves when they handled any materials in the office, and sanitizing the phone and copy machines were a hugely complicated process. If he caught any of them touching a doorknob with their bare hands, he asked them to leave." Only Doug used the bathroom in the office; everyone else had to walk to the fast-food restaurant down the street.

Sandy and Doug are both in their mid-30s. They met when she visited the office to see her sister, a freelance accountant who spent one day a week working for Doug. "My sister would tell me these stories about spraying pens with Lysol and wrapping checks in plastic wrap until he signed them," she says. "I was fascinated; I had to check out this guy."

Sandy thought Doug's symptoms were mere personality quirks until they started dating and his habits began to intrude on their relationship. "He expected me to go along with a long list of restrictions," she says, "all having to do with his contamination fears. Looking back, I think his disorder got worse over the months when we were getting to know each other, because he didn't seem so bad at first."

"Then he started making bizarre demands," she continues, "especially where meal preparation was concerned. Dishes were washed in the dishwasher *before* we ate. Food was scrubbed, sometimes with soap. When I protested or refused to go along, he made references about other women he had discarded from his life, including his own mother, because they wouldn't cave in to his sickness. It was a threat."

One evening when they were arguing, Sandy told him he was being irrational. "He blew up at me," she says, "screaming that he was a successful businessman, that he wasn't crazy—and suddenly I remembered a segment on ABC's *20/20* about people with OCD, who had to go through these strange rituals all the time. They didn't have normal lives anymore because they were compelled to do these behaviors. That show could have been about Doug. I knew then that he had OCD."

Sandy began researching OCD on the Internet and in books, trying to decipher the technical language. She learned that accommodating the OCD sufferer's rituals would only make his symptoms stronger. After a few weeks of trying to persuade Doug to get help for his disorder, Sandy gave him an ultimatum: Either you get treatment or we'll go our separate ways.

Doug went to a local mental health clinic and, after an evaluation, learned that he did in fact have OCD. Sandy was there to give him support. When his therapist outlined a plan for Doug's recovery, though, the resistance started.

"Since his obsessions were about contamination, naturally the ERP exposed him to a lot of dirt," Sandy says. "One week, he was told to remove all plastic coverings from the office. The next week, Doug was supposed to take plates directly from the cupboard and eat from them, without washing them first. That was extremely difficult for him."

Doug started missing appointments with his therapist, then skipping his homework assignments. "It wasn't getting easier for him," Sandy says. "He was losing his motivation; he wanted to quit."

Doug and this therapist discussed what was impeding his progress. In response to Doug's statement that he didn't know of anyone who had OCD, they brainstormed the possibility of his joining a support group. Initially, this seemed to be a good idea, but it turned out that the nearest support group was in a hospital and, given Doug's contamination fears, he felt that this was more than he could handle. Another alternative they discussed was an idea that ultimately kept Doug on track. Doug's therapist suggested that Doug start a blog, an online journal that allows readers to respond with their own comments.

Doug's blog became his new hobby. He could do it independently, without having to attend meetings, but it still gave him interaction with others who experienced the same kinds of obsessions and compulsions—and, in some cases, had conquered the same motivation problem.

Doug was part of a new trend: individuals blogging about their own health problems. His ERP assignments still didn't get any easier, but corresponding online with other OCD patients gave him the mettle to complete them anyway, and he felt stronger each week. It took about six months of blogging before Doug could finally say that he had beaten his OCD symptoms—but, three years later, Doug still writes two or three new blog entries a week, and his symptoms have not returned.

Enhancing Treatment Readiness

Whether you are looking for relief from your own OCD symptoms or concerned about a family member with such symptoms, take comfort in knowing that help is available for countering recovery avoidance. Depending on the circumstances, the therapists in our clinic use a variety of strategies, all of which are potentially effective in boosting patients' treatment readiness:

- If you are a friend or family member of someone who refuses to seek treatment for OCD, talk to a therapist yourself—not about treatment per se, but about getting your loved one *into* treatment. Any clinician experienced in treating OCD will be happy to consult with you and share some techniques that you can try.

- Understand—or try to get the person with OCD to understand—that even though ERP does induce anxiety in a confronting-your-fears way, it is a gradual, controlled approach that ultimately can be easier for patients to handle than the symptoms they've been experiencing. *"Treatment anxiety" is never as bad as the anxiety experienced with untreated OCD.*

- Don't be scared away from treatment by anything you've heard about ERP or medication. Your ERP plan will be custom-designed just for you, your symptoms, and your lifestyle. Your input regarding the speed at which treatment progresses is an important part of the process—treatment will not move forward at a pace that you consider excessive. Likewise, if medication is a component of your treatment, your psychiatrist will make sure that your side effects are minimized. Your feedback about how the medication is working is also important, because everyone's experience with medication is different and your medication management plan will be designed so that you can handle whatever side effects occur.

- Your therapist is your partner in your recovery, so be honest with her about every aspect of your disorder. Think of her as your collaborator; together you are writing the book of your future. She needs to know every detail, as honestly as you can present it, so that OCD will never again be an obstacle for you.

- Before you begin ERP, ask your therapist if you can talk with other patients who have finished their ERP programs. We've found that patients tend to feel more confident about their ability to tackle treatment when they have an opportunity to ask questions of someone who has successfully completed treatment. Indeed, we've seen many instances in which those personal conversations take the edge off new patients' fear and boost their motivation for succeeding.

- If the OCD patient in your life is in denial about the seriousness of his disorder, the therapist may ask him to self-assess the impact that OCD has had on all of your lives. Sometimes, this assessment will involve surveying friends, family members, and co-workers—whose answers may yield surprises for the patient.

- We emphasized this in Chapter 10, "How to Help When a Loved One Has OCD," but it bears repeating here: Supporting the patient, without accommodating his OCD symptoms, is critical—especially early on, when he is just getting into treatment. OCD is the person's·disorder—*it is not the person.*

- As you learn more about your own (or a loved one's) OCD and progress further in your treatment plan, don't hesitate to share with others what you've learned. Volunteer to talk to new patients. If you're comfortable speaking in front of a group, give talks to organizations and mental health support groups. You will find that shifting the focus from your own disorder to helping others will empower you and further boost your self-confidence and motivation to succeed.

- Most OCD patients and their families report that support groups are helpful in their recovery. In Chapter 12, you will find the names of organizations that can guide you to support groups near you. If you're getting help through a mental health clinic, chances are it hosts support groups as well. You also can join online forums where patients and their families discuss OCD, and read and respond to blogs written by OCD patients. You can even start your own blog—an activity that, like keeping a journal, is considered by many to be an effective way to "let off steam." Note that the same chapter lists several resources for learning how to set up a simple blog.

TRY A LITTLE MINDFULNESS

In his landmark book *Wherever You Go, There You Are,* Jon Kabat-Zinn defines mindfulness as "an appreciation for the present moment. . . . It is the direct opposite of taking life for granted. . . . It wakes us up to the fact that our lives unfold only in moments. If we are not fully present for many of those moments, we may not only miss what is most valuable in our lives but also fail to realize the richness and the depth of our possibilities for growth and transformation."

Compared to OCD, whose sufferers sacrifice their current moments to needless rituals and compulsions in an effort to stave off a future catastrophe, mindfulness sounds pretty good, doesn't it? Rather than being obsessed with stubbornly specific outcomes, people who practice mindfulness allow life to unfold. They observe events around them without giving in to obsessions. Minor events throughout the day, such as dressing, shopping, and cleaning house, do not cause them distress or bring about compulsions; they are merely ordinary parts of their lives. In fact, at least one study has shown that mindfulness decreases stress such as that experienced by people with OCD and other anxiety disorders as well as depression.

A cornerstone of mindfulness is meditation. If you've never meditated, you can begin by simply being still for five minutes each morning. Sit in a quiet place in a comfortable chair, place your hands in your lap, close your eyes . . . and be still. Don't think about work, your family, your surroundings—just listen to your breath and let the stillness be all that is happening. All that matters is that quiet, private moment.

In Chapter 12 we've listed several books and other materials that will help you incorporate mindfulness and meditation into your day, with very little effort. Whether you choose to practice mindfulness, meditation, or some form of relaxation, doing so on a regular basis can help you to manage the anxiety associated with OCD and to set aside your rituals for increasingly longer periods of time.

Frequently Asked Questions

Q: I've had OCD symptoms for at least ten years, and now I'm retired. Isn't it too late for me to get treatment?
A: It's never too late to recover from OCD. We've seen patients who have suffered with their obsessions and compulsions for as long as thirty years and didn't realize that they could actually stop ritualizing.

We've also treated older adults whose OCD started well after retirement age. If your rituals interfere with your life, talk to a professional about how to end them. You may need medication initially to get past your anxiety, but with ERP you can conquer your OCD!

Q: My husband says he doesn't need treatment—that if I help him "cut back" on his rituals, our life will be manageable again.
A: Tell your husband that, as of now, you will no longer be involved with his rituals. Remind him that his rituals only make the OCD worse, and that your participation allows him to think his rituals are an acceptable way to live, when in fact they're not. It's up to him to "cut back" on his rituals. If helping him means that you are assisting him in identifying when he is ritualizing and he then practices response prevention, that may be a good strategy. If he's right and life does get back to a manageable level, great! If not, then a condition of your helping him is that he has to see a therapist if his solution doesn't work. Make it a contract—get the plan in writing so there are no excuses if his self-help program doesn't work as well as you both would like.

Q: My wife doesn't actually involve me in her rituals—that is, I don't help her straighten clothes in her drawer for hours or rearrange the bathroom towels. All she asks is that if she takes too long to perform her rituals, I call her boss and tell him she'll be late for work. That's okay, isn't it?
A: What you're doing is accommodating your wife's OCD and making it stronger. It also sounds as if she might be avoiding her recovery by continuing to perform her morning rituals. If you don't want to feed her disorder, you'll need to stop accommodating the OCD and tell her you won't make excuses for her anymore. She probably will beg you to help her just this once, but if you want her to recover, resist her pleas—and reassure her, not the OCD, that when she chooses to recover you will be there to help her.

Q: My boyfriend absolutely believes that his rituals are necessary for his survival, and he won't have anything to do with people who won't enable him. Right now, he isn't speaking to me because I won't accommodate his contamination taboos. How do I convince him to get help?

A: If your boyfriend isn't speaking to you right now, talk to those in his inner circle whom he does trust. Share with them what you know about OCD and how important it is that he seek treatment. Give them something to read on the subject. Sometimes what's most helpful is a group "intervention," whereby all of his family members and friends find a way to communicate to him that they love him and want to support his recovery. The first step is to stop encouraging his OCD behaviors. Understand that he is not accurately assessing the dangers related to his fears. If he is unable to relinquish his rituals, ask him if he will go with you to talk to a professional. Surely he can't be happy in his OCD prison!

Q: Someone recommended I do an "impact analysis" regarding my father's OCD. What does this involve?
A: An impact analysis is an exercise, used by some clinicians, in which the patient lists all of the ways OCD has affected his life—both positive and negative. In some cases, the patient will also be asked to give this survey to family and friends to fill out—with eye-opening results. People with OCD often don't realize how their disorder affects others. In the language of substance abuse treatment, this technique is sometimes referred to as "raising the bottom"—it's a way of preventing the person from "hitting bottom" before he gets help.

Q: What can a family do if a loved one with OCD absolutely refuses to get help?
A: It's always heartbreaking to watch a person you love deteriorate. But when you've researched every aspect of the disorder and tried every means possible to persuade him and he still refuses help, it's time to help yourself. Much like families of alcoholics are taught in Al-Anon, there is a point where you need to decide that you will live a full and happy life in spite of your loved one's OCD. The worst outcome would be for the OCD to ruin two lives. If you and your loved one are approaching this stage, consider talking to a professional yourself so you won't feel guilty about whatever choice you make.

Q: *My fiancé seems willing to get help for his OCD, but so far he's spent six months looking for the "right" program. Why is he so picky about treatment?*

A: This is a surprisingly hard question. Perhaps he's not picky but, instead, is afraid of the ERP or concerned that it will be too difficult. Or, if he's a perfectionist, he might truly be looking for perfection in a treatment provider, afraid to entrust his mental health to someone who's less than perfect. Talk to him about the idea that OCD treatment is a partnership between the clinician and the patient, and assure him that he won't be forced to do anything he really doesn't want to do. On the other hand, there may be no veteran clinicians or OCD treatment programs in your area; despite ERP's proven effectiveness, not that many people are trained in this approach. Likewise, if your fiancé needs an intensive treatment program or an in-patient program, his options may be rather limited as there are only a handful of such programs in the United States. Attending one of these programs may depend on whether it has openings, whether his insurance will pay for it, and so on. In short, he may need to do research.

Q: *My girlfriend is in treatment for OCD and now that she's almost reached the top of her exposure hierarchy, she's starting to relapse. It's almost as though she's doing it deliberately—as though she doesn't want to succeed. What's really going on?*

A: We often see patients who are afraid of success. They've lived with their obsessions and compulsions for a long time and now they have to ask themselves, "What's next? What do I use to replace this part of my life?" Starting anew is both exciting and terrifying. You can be an enormous help to her during this uncertain time. Remind her often that her courage and creativity enabled her to defeat her OCD symptoms, and that she's now free to apply those same qualities to making a new life. Help her explore some new experiences and possibilities for her future.

TWELVE

Resources:
Where to Find More Help

▉ CD IS IMPRESSIVE in its strength—but if you take away any message from this book, we hope it's this: Strong though OCD may be, it can be subdued.

The explanations for why OCD occurs and what perpetuates it can be complicated, and you have to work hard to overcome its symptoms. But if you're motivated, it can be done.

You will recognize success, when it happens, by your ability to once again enjoy new experiences and relationships. You won't be plagued by obsessions or stopped in your tracks by the need to complete rituals. By the time you finish treatment, you will have a vision for your future that doesn't involve OCD. Our hope is that this book will be one tool to help put you on that path, and keep you informed and motivated.

Reading this book is only the beginning of your recovery process. Whether you are experiencing OCD symptoms yourself or you know someone who is, there is a bounty of organizations, books, websites, and treatment centers that can contribute to your understanding of the disorder. If you're an OCD sufferer, remember—you are not alone in your quest for recovery, but you *are* in charge of it!

You will find plenty of help for your OCD out there—and we urge you to explore these resources and take advantage of what they offer.

Organizations and Online Resources

Obsessive-Compulsive Foundation (OCF)

www.ocfoundation.org
112 Water Street, Suite 501, Boston MA 02109
Ph. 617-973-5801

The OCF's website is a good first stop in your quest to learn all you can about OCD. In addition to dozens of articles and other background information, the site points the way to online support groups, intensive treatment centers across the country, and links to separate websites for teens with OCD, parents of OCD patients, and hoarders. Information about clinical trials and how to find a clinician is also on the website. If you are a mental health professional who is interested in pursuing specialized training in treating OCD, the OC Foundation offers Behavior Therapy Institutes where you can get training from the leaders in the field.

The Obsessive Compulsive Foundation also has affiliates and support group listings that may be in your area. You can check the Resources section on its web page or call the Foundation for more information.

National Institute of Mental Health (NIMH)

www.nimh.nih.gov/health/topics/obsessive-compulsive-disorder-ocd/index.shtml

The National Institute of Mental Health is a branch of the National Institutes of Health, the U.S. government agency charged with research and other activities regarding health. This site offers background information on OCD, news updates on the latest research findings, and addresses of treatment centers in your region. You also can order government publications on mental health from the NIMH site.

Association of Behavior and Cognitive Therapies (ABCT)

www.abct.org
> 305 7th Avenue, 16th Fl.
> New York, NY 10001
> Ph: 212-647-1890

ABCT is the primary organization for professionals who are researchers, clinicians, clinical scientists, and educators with interests in cognitive behavior therapy as well as OCD. Its website supplies a downloadable fact sheet on OCD. In addition, you can search its member list in order to find a clinician in your area. If you are a mental health professional, note that ABCT's annual convention offers numerous training opportunities in the area of OCD, hoarding, trichotillomania, and other obsessive-compulsive spectrum conditions.

National Alliance for the Mentally Ill (NAMI)

www.nami.org
> Colonial Place Three
> 2107 Wilson Boulevard, Suite 300
> Arlington, VA 22201
> Ph. 703-524-7600

Type "OCD" in the Search box on NAMI's home page and you'll find numerous articles on a range of OCD topics, from OCD and parenting to fact sheets and workbooks.

American Academy of Family Physicians

www.familydoctor.org
> Type "OCD" in the Search box on the Academy's home page and you'll be directed to an excellent, concise overview of OCD—its symptoms, causes, treatments, and other essential information in a nutshell. This is a good page to forward to a friend who needs basic introductory information on OCD.

Anxiety Disorders Association of America (ADAA)

www.adaa.org
8730 Georgia Avenue, Suite 600
Silver Spring, MD 20910
Ph. 240-485-1001
This site has it all—background information on OCD and other anxiety disorders, how and where to find help, conferences, continuing education for mental health professionals, and resources ranging from a "guide to treatment" to information on clinical trials currently planned or in progress and how to help a family member.

Mental Health America (MHA)

www.mentalhealthamerica.net
2001 North Beauregard Street, 12th Floor
Alexandria, VA 22311
Ph. 703-684-7722
This organization (formerly known as the National Mental Health Association) offers a website featuring fact sheets, information about OCD and other mental illnesses, and links to other organizations. MHA's members run the gamut, including patients, family members of patients, physicians and other clinicians, researchers, and advocates. While this website contains a wealth of information and referral sources, you will need to reread our discussions in Chapters 6 and 7 about how to select a treatment provider in order to make sure that he or she has experience with treating OCD and spectrum disorders.

Tourette's Syndrome Association (TSA)

www.tsa-usa.org
42-40 Bell Boulevard, Suite 205
Bayside, NY 11361
Ph. 718-224-2999

TSA's website is designed for both patients and professionals, and includes background information on Tourette's, recent research, and a help page for the newly diagnosed.

Trichotillomania Learning Center (TLC)

www.trich.org
207 McPherson Street, Suite H
Santa Cruz, CA 95060
Ph. 831-457-1004

It's hard to imagine a trich question (pun intended) that isn't addressed on this website, including how to start a support group. Basic information on trichotillomania, special sections for kids and teens, research, treatment—even a directory of cosmetologists and hair salons experienced in treating trich patients—are all included on this vast site.

American Psychiatric Association (APA)

www.psych.org

The APA site, though primarily intended for mental health professionals, contains information on current research and advocacy efforts that might also be useful for OCD patients and their families, including referrals to psychiatrists.

KidsHealth for Kids

www.kidshealth.org/kid/feeling/emotion/ocd.html

Sponsored by The Nemours Foundation, KidsHealth is a kid-friendly website. Its OCD section explains obsessions, compulsions, the disorder itself, how treatment works—and what it feels like to experience ERP. The website also features non-OCD-specific pages on subjects such as dealing with feelings, growing up, "people/places/things that help me," and other mental and emotional health topics.

Books

Self-Help Books

Obsessive-Compulsive Disorder by Jonathan Abramowitz, Ph.D. Hogrefe & Huber, 2006.

When Perfect Isn't Good Enough: Strategies for Coping with Perfectionism by Martin M. Antony, Ph.D., and Richard P. Swinson, M.D. New Harbinger Publications, 2008.

The Imp of the Mind: Exploring the Silent Epidemic of Obsessive Bad Thoughts by Lee Baer, Ph.D. Plume, 2002.

Rewind, Replay, Repeat: A Memoir of Obsessive-Compulsive Disorder by Jeff Bell. Hazelden, 2007.

The BDD Workbook by James Claiborn, Ph.D., A.B.P.P., and Cherry Pedrick, R.N. New Harbinger Publications, 2002.

Obsessive-Compulsive Disorder: The Facts by Padmal de Silva and Stanley Rachman. Oxford University Press, 2004.

Mastery of Obsessive-Compulsive Disorder: Client Workbook by Edna B. Foa and Michael J. Kozak. Oxford University Press, 1997.

Stop Me Because I Can't Stop Myself: Taking Control of Impulsive Behavior by Jon E. Grand, J.D., M.D., and S. W. Kim, M.D. McGraw-Hill, 2004.

Freedom from Obsessive-Compulsive Disorder: A Personalized Recovery Program for Living with Uncertainty by Jonathan Grayson, Ph.D. Berkley Trade, 2004.

The OCD Workbook: Your Guide to Breaking Free from Obsessive-Compulsive Disorder by Bruce M. Hyman, Ph.D., and Cherry Pedrick, R.N. New Harbinger Publications, 2005.

Help for Hair Pullers: Understanding and Coping with Trichotillomania by Nancy J. Keuthen, Ph.D,, Dan J. Stein, M.D., and Gary A. Christenson, M.D. New Harbinger Publications, 2001.

Overcoming Compulsive Checking by Paul R. Munford, Ph.D. New Harbinger Publications, 2004.

Overcoming Compulsive Washing by Paul R. Munford, Ph.D., New Harbinger Publications, 2005.

Overcoming Compulsive Hoarding by Fugen Neziroglu, Ph.D., A.B.P.P., Jerome Bubrick, Ph.D., and Jose Yaryura-Tobias, M.D. New Harbinger Publications, 2004.

The Hair-Pulling Problem: A Complete Guide to Trichotillomania by Fred Penzel, Ph.D. Oxford University Press, 2003.

Obsessive-Compulsive Disorders: A Complete Guide to Getting Well and Staying Well by Fred Penzel, Ph.D. Oxford University Press, 2000.

The Broken Mirror: Understanding and Treating Body Dysmorphic Disorder by Katherine A. Phillips, M.D. Oxford University Press, 1986.

Overcoming Obsessive Thoughts by Christine Purdon, Ph.D., C.Psych, and David A. Clark, Ph.D., L.Psych. New Harbinger Publications, 2005.

Compulsive Hoarding and Acquiring Workbook by Gail Steketee and Randy O. Frost. Oxford University Press, 2007.

Buried in Treasures: Help for Compulsive Acquiring, Saving, and Hoarding by David F. Tolin, Ph.D, Randy O. Frost, Ph.D., and Gail S. Steketee, Ph.D. Oxford University Press, 2007.

Cognitive Therapy for Obsessive-Compulsive Disorder: A Guide for Professionals by Sabine Wilhelm, Ph.D., and Gail S. Steketee, Ph.D. New Harbinger Publications, 2006.

Feeling Good About the Way You Look: A Program for Overcoming Body Image Problems by Sabine Wilhelm, Ph.D. Guilford Press, 2006.

For Family Members of OCD Sufferers

Freeing Your Child from Anxiety by Tamar E. Chansky, Ph.D. Broadway, 2004.

Helping Your Child with OCD by Lee Fitzgibbons, Ph.D., and Cherry Pedrick, R.N. New Harbinger Publications, 2003.

Loving Someone with OCD: Help for You and Your Family by Karen J. Landsman, Ph.D., Kathleen M. Rupertus, M.A., M.S., and Cherry Pedrick, R.N. New Harbinger Publications, 2005.

Talking Back to OCD: The Program That Helps Kids and Teens Say "No Way"—and Parents Say "Way to Go" by John S. March, M.D. Guilford Press, 2006.

What to Do When Your Child Has Obsessive-Compulsive Disorder: Strategies and Solutions by Aureen Pinto Wagner, Ph.D. Lighthouse Press, 2002.

For Children and Teenagers

Repetitive Rhonda by Jan Evans, M.A. Breath and Shadow Productions, 2007.

Not as Crazy as I Seem by George Harrar. Graphia, 2004.

What to Do When Your Brain Gets Stuck: A Kid's Guide to Overcoming OCD by Dawn Huebner, Ph.D. Magination Press, 2007.

Blink, Blink, Clop, Clop: Why Do We Do Things We Can't Stop? An OCD Storybook by E. Katia Moritz, Ph.D., and Jennifer Jablonsky. Childswork/Childsplay, 2001.

Mr. Worry: A Story About OCD by Holly L. Niner. Albert Whitman & Company, 2004.

A Thought Is Just a Thought: A Story of Living with OCD by Leslie Talley. Lantern Books, 2004.

Up and Down the Worry Hill: A Children's Book About Obsessive-Compulsive Disorder and Its Treatment by Aureen Pinto Wagner, Ph.D. Lighthouse Press, 2004.

OCD Blogs

If you go to Google.com and type "OCD blog" in the Search box, almost 3 million results will appear. We've listed just a few to get you thinking—and perhaps writing! Blogs, if you're not familiar with them, are online journals with a twist: Readers can respond with their own "journal entries." Blogging about one's afflictions and illnesses is a popular Internet trend.

If the idea of blogging about your OCD intrigues you, we recommend that you first spend a little time reading other people's blogs. Then, when you feel ready, respond to a few blogs and get used to putting your ideas "on paper" for other people to read. If you still think you'd like to start your own blog, go to www.blogger.com for some simple instructions on setting up a blog.

Here are the web addresses for a few sample OCD blogs:

- www.theocdblog.com
- www.ocd.healthdiaries.com
- www.oc-illnesses-and-creativity.net/blog.htm
- http://ocdinfo-blog.blogspot.com
- www.thoughts.com

Note: You must register to read blogs on this last site; a simple search will show you the OCD blogs already there. If you like, you can start your own blog as well at this site.

GLOSSARY

ADDICTION: The persistent need for and use of a habit-forming substance, such as alcohol, tobacco, or a narcotic drug, characterized by tolerance and by well-defined physiological symptoms upon withdrawal.

AGGRESSIVE OBSESSIONS: Unwanted, intrusive, and repetitive thoughts about harming others or oneself, wrecking property, or creating a disturbance. *See also* HARMING OBSESSIONS.

ANTIDEPRESSANT MEDICATION: A medication used to prevent or relieve depression. Many antidepressants are also used to treat anxiety disorders, including OCD.

ANXIETY: A physical, emotional, cognitive, and behavioral response to a real or perceived threat. Anxiety may be a normal response to stress or an exaggerated response to a perceived (as opposed to real) fear.

ANXIETY DISORDER: A chronic condition that, unlike a normal response to stress, occurs when the response to a real or perceived threat is maladaptive and causes undue distress or impairs an individual's ability to function effectively. There are several different anxiety disorders (obsessive-compulsive disorder, panic disorder with or without agoraphobia, social anxiety disorder, generalized anxiety disorder, acute traumatic or post-traumatic stress disorder, specific phobia), each of which is associated with a hallmark fear.

AUGMENTATION: In medicine, the taking of one drug along with another, to boost the first drug's effectiveness.

BASAL GANGLIA: A region of the brain composed of four segments that is linked to some forms of OCD and obsessive-compulsive spectrum disorders. Because the basal ganglia enable us to coordinate complex, multiple movements, problems in this region can produce symptoms such as twitches and tremors.

BDD: *See* BODY DYSMORPHIC DISORDER.

BEHAVIORAL THERAPY: An approach for treating psychological disorders, including anxiety disorders, based on principles of reinforcement. These principles involve the extinguishing of undesired behaviors along with the acquisition or learning of new, more adaptive behaviors. Exposure and response prevention (ERP), the gold standard for treating OCD, is a form of behavioral therapy.

BENZODIAZEPINES: Medications, commonly referred to as "tranquilizers," that treat anxiety. Benzodiazepines are often prescribed in the short term for OCD patients whose anxiety may be blocking their ability to perform ERP exercises. Medications such as alprazolam (Xanax) and clonazepam (Klonopin) are examples.

BIOLOGICAL FACTORS: Factors such as genetics or a physiological predisposition that can influence the development of a disorder.

BODY DYSMORPHIC DISORDER: An extreme preoccupation with an imagined or slight body defect, to the point of causing distress and interfering with work or family life.

BRAIN HICCUPS: A term used in the treatment of pediatric OCD, referring to OCD symptoms.

CAUDATE NUCLEUS: Part of the striatum, one of the four basal ganglia. The caudate nucleus functions as a sort of "gate," deciding which impulses and thoughts are appropriate or sufficiently important to pass through and be recognized by the conscious mind.

CBT: *See* COGNITIVE BEHAVIOR THERAPY.

CHECKING RITUALS: Behaviors involving compulsively and repeatedly checking and rechecking things, such as whether a door or window is locked, or the stove is turned off, in order to relieve the fear and anxiety caused by an obsession.

CHILDREN'S YALE-BROWN OBSESSIVE-COMPULSIVE SCALE (CYBOCS): A version of the YBOCS, a widely used symptoms checklist and screening tool, that is used to help diagnose OCD in children and teenagers.

CHRONIC: In medicine, a term that refers to diseases or disorders of long duration.

CLINICIAN: A person qualified in the clinical practice of medicine, psychiatry, psychology, or social work. This term also sometimes refers to nurse practitioners and physicians' assistants.

CODEPENDENCY: A relationship in which one person is controlled or manipulated by the other, who is afflicted with a pathological condition.

COGNITIVE BEHAVIOR THERAPY (CBT): A psychological treatment approach that utilizes both cognitive and behavioral therapy techniques.

COGNITIVE THERAPY: Developed by Aaron Beck, M.D., a form of psychological therapy that emphasizes understanding the initial thoughts, attributions, expectations, and beliefs that influence maladaptive thinking patterns. These patterns are then examined in detail in order to construct more realistic and adaptive strategies for dealing with them, with the goal of altering nonfunctional beliefs and acquiring more functional belief systems or schemas.

COMORBID: A terms referring to a disorder or illness that exists simultaneously with, and usually independent of, another illness.

COMPULSION: An irresistible, persistent urge to perform an act, such as repetitive hand-washing, checking, or "evening up." Compulsions, often referred to as rituals, can be either both behavioral or mental (e.g., thinking a "good" number).

CONTAMINATION OBSESSIONS: Intrusive thoughts, feared by OCD patients, that the patients themselves or people close to them are in immediate danger from germs, viruses, bacteria, or other disease-causing agents. Contamination-related fears can also involve chemicals or other substances (e.g., asbestos). Rituals associated with contamination usually involve washing or avoidance.

CONTROLLING ONE'S THOUGHTS: A phrase referring to the tendency of some OCD sufferers to monitor their thoughts for the presence of obsessions, in the belief that these thoughts are indicative of a catastrophe occurring and, further, that they should be able to control their thoughts as a means of avoiding negative events and distress from occurring,

CYBOCS: *See* CHILDREN'S YALE-BROWN OBSESSIVE-COMPULSIVE SCALE.

DEPRESSION: A psychiatric disorder marked by sadness, hopelessness, lethargy, disinterest, negative feelings toward oneself and others, inactivity, and, in some cases, suicidal thoughts.

DIAGNOSIS: The act of identifying a disease by its signs or symptoms.

DIAGNOSTIC AND STATISTICAL MANUAL OF MENTAL DISORDERS, FOURTH EDITION (DSM-IV): The standard text used by mental health professionals to identify symptoms and their features, prevalence, and patterns so as to enable an accurate diagnosis. The DSM is published by the American Psychiatric Association and is reviewed and updated on a regular basis to ensure that it is in keeping with current knowledge.

DOPAMINE: A neurotransmitter in the brain, linked to voluntary movements and coordination.

DSM-IV: *See DIAGNOSTIC AND STATISTICAL MANUAL OF MENTAL DISORDERS, FOURTH EDITION.*

ENVIRONMENTAL FACTORS: Circumstances outside a person's own self that could influence his or her symptoms and mood, such as relationships, work, studies, and finances.

ERP: *See* EXPOSURE AND RESPONSE PREVENTION.

EXPOSURE AND RESPONSE PREVENTION (ERP): The only behavioral treatment proven effective in treating OCD. Exposure and response prevention involves exposure to, or confronting, the source of the patient's obsessions and fears (e.g., dirt, disorder) while learning to resist the urge to relieve those fears through compulsive behaviors/ritualizing.

EXPOSURE HIERARCHY: *See* HIERARCHY.

FEAR THERMOMETER: A ranking of anxiety-triggering thoughts, actions, and situations, used in treating pediatric OCD. *See also* HIERARCHY.

GAD: *See* GENERALIZED ANXIETY DISORDER.

GENE: A unit of DNA, the molecular basis of heredity (often portrayed as a double-helix woven together and as located on a chromosome) that determines which traits a person will inherit from his or her parents and ancestors. A chromosome is the rod-shaped structure that houses our DNA.

GENERALIZED ANXIETY DISORDER (GAD): Frequent, overwhelming worry sometimes coupled with physical symptoms of anxiety that may not be linked to specific kinds of events; a general state of excessive worry.

GENETIC: Refers to something inherited through the genes.

HABITUATION: In OCD, refers to the ability, through exposure, to tolerate obsession-related fears until the individual can successfully resist the urge to ritualize and not be disabled by the physical sensations of anxiety.

HARMING OBSESSIONS: Harming obsessions relate to beliefs of some OCD sufferers that they may deliberately cause harm to another person by either their action or inaction. A typical obsession might involve not wanting to handle a knife around one's children out of fear that you could lose control and stab someone.

HIERARCHY: A rank ordering of anxiety-producing situations that trigger rituals or avoidance for the person with OCD. These situations are sequenced, thereby enabling a therapist to plan the OCD patient's individualized ERP therapy.

HOARDING: The need to acquire, collect, and/or save things to the extreme, coupled with a fear of discarding objects and a lack of organization.

Hoarding can refer to one type of possession, such as shoes, paper, or even pets, or it can refer to almost everything the hoarder can gather up.

IMAGINAL (OR IMAGINED) EXPOSURE: In ERP, exposure exercises involving the formation of an elaborate mental representation of a feared situation rather than actually taking part in the feared situation (e.g., imaging the stabbing of someone rather than actually harming oneself or another person).

IMPORTANCE OF THOUGHTS: The belief held by some OCD sufferers that if they have a thought it must be important. For these individuals, merely having the thought gives it credibility and increases the likelihood that a feared situation will occur. *See also* MAGICAL THINKING.

INTOLERANCE OF UNCERTAINTY: The tendency of individuals with OCD to be cautious, to take extensive time to make a decision, and to doubt whether their decision was correct. OCD sufferers often have beliefs related to their discomfort over situations that are ambiguous, new, or unpredictable and want to have one right answer.

INTRUSIVE THOUGHTS: Unwanted thoughts that spontaneously arise, produce considerable discomfort, and seemingly force their way into a person's mind. These thoughts, or obsessions, become a focus of attention, which in turn gives them credibility.

IN VIVO EXPOSURE: Exposure to the actual fear-generating object or activity, such as a stove left on or a dirty toilet.

LAPSE: A slipup by a patient during the recovery process. In OCD, this usually involves indulging in a ritual.

MAGICAL THINKING: Obsessions based on superstition, "bad luck," or the patient's presumed ability to make something bad happen if he or she says or does the wrong thing. In the OCD literature this is referred to as "thought-action fusion."

MEDITATION: Engaging in contemplation, reflection, or deep relaxation.

MENTAL COMPULSIONS: Rituals that take the form of a mental activity, such as counting or reciting lyrics or a poem in one's head rather than out loud. Mental compulsions can occur in addition to or instead of behavioral compulsions.

MINDFULNESS: Awareness of present-moment reality, as opposed to going through one's day oblivious to small actions and their significance. Mindfulness involves staying in the moment rather than dwelling on the past or focusing on the future.

MODELING: In ERP, a technique in which the clinician demonstrates or models how an exposure to the anxiety-causing object or event should be conducted. The patient observes the demonstration and then replicates what occurred.

NEUROTRANSMITTER: A chemical compound that carries nerve impulses across synapses, or tiny spaces, between nerve cells in the brain and other parts of the body.

NONCOMPLIANCE: A patient's deliberate refusal to take medications or engage in other aspects of a treatment plan.

OBSESSION: An intrusive, unwanted thought that causes anxiety. In OCD, the obsession is persistent and returns repeatedly.

OBSESSIVE-COMPULSIVE PERSONALITY DISORDER (OCPD): A disorder sometimes confused with OCD because it has certain symptoms in common (e.g., need to control others, perfectionism), but which differs from OCD in that OCPD sufferers (a) do not engage in rituals and (b) see their symptoms as positive and have no desire to stop them.

OBSESSIVE-COMPULSIVE SPECTRUM DISORDERS: A group of disorders, including body dysmorphic disorder, trichotillomania, Tourette's syndrome, and hoarding, that share characteristics with OCD.

OCPD: *See* OBSESSIVE-COMPULSIVE PERSONALITY DISORDER.

OVERESTIMATION OF THREAT: The tendency of OCD sufferers to incorrectly estimate the probability that a negative event will occur as well as the severity of the consequences.

PANDAS. *See* PEDIATRIC AUTOIMMUNE NEUROPSYCHIATRIC DISORDERS ASSOCIATED WITH STREPTOCOCCAL INFECTIONS.

PANIC DISORDER: An anxiety disorder that causes unexpected attacks of intense fear, usually related to thinking that one is dying, going crazy, or losing control, coupled with physical symptoms of anxiety. These attacks are relatively sudden in onset and last for approximately twenty minutes. If the fear of the symptoms extends to the places where the panic attacks occur and avoidance of those places results, then panic disorder with agoraphobia is the diagnosis.

PEDIATRIC AUTOIMMUNE NEUROPSYCHIATRIC DISORDERS ASSOCIATED WITH STREPTOCOCCAL INFECTIONS (PANDAS): A group of pediatric OCD disorders, caused by the antibodies children produce when they have strep throat. The antibodies attack certain parts of the brain, giving rise to OCD symptoms.

PEDIATRIC OCD: Obsessive-compulsive disorder in children and teenagers.

PERFECTIONISM: An overwhelming need to do everything perfectly or, in some individuals, until it feels "just right," often accompanied by fear of some catastrophic consequence if perfection isn't attained.

PHOBIA: An exaggerated, often extreme fear, sometimes initiated when a person experiences or witnesses a traumatizing event. The objects of phobic responses tend to be avoided thereafter. Examples of such objects include animals or insects, environmental events (e.g., lightning storms or tornados), heights, flying, and blood, injury, or injections. Phobias are common in children, most of whom outgrow these fears over the course of their development.

POST-TRAUMATIC STRESS DISORDER (PTSD): A psychological reaction to a highly stressful, traumatic event. Such events can include experiencing or witnessing combat, sexual assault or rape, violence, natural disasters, and motor vehicle accidents.

PROGNOSIS: A clinician's prediction regarding a patient's eventual treatment outcome, based on research as well as on his or her individual progress.

PSYCHIATRIST: A person holding a medical (doctor's) degree who, after completing medical school, has received specialized training to treat mental illness.

PSYCHOLOGIST: A person who has completed a degree in doctoral training (i.e., typically a Ph.D. or Psy.D.) in a clinically related area of psychology and who is licensed to treat patients in the science of cognition, emotion, and behavior.

PSYCHOTIC: A term describing a person who has lost contact with reality, often evidenced by delusions and hallucinations.

PTSD: See POST-TRAUMATIC STRESS DISORDER.

REASSURANCE: A response by family or friends expressing "approval" of an OCD sufferer's ritualizing. Individuals with some forms of OCD can be described as reassurance-seeking.

RECOVERY: The process of combating a disorder. Recovery from OCD occurs when the patient learns how to effectively manage the symptoms.

RELAPSE: The recurrence of symptoms following a period of improvement.

RELIGIOUS OBSESSIONS: Intrusive, repetitive, and unwanted thoughts based on religious teachings, often resulting in guilt.

RESPONSE PREVENTION: The deliberate blocking of ritual responses to obsessions and the learning of more adaptive responses to those obsessions.

RESPONSIBILITY: A belief held by many individuals with OCD that they are responsible for their intrusive thoughts as well as for the perceived catastrophic consequences of those thoughts. Such individuals also feel responsible for preventing harm from occurring (e.g., "I'll be responsible for the house burning down if I don't check the stove").

REUPTAKE: A neuron's reabsorption of a neurotransmitter, following the transmission of a nerve impulse across a synapse.

RITUAL: A compulsive behavior. In OCD, a ritual is a response to an obsession and/or intrusive thought and is intended to relieve or neutralize the fear or anxiety caused by the obsession. *See also* COMPULSION.

SCRUPULOSITY: Collectively, obsessions and compulsions based on the need to be morally perfect. Scrupulosity is typical of religiously based obsessions.

SELF-HELP: Efforts taken to treat one's own disorder with the help of books, websites, CDs and tapes, and participation in support groups, but which do not include the help of a clinician.

SELF-MEDICATION: Attempted treatment of a symptom with alcohol, illegal drugs, prescription medications, or over-the-counter substances.

SEROTONERGIC THEORY: The hypothesis that a dysfunction in transmissions of serotonin between nerve cells in the brain is linked to the development of OCD.

SEROTONIN: A brain chemical (i.e., neurotransmitter) that carries impulses or messages between brain cells.

SEROTONIN REUPTAKE INHIBITOR (SRI): An antidepressant/antianxiety medication that blocks serotonin's reuptake.

SEXUAL OBSESSIONS: Intrusive, repetitive, and unwanted thoughts based on sex, usually in some unpleasant or unacceptable form.

SIDE EFFECT: A secondary, usually adverse effect of taking a drug.

SOCIAL ANXIETY DISORDER: A fear of becoming embarrassed or humiliated or of eliciting disapproval as a result of one's behavior in situations where one is subject to observation or scrutiny by others. In many cases, these situations are then avoided. Fear of public speaking is an example of social anxiety disorder.

SOMATIC OBSESSIONS: Intrusive, unwanted thoughts linked to a feared or imagined illness.

SRI: *See* SEROTONIN REUPTAKE INHIBITOR.

SUPERSTITION: A belief or practice resulting from ignorance, fear of the unknown, trust in magic or chance, or a false idea about the cause of something.

SYMPTOM: An indication of the presence of a physical or mental disorder.

SYNAPSE: The space between two adjacent neurons, or nerve cells, across which nerve impulses are transmitted from one cell to the next.

TIC: A frequently occurring speech or muscle spasm, of which the individual is usually unaware.

TOLERANCE: The gradual resistance to a drug after continual use.

TOURETTE'S SYNDROME (TS): An obsessive-compulsive spectrum disorder characterized by vocal and muscle tics.

TREATMENT RESISTANT: A term referring to a disorder that does not respond to treatment.

TRICHOTILLOMANIA: An obsessive-compulsive spectrum disorder marked by compulsive hair-pulling. A patient with "trich" is likely to pull hair not only from the top of the head but also from the face, arms, and other body parts.

TRYCYCLIC ANTIDEPRESSANT: A group of antidepressants found to be helpful in treating OCD symptoms.

TS: *See* TOURETTE'S SYNDROME.

VESICLES: In nerve cells, tiny pouches at the ends of nerve fibers that store neurotransmitters, such as serotonin, until it's time to release them to other nerve cells.

YALE-BROWN OBSESSIVE-COMPULSIVE SCALE (YBOCS): A popular assessment tool for measuring the frequency and severity of OCD symptoms.

YBOCS: *See* YALE-BROWN OBSESSIVE-COMPULSIVE SCALE.

APPENDIX:
THE YALE-BROWN OBSESSIVE-
COMPULSIVE SCALE (YBOCS)

Check only those symptoms that are bothering you right now. Items marked with an asterisk (*) may or may not be OCD symptoms. To decide whether you have a particular symptom, refer to the description or examples of each item in the right-hand column.

OBSESSIONS
Aggressive Obsessions

____ 1. I fear I might harm myself.

Fear of eating with a knife or fork, fear of handling sharp objects, fear of walking near glass windows.

____ 2. I fear I might harm other people.

Fear of poisoning other people's food, fear of harming babies, fear of pushing someone in front of a train, fear of hurting someone's feelings, fear of being responsible by not providing assistance for some imagined catastrophe, fear of causing harm by giving bad advice.

____ 3. I have violent or horrific images in my mind.

Images of murders, dismembered bodies, or other disgusting scenes.

____ 4. I fear I will blurt out obscenities or insults.

Fear of shouting obscenities in public situation like church, fear of writing obscenities.

____ 5. I fear doing something else embarrassing.

Fear of appearing foolish in social situations.

___ 6. I fear I will act on an unwanted impulse.

Fear of driving a car into a tree, fear of running someone over, fear of stabbing a friend.

___ 7. I fear I will steal things.

Fear of "cheating" a cashier, fear of shoplifting inexpensive items.

___ 8. I fear that I'll harm others because I'm not careful enough.

Fear of causing an accident without being aware of it (such as a hit-and-run automobile accident).

___ 9. I fear I'll be responsible for something else terrible happening.

Fear of causing a fire or burglary because of not being careful enough in checking the house before leaving.

Contamination Obsessions

___ 10. I am concerned or disgusted with bodily waste or secretions.

Fear of contracting AIDS, cancer, or other diseases from public rest rooms, fears of your own saliva, urine, feces, semen, or vaginal secretions.

___ 11. I am concerned with dirt or germs.

Fear of picking up germs from sitting in certain chairs, shaking hands, or touching door handles.

___ 12. I am excessively concerned with environmental contaminants.

Fear of being contaminated by asbestos or radon, fear of radioactive substances, fear of things associated with towns containing toxic waste sites.

___ 13. I am excessively concerned with certain household cleansers.

Fear of poisonous kitchen or bathroom cleansers, solvents, insect spray, or turpentine.

___ 14. I am excessively concerned with animals.

Fear of being contaminated by touching an insect, dog, cat, or other animal.

___ 15. I am bothered by sticky substances or residues.

Fear of adhesive tape and other sticky substances that may trap contaminants.

___ 16. I am concerned that I will get ill because of contamination.

Fear of getting ill as a direct result of being contaminated (beliefs vary about how long the disease will take to appear).

_____ 17. I am concerned that I will contaminate others.

Fear of touching other people or preparing their food after you touch poisonous substances (like gasoline) or after you touch your own body.

Sexual Obsessions

_____ 18. I have forbidden or perverse sexual thoughts, images, or impulses.

Unwanted sexual thoughts about strangers, family, or friends.

_____ 19. I have sexual obsessions that involve children or incest.

Unwanted thoughts about sexually molesting either your own children or other children.

_____ 20. I have obsessions about homosexuality.

Worries like "Am I a homosexual?" or "What if I suddenly become gay?" when there is no basis for these thoughts.

_____ 21. I have obsessions about aggressive sexual behavior toward other strangers, friends, or family members.

Unwanted images of violent sexual behavior toward adult people.

Hoarding/Saving Obsessions

_____ 22. I have obsessions about hoarding or saving things.

Worries about throwing away seemingly unimportant things that you might need in the future, urges to pick up and collect useless things.

Religious Obsessions

_____ 23. I am concerned with sacrilege and blasphemy.

Worries about having blasphemous thoughts, saying blasphemous things, or being punished for such things.

_____ 24. I am excessively concerned with morality.

Worries about always doing "the right thing," having told a lie, or having cheated someone.

Obsessions with the Need for Symmetry or Exactness

_____ 25. I have obsessions about symmetry or exactness.

Worries about papers and books being properly aligned, worries about calculations or handwriting being perfect.

Miscellaneous Obsessions

____ 26. I feel that I need to know or re-member certain things.

Belief that you need to remember in-significant things like license plate num-bers, the names of actors on television shows, old telephone numbers, bumper sticker or T-shirt slogans.

____ 27. I fear saying certain things.

Fear of saying certain words (such as "thirteen") because of superstitions, fear of saying something that might be disre-spectful to a dead person, fear of using words with an apostrophe (because this denotes possession).

____ 28. I fear not saying just the right thing.

Fear of having said the wrong thing, fear of not using the "perfect" word.

____ 29. I fear losing things.

Worries about losing a wallet or unim-portant objects, like a scrap of notepaper.

____ 30. I am bothered by intrusive (neutral) mental images.

Random, unwanted images in your mind.

____ 31. I am bothered by intrusive mental nonsense sounds, words, or music.

Words, songs, or music in your mind that you can't stop.

____★32. I am bothered by certain sounds or noises.

Worries about the sounds of clocks tick-ing loudly or of voices in another room that may interfere with sleeping.

____ 33. I have lucky and unlucky numbers.

Worries about common numbers (like thirteen) that may cause you to perform activities a certain lucky number of times or to postpone an action until a certain lucky hour of the day.

____ 34. Certain colors have special sig-nificance to me.

Fear of using objects of certain colors (e.g., black may be associated with death, red with blood and injury).

____ 35. I have superstitious fears.

Fear of passing a cemetery, hearse, or black cat; fear of omens associated with death.

Somatic Obsessions

___ 36. I am concerned with illness or disease.

Worries that you have an illness like cancer, heart disease, or AIDS, despite reassurance from doctors that you do not.

___*37. I am excessively concerned with a part of my body.

Worries that your face, ears, nose, eyes, or another part of your body is hideously ugly, despite reassurance to the contrary.

COMPULSIONS

Cleaning/Washing Compulsions

___ 38. I wash my hands excessively or in a ritualized way.

Washing your hands many times a day or for long periods of time after touching, or thinking you have touched, a contaminated object. This may include washing the entire length of your arms.

___ 39. I have excessive or ritualized showering, bathing, toothbrushing, grooming, or toilet routines.

Taking showers or baths or performing other bathroom routines that may last for several hours. If the sequence is interrupted, the entire process may have to be restarted.

___ 40. I have compulsions that involve cleaning household items or other kitchen utensils.

Excessive cleaning of faucets, toilets, floors, kitchen counters, or inanimate objects.

___ 41. I do other things to prevent or remove contact with contaminants.

Asking family members to handle or remove insecticides, garbage, gasoline cans, raw meat, paints, varnish, drugs in the medicine cabinet, or kitty litter. If you can't avoid these things, you may wear gloves to handle them, such as when using a self-service gasoline pump.

Checking Compulsions

___ 42. I check that I did not harm others.

Checking that you haven't hurt someone without knowing it. You may ask others for reassurance or telephone to make sure that everything is all right.

___ 43. I check that I did not harm myself.

Looking for injuries or bleeding after handling sharp or breakable objects. You may frequently go to doctors to ask for reassurance that you haven't hurt yourself.

___ 44. I check that nothing terrible happened.

Searching the newspaper or listening to the radio or television for news about some catastrophe you believe you caused. You may also ask people for reassurance that you didn't cause an accident.

___ 45. I check that I did not make a mistake.

Repeated checking of door locks, stoves, electrical outlets, before leaving home; repeated checking while reading, writing, or doing simple calculations to make sure you didn't make a mistake (you can't be certain that you didn't).

___*46. I check some aspects of my physical condition tied to my obsessions about my body.

Seeking reassurance from friends or doctors that you aren't having a heart attack or getting cancer; repeatedly taking your pulse, blood pressure, or temperature; checking yourself for body odors; checking your appearance in a mirror, looking for ugly features.

Repeating Rituals

___ 47. I reread or rewrite things.

Taking hours to read a few pages in a book or to write a short letter because you get caught in a cycle of reading and rereading; worrying that you didn't understand something you just read; searching for a "perfect" word or phrase; having obsessive thoughts about the shape of certain printed letters in a book.

___ 48. I need to repeat routine activities.

Repeating activities like turning appliances on and off, combing your hair, going in and out of a doorway, or looking in a particular direction; not feeling comfortable unless you do these things the "right" number of times.

Counting Compulsions

___ 49. I have counting compulsions.   Counting objects like ceiling or floor tiles, books in a bookcase, nails in a wall, or even grains of sand on a beach; counting when you repeat certain activities, like washing.

Ordering/Arranging Compulsions

___ 50. I have ordering or arranging compulsions.   Straightening paper and pens on a desktop or books in a bookcase, wasting hours arranging things in your house in "order" and then becoming very upset if this order is disturbed.

Hoarding/Collecting Compulsions

___ 51. I have compulsions to hoard or collect things.   Saving old newspapers, notes, cans, paper towels, wrappers, and empty bottles for fear that if you throw them away you may one day need them; picking up useless objects from the street or from garbage cans.

Miscellaneous Compulsions

___ 52. I have mental rituals (other than checking/counting).   Performing rituals in your head, like saying prayers or thinking a "good" thought to undo a "bad" thought. These are different from obsessions, because you perform them intentionally to reduce anxiety or feel better.

___ 53. I need to tell, ask, or confess things.   Asking other people to reassure you, confessing to wrong behaviors you never even did, believing that you have to tell other people certain words to feel better.

___ *54. I need to touch, tap, or rub things.   Giving in to the urge to touch rough surfaces, like wood, or hot surfaces, like a stovetop; giving in to the urge to lightly touch other people, believing you need to touch an object like a telephone to prevent an illness in your family.

___ 55. I take measures (other than checking) to prevent harm or terrible consequences to myself or others.

Staying away from sharp or breakable objects, such as knives, scissors, and fragile glass.

___*56. I have ritualized eating behaviors.

Arranging your food, knife, and fork in a particular order before being able to eat, eating according to a strict ritual, not being able to eat until the hands of a clock point exactly at a certain time.

___ 57. I have superstitious behaviors.

Not taking a bus or train if its number contains an "unlucky" number (like thirteen), staying in your house on the thirteenth of the month, throwing away clothes you wore while passing a funeral home or cemetery.

___*58. I pull my hair out (trichotillomania).

Pulling hair from your scalp, eyelids, eyelashes, or pubic area, using your fingers or tweezers. You may produce bald spots that require you to wear a wig, or you may pluck your eyelids or eyebrows smooth.

YBOCS Score Card

Obsessive Thoughts

Review the obsessions you checked on the Checklist above to help you answer questions 1–5. Please think about *the last seven days* (including today), and check one answer for each question.

1. How much of your time is occupied by obsessive thoughts? How frequently do the obsessive thoughts occur?

   ___ 0 = None
   ___ 1 = Less than 1 hour per day, or occasional intrusions (occur no more than 8 times a day)
   ___ 2 = 1 to 3 hours per day, or frequent intrusions (occur more than 8 times a day, but most hours of the day are free of obsessions)
   ___ 3 = More than 3 hours and up to 8 hours per day, or very frequent intrusions (occur more than 8 times a day and during most hours of the day)
   ___ 4 = More than 8 hours per day, or near-constant intrusions (too numerous to count, and an hour rarely passes without several obsessions occurring)

2. How much do your obsessive thoughts interfere with your social or work functioning? (If you are currently not working, please think about how much the obsessions interfere with your everyday activities.) (In answering this question, please consider whether there is anything that you don't do, or that you do less, because of the obsessions.)

    ___ 0 = No interference

    ___ 1 = Mild, slight interference with social or occupational activities, but overall performance not impaired

    ___ 2 = Moderate, definite interference with social or occupational performance, but still manageable

    ___ 3 = Severe interference, causes substantial impairment in social or occupational performance

    ___ 4 = Extreme, incapacitating interference

3. How much distress do your obsessive thoughts cause you?

    ___ 0 = None

    ___ 1 = Mild, infrequent, and not too disturbing distress

    ___ 2 = Moderate, frequent, and disturbing distress, but still manageable

    ___ 3 = Severe, very frequent, and very disturbing distress

    ___ 4 = Extreme, near-constant, and disabling distress

4. How often to you try to disregard these thoughts and let them pass naturally through your mind? (Here we are *not* interested in knowing how successful you are in disregarding your thoughts but only in how much or how often you *try* to do so.)

    ___ 0 = I always let the obsessions pass naturally through my mind

    ___ 1 = I disregard them most of the time (i.e., more than half the time I try to resist)

    ___ 2 = I make some effort to disregard them

    ___ 3 = I rarely try to disregard the obsessions

    ___ 4 = I never try to disregard the obsessions

5. How *successful* are you in disregarding your obsessive thinking? (Note: Do not include here obsessions stopped by doing *compulsions*.)

    ___ 0 = Always successful

    ___ 1 = Usually successful in disregarding obsessions

    ___ 2 = Sometimes successful in disregarding obsessions

    ___ 3 = Rarely successful in disregarding obsessions

    ___ 4 = I am rarely able to even momentarily disregard the obsessions

Add up the numbers you checked in the five questions above.

Obsession Total: _____

Compulsions

Review the compulsions you checked on the Checklist to help you answer questions 6–10. Please think about the *last seven days* (including today), and check one answer for each question.

6. How much time do you spend performing compulsive behavior? How frequently do you perform compulsions? (If your rituals involve daily living activities, please consider how much longer it takes you to complete routine activities because of your rituals.)

   ___ 0 = None

   ___ 1 = Less than 1 hour per day is spent performing compulsions, or occasional performance of compulsive behaviors (no more than 8 times a day)

   ___ 2 = 1 to 3 hours per day are spent performing compulsions, or frequent performance of compulsive behaviors (more than 8 times a day, but most hours are free of compulsions)

   ___ 3 = More than 3 hours and up to 8 hours per day are spent performing compulsions, or very frequent performance of compulsive behaviors (more than 8 times a day and during most hours of the day)

   ___ 4 = More than 8 hours per day are spent performing compulsions, or near-constant performance of compulsive behaviors (too numerous to count, and an hour rarely passes without several compulsions being performed)

7. How much do your compulsive behaviors interfere with your social or work functioning? (If you are not currently working, please think about your everyday activities.)

   ___ 0 = No interference

   ___ 1 = Mild, slight interference with social or occupational activities, but overall performance not impaired

   ___ 2 = Moderate, definite interference with social or occupational performance, but still manageable

   ___ 3 = Severe interference, substantial impairment in social or occupational performance

   ___ 4 = Extreme, incapacitating interference

8. How would you feel if prevented from performing your compulsion(s)? How anxious would you become?

    ___ 0 = Not at all anxious
    ___ 1 = Only slightly anxious if compulsions prevented
    ___ 2 = Anxiety would mount but remain manageable if compulsions prevented
    ___ 3 = Prominent and very disturbing increase in anxiety if compulsions interrupted
    ___ 4 = Extreme, incapacitating anxiety from any intervention aimed at reducing the compulsions

9. How much of an effort do you make to resist the compulsions? Or how often do you try to stop the compulsions? (Rate only how often or how much you try to resist your compulsions, not how successful you actually are in stopping them.)

    ___ 0 = I make an effort to always resist (or the symptoms are so minimal that there is no need to actively resist them)
    ___ 1 = I try to resist most of the time (i.e., more than half the time)
    ___ 2 = I make some effort to resist
    ___ 3 = I yield to almost all compulsions without attempting to control them, but I do so with some reluctance
    ___ 4 = I completely and willingly yield to all compulsions

10. How much control do you have over the compulsive behavior? How successful are you in stopping the rituals(s)? (If you rarely try to resist, please think about those rare occasions in which you *did try* to stop the compulsions, in order to answer this question.)

    ___ 0 = I have complete control
    ___ 1 = Usually I can stop compulsions or rituals with some effort and willpower
    ___ 2 = Sometimes I can stop compulsive behavior but only with difficulty
    ___ 3 = I can only delay the compulsive behavior, but eventually it must be carried to completion
    ___ 4 = I am rarely able to even momentarily delay performing the compulsive behavior

Add up the numbers you checked in the five questions above.

Compulsion Total: _____

Total Score (Obsession Total + Compulsion Total) = _____

If your score is more than 16, your OCD symptoms fall into the clinical severity range.

11. Check the one statement that best describes what you believe right now. Do you think your obsessions or compulsions are reasonable or rational? Would there be anything besides anxiety to worry about if you resisted them? Do you think something would really happen?

___ 0 = I think my obsessions or compulsions are unreasonable or excessive

___ 1 = I think my obsessions or compulsions are unreasonable or excessive, but I'm not completely convinced that they aren't necessary

___ 2 = I think my obsessions or compulsions may be unreasonable or excessive

___ 3 = I don't think my obsessions or compulsions are unreasonable or excessive

___ 4 = I am sure my obsessions or compulsions are reasonable, no matter what anyone says

12. Check the one statement that best describes how many things you have avoided in the past week. Have you been avoiding doing anything, going anyplace, or being with anyone because of your obsessional thoughts or because you were afraid you would perform compulsions?

___ 0 = I haven't been avoiding anything because of OCD

___ 1 = I have been avoiding a few unimportant things because of OCD

___ 2 = I have been avoiding some important things because of OCD

___ 3 = I have been avoiding many important things because of OCD

___ 4 = I have been avoiding doing almost everything because of OCD

[Note: These last two questions do not need to be scored.]

ACKNOWLEDGMENTS

None of us can advance in our professional lives without the guidance and support of teachers, colleagues, friends, and family. If you are lucky, those categories overlap. I have been exceptionally fortunate.

My graduate advisor at the University of Minnesota, Henry Borow, Ph.D., cultivated my intellectual curiosity and left an indelible stamp on my perspective regarding how to train students and facilitate their education—to say nothing of how to successfully jump the hurdles of graduate school. He also brought me into his family. Henry was an exceptional man and is sorely missed. Barbara Fleming, Ph.D., and Jim Pretzer, Ph.D., my post-doctoral fellowship supervisors, introduced me to cognitive therapy and provided my formal training in this approach. They are both also responsible for encouraging my clinical and research specialization in anxiety disorders. Barb and Jim first introduced me to Aaron Beck, M.D., who, several years later, invited me to become a Beck Scholar. At the time, Dr. Beck was in his 80s, and his enthusiasm for cognitive therapy and comprehensive knowledge and skills were—and remain—a model for anyone who has the desire to become a cognitive therapist. Alec Pollard, Ph.D., has been a colleague and friend, and his expertise in working with OCD patients propelled my interest in this area. Alec, too, provided entrée into the Obsessive Compulsive Cognitions Working Group. OCCWG is an international group of researchers and clinicians who are doing groundbreaking work in facilitating a widespread understanding of OCD. My friends and colleagues within this working group push everyone to stretch the boundaries of their knowledge and to have fun while doing so!

Joseph Flaherty, M.D., who hired me at University of Illinois at Chicago, had the vision to see the importance of a cognitive behavior therapy training program in a department of psychiatry. He has been a source of support during his time as my department head and, more recently, as dean of the College of Medicine. Likewise, Henry Dove, M.D., who has been my interim department head, was my colleague in a joint clinic and has been a fervent supporter of CBT training for our residents. Henry has also been a vocal supporter of mine and a source of sage advice.

On a more personal level, Gayle Beck, Ph.D., has been a trusted friend, a colleague, a source of wisdom, and someone with whom I can always laugh. She has opened any number of doors on my behalf, and for that I am incredibly grateful. My sister, JoAnn, is always there when I need her. An academic herself, she understands the stresses inherent in the job. My longtime friend, colleague, and co-author, Ray Ownby, M.D., Ph.D., M.B.A., has been collaborating with me since I left grad school—far too many years ago to count. Ray does his utmost to keep me busy and out of trouble! And Jeff Howard, who is and will always be my best friend, is there with champagne or a Band-Aid and knows which is needed most.

This book would not have been possible without Lynn Sonberg and Mary Mihaly. You have my gratitude and thanks for involving me in this project and for your expertise in all areas of writing and publishing. I am particularly indebted to Mary for her extensive work on the text.

Finally, I want to acknowledge the patients I have had the opportunity to work with and the students from a number of mental health–related disciplines whom I have trained. As much as you have expressed your appreciation for the contributions I may have made to your lives or careers, it is a two-way street. I learn something from every patient and from every trainee. Thank you for what you have given back.

RESOURCES

CHAPTER 1
OCD: IT'S NO LAUGHING MATTER

Abramowitz, J. S., and A. C. Houts. *Concepts and Controversies in Obsessive-Compulsive Disorder.* New York: Springer Science + Business Media, 2005.

Antony, M. M., C. Purdon, and L. J. Summerfeldt. *Psychological Treatment of Obsessive-Compulsive Disorder: Fundamentals and Beyond.* Washington, DC: American Psychological Association, 2007.

Baer, L. *Getting Control: Overcoming Your Obsessions and Compulsions.* New York: Plume, 2000.

Obsessive-Compulsive Foundation of Metropolitan Chicago: OCD Overview. Available online at www.ocfchicago.org.

Rapoport, J. *The Boy Who Couldn't Stop Washing.* Canada: Plume/New American Library/Penguin Books, 1991.

Steketee, G., and T. Pigott. *Obsessive-Compulsive Disorder: The Latest Assessment and Treatment Strategies.* Kansas City: Compact Clinicals, 2006.

CHAPTER 2
A CLOSER LOOK AT THE MOST
COMMON OBSESSIONS AND COMPULSIONS

Abramowitz, J. S., and A. C. Houts. *Concepts and Controversies in Obsessive-Compulsive Disorder.* New York: Springer Science + Business Media, 2005.

Antony, M. M., C. Purdon, and L. J. Summerfeldt. *Psychological Treatment of Obsessive-Compulsive Disorder: Fundamentals and Beyond.* Washington, DC: American Psychological Association, 2007.

Penzel, F. *Obsessive-Compulsive Disorders: A Complete Guide to Getting Well and Staying Well.* New York: Oxford University Press, 2000.

Steketee, G., and T. Pigott. *Obsessive-Compulsive Disorder: The Latest Assessment and Treatment Strategies.* Kansas City: Compact Clinicals, 2006.

Swinson, R. P., M. M. Antony, S. Rachman, and M. A. Richter. *Obsessive-Compulsive Disorder: Theory, Research, and Treatment.* New York: Guilford Press, 1998.

CHAPTER 3
THE BIOLOGY OF OCD:
WHAT YOU NEED TO KNOW

Foa, E. B., and R. Wilson. *Stop Obsessing! How to Overcome Your Obsessions and Compulsions.* New York: Bantam Books, 2001.

Goodman, W. K., M. V. Rudorfer, and J. D. Maser. *Obsessive-Compulsive Disorder: Contemporary Issues in Treatment.* Mahwah, NJ: Lawrence Erlbaum Associates, 2000.

Grados, M. A., J. Walkup, and S. Walford. Genetics of obsessive-compulsive disorders: New findings and challenges. *Brain & Development* 25 (Suppl.):1–2003.

Landsman, K. J., K. M. Rupertus, and C. Pedrick. *Loving Someone with OCD: Help for You and Your Family.* Oakland, CA: New Harbinger Publications, 2005.

National Institute of Mental Health. How strep triggers obsessive-compulsive disorder—New clues. *Science Update,* October 11, 2006.

National Institute of Mental Health. Mutant gene linked to obsessive-compulsive disorder. *Science Update,* October 23, 2003.

Penzel, F. *Obsessive-Compulsive Disorders: A Complete Guide to Getting Well and Staying Well.* New York: Oxford University Press, 2000.

Schiffer, R. B., S. M. Rao, and B. S. Fogel. *Neuropsychiatry,* 2nd ed. Philadelphia: Lippincott, Williams & Wilkins, 2003.

Storch, E. A., G. R. Geffken, and T. K. Murphy. *Handbook of Child and Adolescent Obsessive-Compulsive Disorder.* Mahwah, NJ: Lawrence Erlbaum Associates, 2007.

Storch, E. A., A. Lewin, G. Geffken, W. Goodman, and T. Murphy. A neuropsychiatric review of pediatric obsessive-compulsive disorder: Etiology and efficacious treatments. *Neuropsychiatric Disease and Treatment* 2:1 (2006).

CHAPTER 4
A STEP-BY-STEP GUIDE
TO GETTING A DIAGNOSIS

American Psychiatric Association. *Diagnostic and Statistical Manual of Mental Disorders, Fourth Edition.* American Psychiatric Association, 2000.

Baer, L. *Getting Control: Overcoming Your Obsessions and Compulsions.* New York: Plume, 2000.

Barlow, D. H. *Anxiety and Its Disorders: The Nature and Treatment of Anxiety and Panic,* 2nd ed. New York: Guilford Press, 2002.

Foa, E. B., and R. Wilson. *Stop Obsessing! How to Overcome Your Obsessions and Compulsions.* New York: Bantam Books, 2001.

Frost, R. O., and G. Steketee. *Cognitive Approaches to Obsessions and Compulsions: Theory, Assessment, and Treatment.* New York: Pergamon, 2002.

National Institute of Mental Health. Half of adults with anxiety disorders had psychiatric diagnoses in youth. *Science Update*, February 7, 2007.

Schiffer, R. B., S. M. Rao, and B. S. Fogel. *Neuropsychiatry,* 2nd ed. Philadelphia: Lippincott, Williams & Wilkins, 2003.

Storch, E. A., G. R. Geffken, and T. K. Murphy. *Handbook of Child and Adolescent Obsessive-Compulsive Disorder.* Mahwah, NJ: Lawrence Erlbaum Associates, 2007.

CHAPTER 5
IF IT ISN'T OCD: UNDERSTANDING RELATED DISORDERS, COMORBIDITY, AND THE OBSESSIVE-COMPULSIVE SPECTRUM

Abramowitz, J. S., D. McKay, and S. Taylor. *Obsessive-Compulsive Disorder: Subtypes and Spectrum Conditions.* New York: Elsevier, 2007.

Abramowitz, J. S., D. McKay, and S. Taylor. *Clinical Handbook of Obsessive-Compulsive Disorder and Related Problems.* Baltimore: Johns Hopkins University Press, 2008.

Abramowitz, J. S., and A. C. Houts. *Concepts and Controversies in Obsessive-Compulsive Disorder.* New York: Springer Science + Business Media, 2005.

American Psychological Association. *Answers to Your Questions About Panic Disorder.* Washington, DC: American Psychological Association, 2008.

Antony, M. M., C. Purdon, and L. J. Summerfeldt. *Psychological Treatment of Obsessive-Compulsive Disorder: Fundamentals and Beyond.* Washington, DC: American Psychological Association, 2007.

Deckersbach, T., S. Wilhelm, and N. Keuthen. Self-injurious skin picking: Clinical characteristics, assessment methods, and treatment modalities. *Brief Treatment and Crisis Intervention* 3:2 (Summer 2003):249–258.

Mansueto, C., P. T. Ninan, and B. O. Rothbaum. *TTM Treatment in Adults: A Guide for Clinicians.* Trichotillomania Learning Center, 2008.

National Women's Health Information Center. *Body Dysmorphic Disorder (BDD).* Available online at www.MedicineNet.com.

Phillips, K. A. *The Broken Mirror: Understanding and Treating Body Dysmorphic Disorder.* New York: Oxford University Press, 1986.

Swinson, R. P., M. M. Antony, S. Rachman, and M. A. Richter. *Obsessive-Compulsive Disorder: Theory, Research, and Treatment.* New York: Guilford Press, 1998.

CHAPTER 6
THE GOOD NEWS ABOUT TREATMENT:
WHAT WORKS BEST

Abramowitz, J. S., and A. C. Houts. *Concepts and Controversies in Obsessive-Compulsive Disorder.* New York: Springer, 2005.

Abramowitz, J. S., D. McKay, and S. Taylor. *Clinical Handbook of Obsessive-Compulsive Disorder and Related Problems.* Baltimore: Johns Hopkins University Press, 2008.

Antony, M. M., C. Purdon, and L. J. Summerfeldt. *Psychological Treatment of Obsessive-Compulsive Disorder: Fundamentals and Beyond.* Washington, DC: American Psychological Association, 2007.

Baer, L. *Getting Control: Overcoming Your Obsessions and Compulsions.* New York: Plume, 2000.

Landsman, K. J., K. M. Rupertus, and C. Pedrick. *Loving Someone with OCD: Help for You and Your Family.* Oakland, CA: New Harbinger Publications, 2005.

Mental Health: A Report of the Surgeon General. Available online at http://www.surgeongeneral.gov/library/mentalhealth/home.html.

Nathan, P. E., and J. M. Gorman. *A Guide to Treatments That Work.* New York: Oxford University Press, 2007.

Steketee, G, and T. Pigott. *Obsessive-Compulsive Disorder: The Latest Assessment and Treatment Strategies.* Kansas City: Compact Clinicals, 2006.

CHAPTER 7
WHAT TO EXPECT FROM TREATMENT,
STEP BY STEP

Abramowitz, J. S. *Obsessive-Compulsive Disorder.* New York: Hogrefe & Huber, 2006.

Antony, M. M., C. Purdon, and L. J. Summerfeldt. *Psychological Treatment of Obsessive-Compulsive Disorder: Fundamentals and Beyond.* Washington, DC: American Psychological Association, 2006.

Franklin, M. E., and E. B. Foa. Obsessive–compulsive disorder. In D. H. Barlow (ed.), *Clinical Handbook of Psychological Disorders* (pp. 164–215). New York: Guilford Press, 2007.

Wilhelm, S., and G. S. Steketee. *Cognitive Therapy for Obsessive-Compulsive Disorder: A Guide for Professionals.* Oakland, CA: New Harbinger Publications, 2006.

CHAPTER 8
THE ROLE OF MEDICATION IN RECOVERY

Baer, L. *Getting Control: Overcoming Your Obsessions and Compulsions.* New York: Plume, 2000.

Foa, E. B., M. R. Liebowitz, and M. J. Kozak et al. Randomized, placebo-controlled trial of exposure and ritual prevention, clomipramine, and their combination in the treatment of obsessive-compulsive disorder. *American Journal of Psychiatry* 162 (2005):151–161.

Goodman, W. K., M. V. Rudorfer, and J. D. Maser. *Obsessive-Compulsive Disorder: Contemporary Issues in Treatment.* Mahwah, NJ: Lawrence Erlbaum Associates, 2000.

Penzel, F. *Obsessive-Compulsive Disorders: A Complete Guide to Getting Well and Staying Well.* New York: Oxford University Press, 2000.

Steketee, G., and T. Pigott. *Obsessive-Compulsive Disorder: The Latest Assessment and Treatment Strategies.* Kansas City: Compact Clinicals, 2006.

Swinson, R. P., M. M. Antony, S. Rachman, and M. A. Richter. *Obsessive-Compulsive Disorder: Theory, Research, and Treatment.* New York: Guilford Press, 1998.

Zeltner, B. Making headway. *The Plain Dealer*, March 25, 2008.

CHAPTER 9
CHILDREN AND OCD

Antony, M. M., C. Purdon, and L. J. Summerfeldt. *Psychological Treatment of Obsessive-Compulsive Disorder: Fundamentals and Beyond.* Washington, DC: American Psychological Association, 2007.

March, J. S. *Talking Back to OCD.* New York: Guilford Press, 2007.

Storch, E. A., G. R. Geffken, and T. K. Murphy. *Handbook of Child and Adolescent Obsessive-Compulsive Disorder.* Mahwah, NJ: Lawrence Erlbaum Associates, 2007.

CHAPTER 10
HOW TO HELP WHEN
A LOVED ONE HAS OCD

Baer, L. *Getting Control: Overcoming Your Obsessions and Compulsions.* New York: Plume, 2000.

Landsman, K. J., K. M. Rupertus, and C. Pedrick. *Loving Someone with OCD: Help for You and Your Family.* Oakland, CA: New Harbinger Publications, 2005.

Penzel, F. *Obsessive-Compulsive Disorders: A Complete Guide to Getting Well and Staying Well.* New York: Oxford University Press, 2000.

Steketee, G., and T. Pigott. *Obsessive-Compulsive Disorder: The Latest Assessment and Treatment Strategies.* Kansas City: Compact Clinicals, 2006.

Swinson, R. P., M. M. Antony, S. Rachman, and M. A. Richter. *Obsessive-Compulsive Disorder: Theory, Research, and Treatment.* New York: Guilford Press, 1998.

CHAPTER 11

WHAT TO DO WHEN SOMEONE YOU LOVE ISN'T READY TO BEGIN TREATMENT

Antony, M. M, C. Purdon, and L. J. Summerfeldt. *Psychological Treatment of Obsessive-Compulsive Disorder: Fundamentals and Beyond*. Washington, DC: American Psychological Association, 2007.

Kabat-Zinn, J. *Wherever You Go, There You Are: Mindfulness Meditation in Everyday Life*. New York: Hyperion, 1994.

Landsman, K. J., M. A. Rupertus, and C. Pedrick. *Loving Someone with OCD: Help for You and Your Family*. Oakland, CA: New Harbinger Publications, 2005.

Penzel, F. *Obsessive-Compulsive Disorders: A Complete Guide to Getting Well and Staying Well*. New York: Oxford University Press, 2000.

Steketee, G, and T. Pigott. *Obsessive-Compulsive Disorder: The Latest Assessment and Treatment Strategies*. Kansas City: Compact Clinicals, 2006.

APPENDIX:

THE YALE-BROWN OBSESSIVE-COMPULSIVE SCALE (YBOCS)

Goodman, W. K., L. H. Price, and S. A. Rasmussen et al. The Yale-Brown Obsessive-Compulsive Scale. *Archives of General Psychiatry* 46 (1989):1006–1011.

INDEX

sexual obsessions, 175–176, 183
somatic obsessions, 176–177, 185–186
speaking of OCD in third person, 184, 189, 192
Steffie's story, 185–186
superstition/magical obsessions, 176
support from family, 188–190, 194
treatment noncompliance, 187
Choline, 52–53
Citalopram (Celexa), 159, 160, 165, 179
Cleaning compulsion. *See* Contamination issues
Clinical trials information, 242, 244
Clomipramine (Anafranil)
description/side effects, 158, 160–161, 162, 169
neurotransmitters and, 51, 52
Cocaine, 56
Cognitive behavior therapy. *See* CBT (cognitive behavior therapy)
Comorbidity and OCD
description, 55, 76, 81, 82–83
diagnosing OCD and, 76–77, 82–83, 103–104
disorders overview, 83–95
frequently asked questions, 104–106
medications and, 153
occurrence, 81, 82
See also specific disorders
"Complex" genetic disorders, 54
Compulsions
definition/description, 2, 6, 13
frequently asked questions, 42–44
habits/upbringing and, 57
mental rituals, 38
relief and, 14, 43, 97, 113, 120
role of, 13, 36, 41, 42–43
See also specific types
Compulsive gambling, 42, 96, 97, 105, 120

Compulsive sexual behavior, 42, 97, 120
Compulsive shopping, 42, 96, 97
Compulsive slowness, 39–40
Constipation side effect, 158, 159, 164
Contamination issues
bullying example, 21–22
children, 21–22, 175, 177–179
description/examples, 17, 18–22
fears with, 16, 18, 21
overview, 17–22
Sarah's story, 18–20, 47, 56, 73–75, 117–118
Contributing factors
cause vs., 57
overview, 55–57
Cortico-striato-thalamic regions of brain
description/function, 48–49
with OCD, 49–50
Coulter, Anne and OCD
checking symptoms, 9, 24–25
depression and, 77
diagnosis, 77–78
medications, 156–157
story summary, 9–10
treatment, 10, 109–111, 156–157
Counting/repeating, 37

D-cycloserine, 170
Deal or No Deal (TV show), 12
Decision-making areas of brain, 48, 50
Deep brain stimulation (DBS), 166, 170
Denial
recovery avoidance and, 228, 235–236, 238
supporting OCD sufferers and, 197–198, 199, 202
Depression and OCD
BDD and, 98
description, 76, 83–84
major depressive disorder (MDD), 7, 62, 76, 82, 98

Escitalopram (Lexapro), 160
"Evening-up" compulsion, 3, 29, 31, 57, 196, 198–199
Executive function, 48
Exposure and response prevention. *See* ERP (exposure and response prevention)

Fatigue side effect, 158, 159, 163, 169–170
FDA (Food and Drug Administration), 158, 160, 166, 170
"Fear thermometer," 182, 184, 187–188, 189, 191, 192, 193, 194
Fluoxetine (Prozac), 78, 156–157, 158–159
Fluvoxamine (Luvox), 157, 158
fMRI (functional magnetic resonance imaging), 47, 48
Foa, Edna B., 74–75
Food and Drug Administration (FDA), 158, 160, 166, 170
Freud, Sigmund, 73
Freudian ideas on OCD, 44, 45
Functional magnetic resonance imaging (fMRI), 47, 48

GABHS (hemolytic streptococcus infection), 173–174
GAD (generalized anxiety disorder), 91–93, 104–105
Generalized anxiety disorder (GAD), 91–93, 104–105
Genetics
    obsessive-compulsive spectrum disorders, 54–55
    panic disorders, 84
Genetics and OCD
    about, 53–55, 58, 223
    evidence for, 47
    frequently asked questions, 58, 223
    statistics on, 58
    studies, 53–54
    twins studies, 54

Globus pallidus, 50
Glutamate, 54
Group "intervention," 239

Habit reversal treatment, 99, 100
Habits and OCD development, 56–57
Habituation, 115–116
Half-life of drugs, 169
Harm-related obsessions/checking compulsions
    Anne Coulter's story, 24–25
    avoidance and, 26, 27, 28, 39
    children, 175
    fears with, 16, 22, 23, 24
    Jonathan's story, 66–67, 68, 109, 112, 113–115, 215–217
    overview, 22–25
    uncertainty and, 23
Headaches side effect, 158, 159, 164–165
Health insurance, 12, 69, 231
Hemolytic streptococcus infection (GABHS), 173–174
Hoarding
    children, 176
    definition/description, 33–35, 100–102, 105
    examples, 34, 35, 57, 102–103, 224
    fears and, 35–36
    health risks, 34–35, 101
    Kenny's story, 102–103
    OCD and, 33, 81–82
    OCD vs. impulse control disorder, 33, 35–36
    overview, 33–36
    resources for, 242, 243
    symptoms, 34
    treatment, 101–102, 120
Hollywood and OCD, 1, 2
hSERT gene, 53
Hughes, Howard, 12, 17

Imipramine (Tofranil), 158
Impact analysis, 239

Relationships and OCD. *See* Supporting OCD sufferers

Relaxation log, 128chart

Relaxation techniques, 125, 127–128, 128chart, 136, 237

Religious obsessions
children, 177
fears/worries with, 31–33
historical examples, 11
overview, 31–33
thought-action fusion and, 31
uncertainty and, 33
See also Scrupulosity

Repeating/counting, 37

Repetitive transcranial magnetic stimulation (rTMS), 166, 170

Resources
blogs, 248–249
for children/teenagers, 242, 245, 248
clinical trials information, 242, 244
for family/friends, 242, 244, 245, 247–248
finding a clinician, 69, 80, 148, 242, 243, 244
organizations/online resources, 80, 242–245
overview, 241–249
self-help books, 246–248
See also Support groups

Responsibility, inflated, 22–23, 39–40, 64–65, 112–113, 114, 144–145, 146chart, 175, 197, 198

"Reuptake" of serotonin, 51

Reward/punishment sensitive areas of brain, 48

Rituals. *See* Compulsions

rTMS (repetitive transcranial magnetic stimulation), 166, 170

Rubbing/tapping/touching symptoms, 36–37

SAD. *See* Social anxiety disorder (SAD)

SAPAP3 gene, 54

Scarlet fever, 173

Scrupulosity, 11, 17, 32–33, 177
See also Religious obsessions

Secrecy
diagnosing OCD and, 61, 67, 68, 77, 78
with OCD, 1, 9, 10, 11, 15, 34, 61, 67, 68, 77, 78, 215

"Segregation" in the brain, 54

Self-help books, 246–248

Serotonergic theory, 50–52

Serotonin
function, 51
reuptake, 51
substance abuse and, 56

"Serotonin poop-out," 168

Serotonin reuptake inhibitors (SRIs)
description, 52, 145, 153
uses, 52, 145, 153
See also specific SRIs

Sertraline (Zoloft), 159

Serzone, 165

Sexual addiction, 42, 97, 120

Sexual/aggressive obsessions
avoidance and, 39
children, 175–176, 183
compulsions with, 28
examples, 27, 28
fears with, 25–26, 27–28
overview, 25–28
symptoms, 26–27
thought-action fusion and, 26

Sexual effects of medications, 158, 165, 183

Skin-picking
genetics and, 55
overview/treatment, 81–82, 99–100

Slowness, compulsive slowness, 39–40

Social anxiety disorder (SAD)
overview, 89–91
treatment, 91, 153

Somatic obsessions
children, 176–177, 185–186
See also Body dysmorphic disorder (BDD)